The Conditions of Hospitality

Series Board

James Bernauer

Drucilla Cornell

Thomas R. Flynn

Kevin Hart

Richard Kearney

Jean-Luc Marion

Adriaan Peperzak

Thomas Sheehan

Hent de Vries

Merold Westphal

Michael Zimmerman

John D. Caputo, *series editor*

Perspectives in
Continental
Philosophy

Edited by THOMAS CLAVIEZ

The Conditions of Hospitality
Ethics, Politics, and Aesthetics on the Threshold of the Possible

FORDHAM UNIVERSITY PRESS
New York ▪ *2013*

Copyright © 2013 Fordham University Press

All rights reserved. No part of this publication may be reproduced, stored in a retrieval system, or transmitted in any form or by any means—electronic, mechanical, photocopy, recording, or any other—except for brief quotations in printed reviews, without the prior permission of the publisher.

Fordham University Press has no responsibility for the persistence or accuracy of URLs for external or third-party Internet websites referred to in this publication and does not guarantee that any content on such websites is, or will remain, accurate or appropriate.

Fordham University Press also publishes its books in a variety of electronic formats. Some content that appears in print may not be available in electronic books.

Library of Congress Cataloging-in-Publication Data

The conditions of hospitality : ethics, politics, and aesthetics on the threshold of the possible / edited by Thomas Claviez. — First edition.
     pages cm
  Proceedings of a conference held in Sept. 2008 in Stavanger, Norway.
  Includes bibliographical references (pages   ).
  ISBN 978-0-8232-5147-6 (cloth : alk. paper) — ISBN 978-0-8232-5148-3 (pbk. : alk. paper)
  1. Hospitality. I. Claviez, Thomas.
  BJ2021.C66 2013
  177'.1—dc23
                                                                                          2012043899

Printed in the United States of America

15 14 13 5 4 3 2 1

First edition

Contents

Introduction: "Taking Place"—Conditional/Unconditional Hospitality
Thomas Claviez   *1*

The Ethics of Hospitality

Hospitality—Under Compassion and Violence
Anne Dufourmantelle   *13*

Transcending Transcendence, or: Transcend*ifferances*: Limping toward a Radical Concept of Hospitality
Thomas Claviez   *24*

Toward a Mutual Hospitality
Luce Irigaray   *42*

The Politics of Hospitality

To Open: Hospitality and Alienation
Pheng Cheah   *57*

Frictions of Hospitality and the Promise of Cosmopolitanism
Thomas Hylland Eriksen   *81*

Proximity and Paradox: Law and Politics in the New Europe
Bonnie Honig   *94*

Conditions for Hospitality or Defence of Identity? Writers in Need of Refuge—A Case of Denmark's "Muslim Relations"
   Ulrik Pram Gad   *111*

THE AESTHETICS OF HOSPITALITY

Conviviality and Pilgrimage: Hospitality as Interruptive Practice
   Mireille Rosello   *127*

Hospitality and the Zombification of the Other
   Nikos Papastergiadis   *145*

The Art and Poetics of Translation as Hospitality
   Paola Zaccaria   *168*

Notes   *185*

Works Cited   *199*

List of Contributors   *211*

The Conditions of Hospitality

Introduction

"Taking Place"—Conditional/Unconditional Hospitality

THOMAS CLAVIEZ

The essays assembled in this volume represent the collected contributions to a conference held in Stavanger, Norway, in September 2008, with the title "The Conditions of Hospitality." It was designed to commemorate and contemplate the lasting influence and heritage of the works of Emmanuel Levinas and the late Jacques Derrida, which have allowed us to think about hospitality in new ways.[1] The conference papers have been complemented by selected essays from renowned scholars that attest, in their disciplinary and theoretical variety, to the multifaceted way in which this concept has been received, and worked into, various scientific realms and disciplines, such as philosophy, politics, psychoanalysis, anthropology, aesthetics, ethics, and translation studies. If Jacques de Ville in his 2011 book *Jacques Derrida: Law as Absolute Hospitality* has very lucidly traced the different discursive regimes that have contributed to the genealogy of the concept of radical hospitality that the late Derrida has bequeathed upon us, this collection might be read as the attempt to return this aporetic gift to the disciplines that went into its making.

Stavanger was a fitting place to host this conference on hospitality. It was the city host to all of Europe as its "Capital of Culture" in 2008 and is also the headquarters of the International Cities of Refuge Network (ICORN), a vital contributor to the "Arts of Hospitality" project. This project was a main Stavanger2008 event, of which the conference was a part. Special thanks go out to Helge Lunde from ICORN, and the former and the current head of Sølvberget, Stavanger Cultural Center, Trond Lie and Marit Egaas, for initiating the "Arts of Hospitality" project and entrusting the academic part of the conference to me, and to project manager Eirik Bø, who not only took me in as co-organizer of the conference, but whose enthusiasm and logistic talent were essential to make it all happen. I also want to express my gratitude to my assistant, Viola Marchi, for her patience and expertise in editing and revising the manuscript, as well as to Christina Rickli, Nora Escherle, Annie Cottier, and Alyssa Emch-McVey, who helped put it together.

The idea to form an association of cities that offers—if not refuge, then at least "conditional" hospitality—to persecuted artists, authors, or journalists is the subject of one of the most influential texts on hospitality (and its close conceptual ally, cosmopolitanism): *On Cosmopolitanism and Forgiveness* (2001a) brought together two essays of Jacques Derrida, one of which is the transcription of an address to the International Parliament of Writers in 1996. In this address, he refers to the idea of "open cities" (*villes franches*, or, in Norwegian, *fribyer*), an idea that has found its material manifestation in the International Cities of Refuge Network, the history of which Emmanuel Levinas (1994) had addressed in his essay "Cities of Refuge" in *Beyond the Verse*, which Derrida (1999a), in turn, had commented upon in "A Word of Welcome" in *Adieu to Emmanuel Levinas*.

One of the most categorical definitions that Derrida (2001a, 16) gives of hospitality in his essay "On Cosmopolitanism" is the following: "Hospitality is culture itself." Against the assumptions that currently reign in Europe and beyond, and which still manifest themselves in school and university curricula all over the world—that culture is closely connected to, and an organic outgrowth of, the nation that produces it—Derrida's definition of hospitality as (being) culture, and thus culture as (being) hospitality, should give us reason to pause. It points to the fact that culture, and all the artifacts, discourses, institutions, genres, and media it is taken to comprise, not only defies the homogeneity that its (allegedly) national moorings try to preserve, but that culture itself, as Homi Bhabha (1994, 114) has put it, should not be considered "as the source of conflict—different cultures—but as the effect of discriminatory practices." Culture, that is, is a (power-ridden) negotiation of differences that always transcends—and historically always has transcended—national boundaries, and thus steadfastly subverts the homogeneity that a national(istic) concept of culture implies.

The faculty that helped to imagine, in Benedict Anderson's (1991) words, the community of the nation, is now asked to envisage a different space/place where an encounter between the same and the other can take place—which would be nothing else but a place for/of culture. In his address, Derrida (2001a, 8) asks: "Could the city, equipped with new rights and greater sovereignty, open up new horizons of possibility previous undreamt of by international state law?" To turn to the city as such a space/place that offers an alternative to the exclusionary practices of the nation-state is not devoid of a certain historical irony, since the Greek *polis*—and its presumed homogeneity that forms the basis of, for example, Aristotle's ethics—has rather served as the point of resistance against which the tradition of cosmopolitanism has explicitly defined itself, starting with the Stoics.[2] But the question is even larger: Can a place possibly be imagined where unconditional hospitality, which both Levinas and Derrida helped us think, can play a role—let alone be exercised—or does such an idea of hospitality represent a genuine utopia: a *u-topos*, a nonplace, in which, by definition, nothing can "take place"?

What unites the essays assembled in this volume is not only the concept of hospitality as such but also the recurring question about the possible location that would allow a hospitable (or, for that matter, "hostipitable") encounter to actually "take place." Such a place sometimes seems to be co-extensive with the very nonplace—the abyss—that separates Derrida's unconditional and conditional hospitality, as much as it does Levinas's Saying from the Said; if anything, the shifting "fault line" between the two is mirrored in these essays as well. However, to think together mutual dependency and radical alterity, reciprocity and irreciprocity, justice and the law—all of which characterize the relationship between these binaries—is exactly what any encounter with an other (or Other) will always require us to do.

We might, indeed, have entered an era that forces us to think about space and place in different terms—in terms of a "heter-u-topia" that defies the homotopia the nation-state was so desperate to claim and proclaim. As Michel Foucault (1998, 174) once remarked: "The present age might be the age of space.... We are in an era of the simultaneous, of juxtaposition, of the near and far, of the side by side, of the scattered." The decisive question is how we conceive of the "heter-u-topia" that allows for such a simultaneity of differences to (co)exist. Does it have to be a threatening one in which we lose our moorings and orientation? Does it have to be a geographical space/place? As Anne Dufourmantelle suggests in her contribution to this book, neither possibility is a necessity, since one of the very spaces in which such an encounter takes place "is the space of thinking itself. To think is to invite, to offer a shelter to the other, within ourselves; the other as the possibility to be(come) yourself." This, as she correctly points out, is partly due to the fact that "the first condition of humanity is exile," and that we are thus forced to engage with the other—for better or worse—in order to become full human beings at all. That such an engagement might be either threatening or exhilarating, and create both fear and potential, may not be more than a scholastic *aperçu*; the latter one, however, is all too often forgotten, which, in turn, leaves us with what Levinas (1986, 346) has called the "allergic reaction toward the Other." This also has repercussions on the lively discussion about recognition that, in my view, still fails to sufficiently take into account the very *paradoxon* at the heart of recognition: that it always has to come from another, or even an Other in the Levinasian sense, and that it consequently also entails "other" forms and mechanisms of recognition. This fact enormously problematizes the entire dynamics of recognition, but if alterity is not accounted for in all facets of social life—not as a concept, but as the arché-experience of sociality—we will never get a grip on the "social" as such. In fact, I would venture to say that only thinking that conceives of itself as such an opening up toward the new, the unknown, the incalculable, and alterity as such deserves to be called thus. Such thinking, then, would indeed constitute a kind of promise: the promise, in Dufourmantelle's (Derrida and Dufourmantelle 2000, 32) words, of "giving place to the place," the place in which we might receive the other/Other.

Thinking as such is then a form of transcendence—but what is it that we transcend? Does the negotiation of different particulars in the light of a "solution" imply a peaceful realm of the third that escapes the meshes of singularities? Or one that forces incompatible and irreducible singularities under a sameness that blots out their very singularity? If culture and its manifestations show us anything, it is that, more often than not, the latter is the case, and that we, as I suggest in my own contribution, might have to rethink the entire (rather static) concept of transcendence as a processual transcend*ant*—or even a limping transcen-*dance*—that, finally acknowledged as transcen*différance*, still provides a space/place for singularities to be exposed to each other in the sense that Jean-Luc Nancy gives to the term in *The Inoperative Community*.

Perceived as such, it comes close to the place and the transcendence that Luce Irigaray refers to in her essay "Toward a Mutual Hospitality." The space she asks us to envisage is a "spatial third, which does not belong to one gender or the other but happens through the between two, without it being possible for this third to be appropriated by or to the other gender," and one "beyond the space defined by any culture." Contrary to Levinas, however, Irigaray repeatedly defines the hospitality offered by and within this space as explicitly "reciprocal," which, as I take it, contains echoes of the critique she has voiced against Levinas's gendered "other" (Irigaray 1991) and the highly problematic irecipocity that the gender question "engenders." Consequently, the transcendence she argues for is one "respectful toward our self-affection and shareable by the whole of humanity." The placenta is one physical place she suggests that permits such a coexistence of the one and the other.[3]

In "To Open: Hospitality and Alienation," Pheng Cheah provides a critical juxtaposition of Derrida's radical hospitality with the works of Hannah Arendt and Karl Marx. Arendt, in her insistence on the "right to have rights," also points out that such a right is inextricably connected to a place, as it is having "a place in the world which makes opinions significant and actions"—and, for that matter, having rights—"effective." Cheah distinguishes between a conditional hospitality implicit in the works of Marx and Arendt that allows the host and the guest to return from their mutual encounter unscathed and to reenter a sphere of what is "proper" to each one—such hospitality always being "limited and conditioned by this proper"—and a "deconstructive idea of hospitality so radical . . . that it breaks away from this schema of the proper and envisions an improper hospitality where the opening is that of the human host's structural vulnerability to a non-human other instead of a power that co-belongs with humanity." If we, however, envisage a hospitality open to whomever or even whatever may come, Cheah reminds us that, in a globalized market economy, we consequently would also have to take into account what he calls a "primal scene" of hospitality—that of "capital flows," which precedes the secondary one of the people.

Another conceivable, "primal" scene of hospitality is evoked by Thomas Hylland Eriksen in "Frictions of Hospitality and the Promise of Cosmopolitanism." While Derrida's notion of an unconditional (and irreciprocal) hospitality asks us to welcome the other without "the question," without the requirement to identify him/her/itself, Eriksen, who conceives of hospitality as strictly reciprocal (though he distinguishes between a "balanced" and a "generalized" reciprocity), insists on the fact that *not* asking anything of the guest might also be experienced by the latter as an act of inhospitality, since a "lack of interest in one's guests may in fact be a more serious impediment to integration than is commonly assumed." What we have almost forgotten in the post-9/11 times of burning *banlieues* and the alleged clash of civilizations is that the guest—any guest—that appears at our (or any) door is always also an offer. Moreover, what Eriksen's discussion of the "primal scene" of hospitality—be it the offering of a glass of water or a cup of coffee—points to is the fact that, far from being a demand that potentially surpasses all the facilities available to the host, an ethics of hospitality actually can manifest itself (to rephrase another famous term of Hannah Arendt) in a certain "banality of goodness" embodied in the simple offer of a glass of water.

If such an act might be "banal," it is also always a political act—even more so in a time when "harboring unwanted elements" is turned into a crime.[4] In her essay "Proximity and Paradox: Law and Politics in the New Europe," Bonnie Honig takes issue with Seyla Benhabib's insistence on a highly formalized cosmopolitanism based upon presumably universal values, as such an approach "insulate[s] us from the urgencies of contingency and contiguity out of which solidaristic progressive politics often arise." The experience of "contingency and contiguity"—which might safely be called the hallmark of modernity as such—forces us to rethink universalism (as one instance of a transcendence that has become highly problematic), and consequently also what Benhabib has called "democratic iterations." Such iterations only avoid becoming liturgical repetitions if we define democracy, as Derrida has urged us to do, as always "to come"; that is, as an event that actually might force us to radically rethink what we sometimes consider "achieved" democratic structures.[5]

What is asked for, in Honig's view, is a politics of the "double gesture," one that acknowledges the very paradox and aporia between a structured, conditional hospitality and the eventfulness of the singular encounter with the Other, which a pure, universal formalism does not offer a place for.

That Europe, as Benhabib has repeatedly suggested, might be the exemplary "theater" in which universal norms engender tangible politics, is a result of an optimism that might be misplaced, as Etienne Balibar (2003)[6] has pointed out repeatedly, and as Ulrik Pram Gad's case study of the political debate surrounding ICORN in Denmark confirms. Gad rightly insists that utopian dreams about achieving a radical hospitality alone will not do, and that we "have to make ourselves familiar with the strategic terrain we intend to intervene in" in order to arrive at the "concrete politics and ethics of hospitality" that Derrida himself called for in *On Hospitality*. However, a closer look at just such a concrete strategic terrain as provided by said debate leads one on quicksand. What we find there might also be termed a politics of the "double structure," but most probably not the one Honig has in mind: a double standard—and here Denmark certainly is not an exceptional case—in which, with a self-righteousness bordering on cynicism, a state offers "refuge" to writers who "write or in other ways express themselves about something that is not accepted where they live," just to make sure that these writers sign an agreement that basically asks the same of them in the hosting country. If Gad's essay makes one thing clear, it is that the experience of contingency and contiguity is not something that pertains to the arrival of the guest or immigrant exclusively: It can be found in any kind of politics right at home.

As Mireille Rosello's contribution "Conviviality and Pilgrimage: Hospitality as Interruptive Practice" shows, however, it usually takes a "place outside" one's own comfort zone to actually learn how to reassess the very borderlines of this zone. Reading Paul Gilroy's (2004) concept of "conviviality"—as developed in his book *After Empire*—against Coline Serreau's wonderful 2005 movie *Saint-Jacques la Mecque*, Rosello asks the question: "Would it not be more productive to look for what exactly, in our thinking about hospitality, emphasizes practices rather than identities?" Pursuing this direction in her analysis of Gilroy and Serreau, it becomes apparent that what Gayatri Spivak (1988, 289) has called the "romanticization of the other" leads a problematic and complicated, but sometimes also comic coexistence, with the rather noisy and messy state of neighborliness. Not unlike the banality of a glass of water offered to the stranger, Gilroy's "conviviality" also entails "a liberating sense of the banality of intermixture and the subversive ordinariness of . . . convivial culture in which 'race' is stripped of meaning and racism." Rosello's definition of conviviality as "a hospitality based on togetherness rather than sameness or belonging" brings to the fore once again a concept of space not yet saturated by notions of sameness or what we share.

Tropologically speaking, one could define such a space (and the community within it)—in which contingency and contiguity characterize the relationship between its parts—as metonymical, in contrast to a place and a community conceived of as metaphorical, that is, defined by an essential and shared "third" that connects its parts. Consequently, conviviality is not a given, but an arduous process, an "exception that results from a long and difficult learning process. Convivial practices interrupt the norm."[7]

No such thing as conviviality can evolve if the (segre)gated places to which we confine both ourselves and the other harden into the front lines between ghettoes. In his essay "Hospitality and the Zombification of the Other," Nikos Papastergiadis shows that we have moved beyond the concept of the "proper" in the sense that Cheah uses it. The so-called "guest workers" that came to Western European cities in the '60s, '70s, and '80s were, according to Papastergiadis, described with the metaphor of the "cog in the machine"—denoting "the general form of alienation under capitalism." Today, the youths peopling the ghettoes known in France as *banlieues* (a term that, etymologically speaking, evokes both neighborhood or quarter as it does "fringed" or "banned" areas) have taken on the spectral identity of "mad dogs," since they do not even represent "object[s] for use and exploitation" anymore, but have acquired the (non)qualities of "a redundant and purposeless thing." Not having left anything "proper" to them—not even the "purpose" and propriety of the exploited "cog in the machine"—they are left outside any social contract and haunt the precincts of their host nation as "zombies," a scenario taken up and aesthetically gauged more than seventy years ago in Richard Wright's powerful novel *Native Son*. Taking up Giorgio Agamben's notion of the *homo sacer*, Papastergiadis argues that, although there might be some parallels between the *banlieues* and the camps, which, for Agamben, constitute the (if extreme) paradigm of modern existence in an era of biopolitics, only a politics of translation can help us to get out of this stalemate. To "translate" a (mostly second) generation of immigrants into an anonymous mass of spectral zombies will turn out to be a self-fulfilling prophecy—a prophecy that, if it turns into reality, will not leave us much time to celebrate that we have been correct.

Europe, translation, and the relationship of both to hospitality is also the subject of the final essay, Paola Zaccaria's "The Art and Poetics of Translation as Hospitality." Sparked by the experience of the inhospitable welcome extended to refugees from Albania in the harbor of Bari in 1991—a scenario, however, that has repeated itself endlessly on the shores of the Mediterranean—Zaccaria claims that any act of translation as such always constitutes (or at least should constitute) an "act of hospitality." The limits of a "hospitable translation," however, become evident when we have a look at the term used for the "holding centers" that the refugees were cooped into under the burning, South Italian sun: The name *Centri di Permanenza Temporanea*—even if we take into account that *permanenza* in Italian simply means "stay"—unwittingly dramatizes the fact that "staying somewhere" and "permanence" have become hopelessly disentangled in a globalized world.

Translated literally, "temporary permanence" might actually capture the paradoxical form of our spatial existence in and experience of such a world. To conceive of such places as "centers," moreover, might just add a dose of supplemental irony—or uncanniness, if read against Agamben's camp.

If, as Zaccaria claims, there is, in the case of translation, a "promise and exhilaration in letting oneself be touched by these brave new wor(l)ds," one has to keep in mind that this touch might take diverse, and sometimes threatening and belligerent turns. However, to use such eventualities in order to raise the popular question "what if the other turns out to be a Trojan Horse" and to categorically subject any other to a general suspicion (in order to retain the right to identify him or her), one should remind oneself that said Trojan Horse was a product of a war. If we take that metaphor, in a Hobbesian way, to define all of our (co)existence, we do not even need to take into account any form of "unconditional" or "radical" hospitality.[8]

One would think, however, that we have progressed beyond that. This insight is neatly summed up in the following quote of Zaccaria: "The declaration of the impossibility of an absolute hospitality which gives shape to the aporia of conditional/unconditional hospitality excludes any possibility to devise new models of living together through hospitality, because the assumption of ownership of and belonging to a house-space-land-country—however tolerant or hos(ti)pitable it might be—will forever maintain the newcomer in a position of distance." This turns out to be another self-fulfilling prophecy, which boils down to the rather banal implicit assumption that my neighbor may turn out to be a monster (as Slavoj Žižek wants to convince us), but at least I knew he/she/it would . . .

Taken together, the essays collected here resonate richly with each other in a productive and dialogic way, and since the aporia at the heart of the paradoxical character of hospitality, as defined by Levinas and Derrida, cannot be solved, and will not go away so as not to bother us anymore, a fruitful and open dialogue—and, as Dufourmantelle reminds us, thinking as such—is one of the places where this aporia can "take place."

The Ethics of Hospitality

Hospitality—Under Compassion and Violence

ANNE DUFOURMANTELLE

I

Hospitality has become the gateway to hell. I am aware that this might sound hyperbolic—I do, however, mean it seriously. One could picture Cerberus, in the antique representations of hell, guarding the entry to the netherworld, or Horus, in Egyptian mythology, weighing the good and bad actions as they are presented to him by those newly arrived, as figures of radical hospitality, since they are the ones that separate the living from the dead. In the face of today's political rules, hospitality is not an invitation for a better life—at most, it offers a shelter—but a fully armed technological gate, serving as a limit and a threshold: "Here the civilized world begins: *no trespassing*!" Hence, hospitality is no longer a private gesture but an issue for a whole society anxious to close its frontiers to illegal immigrants and refugees, the solicitants of this world. Questioning ourselves on the conditions of hospitality has never been more important. But before I continue to inquire further into a possible interpretation of these conditions, I would like to recall how Derrida forever opened the *question* of hospitality.

Before becoming a thought or an idea, hospitality is an experience, a pure event. "Come in and be in my home as if it were yours; be my guest, you whom I don't know." Can hospitality, like forgiveness, be offered to the other unconditionally? Hospitality describes a figure, a space that allows a gesture of invitation to take place. That is, I believe, the space of thinking itself. To think is to invite, to offer a shelter to the other within ourselves, the other as the possibility to be(come) ourselves. As the experience of an encounter and a recognition, hospitality is present both in the Hellenic world and the Hebraic one. It holds together, as separated, the profane and the sacred. As such, it could take the figure of a *theoxenie* (visitation of a god in a house of mortals). Inhospitality to a god was severely punished. This is how the idea of hospitality as sacred gesture originates, the hosted guest being the mediator between two divided spheres, the one that allows a community to grow, coming both as a threat and as a gift. But the threshold has turned out to be an unnamed void for us, haunted subjects who, unlike the Hellenic hero or the Cartesian subject, do not belong to the realm of an ordered space anymore, but are condemned to seek in a much darker night the possibility of a relation to the other, without a guarantee that the hospitality we are called upon to give has a sense anymore.

Hospitality, in its essence, is unconditional, contrary to all other forms of human society that depend on conditions—laws. Derrida was the first to urge us to reconsider this unresolved tension between unconditional hospitality and the conditions imposed upon the act of hospitality.

Why is it that the law of unconditional hospitality arose in almost all primitive societies? Doubtlessly because one of the laws that built all civilization is the incest taboo, which means, as Lévi-Strauss has demonstrated so lucidly, that a society functioning in an endogamic way is doomed. The acceptance of the other to the point of the dissolution of self-enclosed tribes or groups—of which the hospitality to a stranger is an integral part—is in that sense the condition of the survival of all human societies. This immemorial law of hospitality also reminds us that the first condition of humanity is exile. The first human societies were nomadic, a state in which the human being leads a displaced, fragile existence. It was only much later that sedentary cultures and lifestyles evolved. The rule of unconditional hospitality may well concretely remind us of the fact that the one who takes in, the host, may well be, from one day to another, cast on the road and in need of refuge him- or herself. In nomadic cultures, people came and went; they did not mean to stay. The main problem was not one of immigration, but of translation. When we refer to "primitive" rules of hospitality, we are not speaking about charity or condescendence; to give bread to the poor is not offering hospitality. Such was the unwritten rule: that the foreigner be received and honored like a king. This primordial directive invokes something similar to the Bakhtinian carnivalesque, as the poor and needy can turn into masters, and even prevail, if temporarily, over the latter. In this sense, one could call the act of hospitality the first political act.

The etymological, Latin roots of the word suggest that much: *hostis* comprises both the "inviting" master and the "invited" guest. However, it has also developed into "hostility" and the enemy. Thus host and hostility have a common root in our language—the host is de facto always a potential enemy. Derrida (1998) coined the term *hosti-pitalité* to capture this ambivalence. The foreigner excites the fantasy as one who might come in order to dispose of you or of your property, or to seduce you. Derrida (2001a, 7) compared the question of unconditional hospitality to the one of parricide: The father is the host of the house, while the foreigner, from the moment the door is opened to him, enjoys all rights—even the right to take the master's place (many fears nowadays dealing with the actual question of illegal immigration can be related to this question). I want to point out that unconditional hospitality is an obligation to welcome the other without asking him anything: neither about his identity nor where he comes from or where he lives. Derrida shows very convincingly that this law of "unconditional hospitality" cannot be turned into a policy, because as such it would be utterly radical. No economy can be reasonably deduced from it, since unconditional hospitality radically subverts the rules of a social tissue based upon exchange and reciprocity (i.e., a certain symmetry/reciprocity): I invite you, and in exchange I expect you to offer at least your identity and your origin of birth; then let us see what other exchanges we might engage in.

The occidental economic society based on exchange was pressured to reorganize the rules of hospitality. All public places that arose in Europe from the fourteenth century on (churches, hospitals, etc.) started to reconsider the rules of hospitality. What would be the minimum information required from a poor person, a refugee, someone wounded? Thus, the intrusion of the foreigner into the "home"—which figures so strongly in the process of unconditional hospitality—would be subjected to certain conditions, rules pertaining to the concept of hospitality: Whom are we going to open our door to, and under what circumstances? How can the one hosting a foreigner protect himself against the violation of his home, or even violence as such? It was these questions that instigated the moral reflections of Kant as well as of Diderot and the Encyclopedists. At a time of massive colonial conquests, what hospitality could or should be offered the "savage," the stranger arriving with his or her own unfamiliar codes and culture? What right do we have to ask strangers to abandon their rules and adopt ours?

When unconditional hospitality turns into civil law—with its own rules, rights, and duties—it creates a common space. But does asking the other to come toward us into a common space not already constitute a sort of violence? Can this still be called *hospitality*? It is of eminent importance to be able to conceptualize the consequences of such violence, since it is here that the question of space—thought of as common achievement, as architecture and language—emerges.

To resort to the image of the house, it takes walls not only to build a protection, but also to imagine a "containing space" (for oneself and the other) and openings (doors, windows) between the inside and the outside. Violence too often results from our inability to recognize the so-called "otherness" of the "other" as in fact very close to us: a part of ourselves. Someone personally invited into a space where not even a moment of recognition (nor language, nor identity, nor mutual understanding) is offered, might be tempted to commit an act of violence, as the welcome manifests itself as violence. Hospitality is not a *mise en demeure* (cf. Derrida, 1998).

II

Hospitality has become the gateway to barbarism; how could this happen? Hospitality has been at the roots of all primitive human societies, because you could immediately become the very stranger that you opened your door to: The condition of exile could easily revert at an instant. The minute this is lost sight of—the minute we assume that we are the ones who belong, while the other does not, because he or she is "the other," the stranger, the one who asks (for citizenship, protection, work, recognition, etc.), a power game sets in, in which hospitality becomes something that one can choose to offer or withhold—a worthless card in a dovetailed game. The gateway to hell begins when hospitality turns into a question of who deserves and who does not. To whom will we extend our pity, our acknowledgment—or, for that matter, our contempt? Hospitality simply becomes another item in an arsenal that the host commands—no return expected.

The problem might be that hospitality actually denotes an almost mystical experience, a borderline concept that only Derrida has come close to when thinking about humankind approaching its "other." Not even Levinas realized that in order to assume the responsibility for the other, I will have to confront her in my world, and what such a "revolution" entails. In our social economy, where possessions and belongings have come to constitute an ethics of their own, the danger of having everything taken away from you is just unbearable, and the act is considered criminal—especially when that comprises our "place," our "right" to have a home. So we suppose we have a "right to belong" somewhere, somehow. But have we not forgotten, in that process, that only someone who has not forgotten that he or she is a dweller—and thus, potentially, a host—can genuinely "belong"? That there is not such "right" if you do not grant it to hospitality first?

Hospitality, then, is an experience rather than a concept. Levinas wrote that he preferred the term *épreuve* to "experience," because the former (which means "test") implies both the idea of life and its critical verification, something that overwhelms the self by challenging its endurance (Malka 1984, 108). He opts for a kind of trial: a test site in which the self is placed at absolute risk. The call for "verification"—the provisional character of which is betrayed by its quotation mark—indicates a life submitted to incessant probation and perpetual revision.

There are two events—or, rather, two experiences—that, as subjects (egos), we cannot "think" completely: our birth and our death. If at all, we can only conceptualize them as general, but certainly not as personal, human experiences. Our birth in fact constitutes the first act of hospitality—offered to, not by, us—and not a psychological, but an ontological, existential problem: We come from a mother's womb, we begin our beings as cells splitting and growing, until we finally part, indeed "disassemble" ourselves from another human being who has nourished and (preferably) loved us, but at least carried us long enough to be born.

In this special case, hospitality actually is the precondition to life. Usually, the body does not accept any form of unrecognized otherness; as such, the latter constitutes a threat to the organism to be fought and destroyed. A baby, on the contrary, is a result of a process of differentiation that has made him or her an other. However, right from the beginning, death looms, and if hospitality is about a threshold, an act of trespassing, death makes us aware that our finitude confines us to the status of visitors here on earth—a status that, in turn, forms the precondition for hospitality as such. Hospitality, consequently, is rooted in the experience of death, of letting go, of abandoning everything you have loved, acquired, and imagined. Hospitality, then, is by necessity based upon the exilic condition of humankind as such and relates to the possibility of death and the experience of mourning, which offers hospitality to the dead, their language, and their memory. In every so-called "primitive" culture, offering burial to the dead bodies and hospitality to the stranger were among the most important rules shared by the living.

Our world no longer believes in eternal life but in endlessly repeated moments of (indefinite) survival, as it believes in endlessly repeated moments of betrayal. Our world can no longer accept death as the final mystery of the world, the ultimate liberation, as it no longer can consider death a proof of extreme love. It can only consume the product of death; it has no other option than to betray it. It cannot take it for that which friendship respects, simultaneously surpasses, and finally transcends. Our world has become the merchant of death.

The question of the border, the limit, the threshold, the step beyond the limit, recurs ever so often in Derrida's language, as if the impossibility of marking out a stable territory where thought could be established constitutes a provocation to thought itself. In order to "offer hospitality," he wonders,

> is it necessary to start from the certain existence of a dwelling, or is it rather only starting from the dislocation of the shelterless, the homeless, that the authenticity of hospitality can open up? Perhaps only the one who endures the experience of being deprived of a home can offer hospitality. (Derrida and Dufourmantelle 2000, 56)

According to the Czech philosopher Jan Patočka,

> man enters into amplitude upon submitting to the fascination of the limits that press upon our lives. He is compelled to confront these limits to the extent that he aspires to truth. He who seeks truth cannot allow himself . . . to be lulled by the quietude of everyday harmony; he must allow to grow within himself the disturbing, the unreconciled, the enigmatic, that from which ordinary life turns away in order to deal with the order of the day. (Patočka 1990, 36)

Night for Patočka is "the opening onto what disturbs." (Patočka 1983, 59). It asks us to traverse the experience of the loss of meaning, an experience that engenders the authenticity of philosophical thinking. If we take into account Patočka's reflection on his experiences at the front lines in World War I, these might seem impossibly far removed from any concept of hospitality, as war is prone to aggravate distinctions into binary oppositions. However, in this night-experience on the front, the adversary is no longer the same, he is "our accomplice in the disturbance of the day. So here is what the abyssal domain of prayer for the enemy opens to us: the solidarity of the shaken." (Patočka 1996, 131). To die so that a truth of the questioning of meaning may survive, and not elevate that act to the arrogance of a response, is to accord night its reality, the opposite of an abdication.

The condition of our native exile is our inability to have a land of one's own. The "night" of hospitality—according to Patočka, the question of the "nonplace," of an impossible dwelling—makes sense only if the act of hospitality "belongs" neither to the host nor to the guest, but to the gesture by which one of them welcomes the other.

This is why the distinction between unconditional hospitality and the laws of hospitality is quintessential, for unconditional hospitality threatens a society that has chosen transparency as a method to totalize power through fragmenting responsibility. The question that the foreigner poses to us resounds in "utopia," in the Greek sense of the *a-topos*, the nonplace, prophetically conceived by Thomas More, which nowadays would designate the "out of place" from which the question of hospitality is (im)posed on us. However, nowadays *homo politicus* strikes a note of sovereign insolence, to the extent that our culture relegates the political entirely to theatrical effect; there exist only a few people who—by virtue or by the power conferred onto them by others—are intent to rein in or even suspend economic processes by means of values that are not measurable. But has not the madness of political utopia wreaked enough havoc in the twentieth century for us to beware of our economic future? In fact, by turning into ideology, utopia has acquired a language linking it to the implacable logic of economic "efficiency," which it once was designed to counter. Utopias from Marxism to fascism that are inscribed in the reality of a place, a country, a power, collapse at the very core, transfixed by a nostalgia for a timeless fixity they assume, indeed presuppose, to work at all. Right in our face, the political has disintegrated into the subtle coils of economic efficiency, extinguishing its traces behind it.

Today, starting from that radical unfamiliarity of language and death in a foreign land, as both Derrida and Levinas evoke them, should we not rightfully expect from political utopia a "placelessness" which opens the possibility of a human (cosmo)polis? A utopia that has become audible nowadays because it acknowledges the other, that unexpected and always disturbing guest that might well constitute one of the spectral appearances of our times. If "creating time" is equivalent, in Hebrew, to "invitation," what does it mean that, in order to produce time, there have to be two? Does that not indicate that there has to be some kind of otherness, an intrusion of a genuine other into the "normal," mathematical time frame that does not allow for time to be "created"—let alone by some "other"? The future—the not-yet, not-here—is given to us as that which comes to us from the other, from what is absolutely surprising, new, incalculable—untimely.

Hospitality confronts us with the difficulty of thinking about radical otherness and of welcoming it. Does it begin, Derrida wonders,

> with the unquestioning welcome, in a double effacement, the effacement of the question *and* the name? Is it more just and more loving to question or not to question? to call by the name or without the name? to give or to learn a name already given? Does one give hospitality to a subject? to an identifiable subject? to a legal subject? Or is hospitality *rendered*, is it *given* to the other before they are identified, even before they are (posited as or supposed to be) a subject, legal

Hospitality—Under Compassion and Violence ▪ 19

subject, and subject nameable by their family name, etc.? (Derrida and Dufourmantelle 2000, 29)

"The question of hospitality thus is the question of the question," Derrida concludes, and he adds:

> We have alluded to this: the difference, one of the subtle and sometimes ungraspable differences between the foreigner and the absolute other is that the latter cannot have a name or a family name; the absolute or unconditional hospitality I would like to offer him or her presupposes a break with hospitality in the ordinary sense, with conditional hospitality, with the right to or pact of hospitality. In saying this, once more, we are taking account of an irreducible pervertibility. The law of hospitality [but we might as well say the conditions of hospitality], the express law that governs the general concept of hospitality appears a paradoxical law, pervertible or perverting. It seems to dictate that absolute hospitality should break with the law of hospitality as right or duty, with the "pact" of hospitality. To put it in different terms, absolute hospitality requires that I open up my home and that I give not only to the foreigner (provided with a family name, with the social status of being a foreigner, etc.), but to the absolute, unknown, anonymous other, and that I give place to them, that I let them come, that I let them arrive and take place in the place I offer them, without asking of them either reciprocity (entering into a pact) or even their names. The law of absolute hospitality commands a break with hospitality by right, with law of justice as rights. Just hospitality breaks with hospitality by right; not that it condemns or is opposed to it, and it can on the contrary set and maintain it in a perpetual progressive moment; but it is as strangely heterogeneous to it as justice is heterogeneous to the law to which it is yet so close, from which in truth it is indissociable. (25–27)

III

So what happens when our eyes rest on these words: hospitality, proximity, enclave, hate, foreigner? Even if we may for an instant find some "elsewhere" in them, they are soon assimilated into a landscape marked by the seal of our habitus of thinking and memorizing, provoking a fear caused by our incursion into an unknown place whose strangeness freezes us stiff before we get used to it step by step. Is the anguish that it provokes enough to keep us alive—in other words, to prevent us from getting accustomed (which, not surprisingly, shares etymological roots with the border patrol known as "customs")? Is it really possible to speak of alterity, let alone to think it, without the thought being instantly put to a test? Usually it is not; usually, it screens "the other" (the guest) and then moves on to examine another question. However, sometimes—and Levinas was very much aware of this—thinking allows itself to loosen its bearings. One of the terms to designate this "being at loss" philosophically is "astonishment," or, actually, philosophy itself. But it is this very astonishment that Derrida urges us to think—and not only to rethink something we are already familiar with.

Our anxiety grows out of the questions: What/who is the foreigner? What does he/she/it mean? Where do you come from; where are you going? What are your intentions? What is it you want from me? The foreigner, indeed, does not pose the question—he/she/it is the question—a question that begs my response and my responsibility. How to respond to, and thus be responsible for, them? Respond to a question that actually comprises a demand, many demands, and even prayers? In what language can the foreigner address his or her question? Receive our response and responsibility?

Speaking about language, about what Derrida has shown us, and about pervertibility, I want to point out that in French the word "question" also means "torture." To "pose a question" and to "put somebody into question" (*soumettre quelqu'un à la question*)—as when you torture someone—are thus closely related. The extent to which the sublimated scenes of torture have left traces in the way we arrange our practices and institutions with regard to "truth" thus also "begs the question"—maybe a tortuous one.

Testing traverses the experience of hospitality when it comes to determining the laws and conditions of hospitality. Still, a history of lacerated disclosure begins with the Greek notion of *basanos*, relating truth to torture, as Avital Ronell reminds us (cf. Ronell 2005). Slaves would be tortured in order to disclose the truth (e.g., about the plans that their masters entertained), since the masters themselves—being free persons—could not be subjected to such torture "testing." If we can agree that murder and hate designate everything that excludes closeness, it is insofar as they ravage an original relationship to alterity. The *hostis* responds to hospitality in the way that the ghost recalls itself to the living—by not allowing them to forget. To the pacified reason of Kant, Derrida (cf. Derrida and and Dufourmantelle 2000, 4) opposes the primary haunting of a subject prevented by alterity from closing itself off peacefully. On the contrary, we have two regions in which "we rediscover the open question of the relationship between hospitality . . . beginning with the name, the question of the name, or else opening up without questions . . ." (12). It is this "giving place to the place" that constitutes a promise to be kept. It makes us realize that the question of hospitality is a fundamental question, founding the history of our culture, of thinking proper but, as yet, still remains unthought itself. Once we realize that the subject—every single one of "us"—is bound by the unconditional law of hospitality to "the other" before we can claim whatever "right" for ourselves, we are consenting to an existential exile, in other words, a relationship, a place, a dwelling, which is both native (I almost daresay maternal), but never complete. It would allow us to think the subject—indeed and foremost, ourselves—first of all as a guest, even in our own home.

It is only when I meet and recognize the other as preceding me and my knowledge that the possibility of true hospitality emerges: hospitality as joy.[1] For Levinas, the other is revealed precisely by his otherness, not as a negative impact to the self, but as the phenomenon of "kindness." This other, who might be the agent of the utmost violence—who, if he chooses to, can kill me, destroy me, alienate me—how am I to welcome him without reserve? The transcendent quality of hospitality (neither religious nor purely political) constitutes this point where the other impacts our inner selves, urging us to give shelter to the other within our self. The other as the possibility to be(come) oneself is, since the Freudian revolution, a pact with a possible insanity within. Foucault has, in his own way, analyzed how the way society treated and relegated the "insane" reveals its relation to the necessity of repression and censorship in general. What is at stake here is the very question of hospitality extending beyond madness to the disorders of "otherness."

The situation has never been more threatening than today. The way mentally disordered people are treated today in psychiatric hospitals (a space that, alas, only etymology relates to hospitality, engulfed in a medicated silence) is the signature of our oblivion, of our denial, of our collective forgetting that madness is the question that we, haunted subjects of desire, want to elude as a frightening guest, or spectral guest, maybe returning to us from a traumatic past. Wilfred Bion, the brilliant English psychiatrist who nearly died in 1917 in the Battle of the Somme, spent his life taking care of the insane and of traumas caused by the war and wrote about them. For him, thinking is a machine for swallowing wild thoughts, thoughts that present themselves to the intellect. And in this intimate struggle between madness and thought, it is wild thought that wins. But it wins in secret; it takes refuge in folded papers, twisted words, dreams, stammerings emanating from the memory of death. It is a childhood language that suddenly reappears. In this sense, in Bion's view, "wild thoughts," thoughts without a thinker, have indeed something to do with hospitality to madness, for they submerge our patiently consolidated beliefs.

If to philosophize is also to learn to die, then night makes room, in our ever-so-"diurnal" world, for the memory of those dead souls that come back to us with their language and their history, with barbarism, suffering, wars, alliances, and betrayals, when one suddenly hears the echo of their voices come to free us a little of the burden weighing down our souls. What is transmitted in them is a secret order to make way for a hospitality toward the traumatic eras of our common history.

Hospitality is a *kairos*: the instant of grace or the right moment. Nothing can be elevated to the power of the idea but the idea itself. Thinking philosophically about hospitality, there can be no slippage from one subject to another, from one utterance to another: The philosopher has to stay aware. Today, we no longer believe in the enchantments so well staged by Nietzsche. We organize mystifications; we build the future chambers where we will be spellbound. Between enchantments and spells, there is the crypt: the vaulted chamber from which no one exits, the place where the body is enclosed. Here there is no trespassing, and the possibility of hospitality is only the realm of compassion for what is already lost or at loss, that is the recognition of the other as such. Hospitality begins when the subject is not imprisoned by his own echo anymore, just someone who is there, a guest presenting itself in that indefinite space of the present that is the space of every true event. An event is an encounter that has an infinitesimal likelihood of occurring but that takes place nevertheless. It does nothing but express this, the opening of the present to the unhoped-for, to the "over-and-above," or to what one would still like to call grace. If philosophy has resolved—with the help of Wittgenstein in particular—to seek in language itself the conditions of possibility of conceptualizing the world, in that language it has encountered the unsayable, the untranscribable, the pure signifier, as Lacan would say—that is, a place for the Other.

Hospitality under compassion and violence—that is to say, hospitality under the violence of radical ethics, caused by radical (com)passion—is unconditional hospitality. Only then, and at this price, are we able to think about the rules of hospitality.

Transcending Transcendence, or: Transcend*ifferances*
Limping toward a Radical Concept of Hospitality

THOMAS CLAVIEZ

I

Transcendence has recently come under attack. It has come under suspicion in the entire debate about our globalized world, in theoretical discussions about cosmopolitanism, and in political manifestos that debate how to deal with the global village we have perceived our planet to be. And in a village, as is well known, everybody is each other's neighbor.

In both the theoretical discussions and the political debates, what gives rise to said suspicions is that transcendence somehow seems to team up with universalism, whose imperial implications and effects have been scrutinized to an extent that makes it unnecessary to lay them out in detail. What causes this alleged connection between transcendence and universalism is that both, if in different ways, move beyond—transcendence designating just such a moving beyond—the local, the singular, the historically contingent. The last philosophical attempt to try to keep these two strands dialectically woven together has arguably been Hegel's. His goal to safeguard reason from the ethereal timelessness it inhabits in Kant's thought and to tie it to history unfolding is, however, bought at the price of projecting some unifying, transcendent teleology to prevent it from being swallowed up in the particularities of history, to avoid it being entirely subjugated to the microscopic forces of the daily, the political, or what Kant would have called the realm of the anthropological.

The allergic reaction of theory against universalism and transcendence, however, has not been fed by political considerations alone: the *locus classicus* being Marx's insistence not to explain the world, but to change it. It also has been tackled on its home turf by a philosophical trajectory that we all are familiar with, one stretching via the landmarks of Nietzsche and Heidegger, and then bifurcating into either the American variety of pragmatism or the European forms of poststructural thinking.

The premonitions voiced by either of these strands can be roughly classified as follows: While poststructuralism has tried to deconstruct the axioms and premises of the (phal)logocentrics of Enlightenment—though still holding on to an ever so precarious strategy or remnant of emancipation and a (transcendent?) alternative to reason as transcendence—American pragmatism has advised philosophy to completely give up even on such a minimalist strategy, to rid itself from such idealistic remnants, and to acknowledge and tackle a reality that is not unfolding along the teleological lines of Hegelianism. The debate between Richard Rorty and Jacques Derrida might serve as an example here;[1] its relevance for our purposes lies in the fact that Rorty openly admits that doing away with any claims toward transcendence leads to a form of ethnocentrism—an ethnocentrism, however, unaffected by the bad conscience the term might induce, happily but modestly acknowledging and endorsing its own limits: parochialism rehabilitated.[2]

In view of the problems facing the Western world and its metaphysical foundation, this in fact seems, at first sight, not only a feasible, but even a recommendable, strategy to pursue. Purged of any kind of aspiration to go, look, or see beyond, uninhibited by restraints of bad conscience or even, famously, of logical consistency (the latter being the "hobgoblin of little minds," as Emerson [2007, 141] so famously put it), our forces and wo/manpower can be dedicated to managing the urgent, the practical, the contingent—which undoubtedly would be enough to keep us busy. But what, then, does transcendence mean, and why exactly has it fallen into disrepute? Could we simply do away with it, or might we be able to—dare I say—transcend it? Can one transcend transcendence without giving way to a jolly celebration of inconsistency? Or aporia? Does one follow from the other? What is the price of either dumping transcendence, or transcending it? These are some of the questions I would like to address in conjunction with what has been considered the radicalism, if not hyperbole, of the ethics of hospitality as they have been outlined by Jacques Derrida and Emmanuel Levinas.

II

In order to do so, let me offer some working definitions in order to clarify what we are talking about when we discuss transcendence, radicalism, and hyperbole.

Let us define transcendence as that which goes beyond the given, beyond the status quo of certainties, assumptions, and interpretations of what is. Let us call radicalism the political implications that the claim to transcendence—if to different degrees—carries with it; to call a philosophy radical is not a philosophical, but always a political, statement. Let us, finally, call hyperbole the rhetorical figure in which the politically radical implications of some form of philosophical transcendence find their expression.

Let us furthermore assume that transcendence has both a descriptive and a normative aspect to it. Although these two are notoriously difficult to keep apart, they cannot be completely disentangled. One of the recent philosophical attempts to do so might be Lyotard's philosophy of language regimes, which, in the final instance, results paradoxically in the prescription that prescriptive sentences should be considered and kept apart from other sentence regimes, but that they do not enjoy a special status—an assumption that, as I have shown elsewhere, he shares with Paul de Man.[3] A similarly troubled relationship could be claimed for the political and the philosophical realms, be they viewed as language regimes, discourses, practices, or disciplines. The political, unimbued by any considerations beyond what is, would be reduced to sheer administration, bureaucracy, management, or human engineering—though I am hesitant to even use the term "human" in this connection. Such a Weberian scenario would turn into a Kafkaesque, barren, static, and in the double sense of the word unmoved/unmovable structure. The philosophical, in turn, untouched by any consideration of the pragmatics and practice of the political, would end up as so many metaphysical castles in the air.

Let me follow up on the difference between transcendence as descriptive and normative or even prescriptive. Transcendence can be purely descriptive by claiming that a certain realm transcends a certain other one; this transcendence, moreover, can be either factual or projected. While to call a projected or imagined transcendence descriptive might arouse first objections, let me just add that even if such transcendence transcends the given, it might do so on purely quantitative terms, as embedding the particular in something larger (spatially) and something either to come, something that could have been, or something that will have been. That this is not by definition and default also prescriptive might be ascertained by the existence of the many dystopias that literary and philosophical history provides us with, although one could claim that such dystopias always also transport normative points of view.

III

All of these points are mirrored, accumulated, and merged in what is arguably the most radical—and, by default, hyperbolic—definition of Derridean/Levinasian ethics of hospitality to date. In *Of Hospitality*, Derrida defines what he calls the "categorical imperative of hospitality" (Derrida and Dufourmantelle 2000, 81)—an imperative without an imperative, as he later qualifies—as follows:

> Let us say yes to who or what turns up, before any determination, before any anticipation, before any identification, whether or not it has to do with a foreigner, an immigrant, an invited guest, or an unexpected visitor, whether or not the new arrival is the citizen of another country, a human, an animal, or divine creature, a living or a dead thing, male or female. (77)

It is not by accident that Anne Dufourmantelle's commentaries that accompany this passage turn to the concept of hyperbole exactly at this point. But let us first of all consider how far Derrida can be said to indeed gauge or even transcend certain limits or concepts, as Dufourmantelle claims (80).

He first of all transcends what seems to be the realm of the human proper, and thus seemingly also the realm of the political—though I am not sure whether collapsing so nonchalantly these two categories is legitimate. To include animal and divine creatures (and even dead things!) into the realm of hospitality certainly implies a transcendence of the realm of the human. From an exclusively philosophical point of view, I would argue, this is per se nothing radical. Seen from a political point of view—and from the practical implications that the prescriptive aspect of his transcendence, to which I'll turn below, entails—to enlarge the scope of those to whom or to which hospitality ought to be offered to such a degree would simply appear scandalous. This outcry, however, turns out to be a bit hypocritical, considering the fact that divine and animal creatures, as well as dead things, have played and probably, for some time to come, will play an enormous role in politics, as we all know—all disenchantment of politics turned into bureaucracy, as Max Weber diagnosed it, notwithstanding. Thus we realize that the political is not, and never has been, purely devoted to the realm of the human; it has, in a spectral way, always been inhabited by realms of the nonhuman. In this regard, we might indeed, as Bruno Latour (1993) has argued in his book of the same title, "have never been modern," since

> [n]o one has ever heard of a collective that did not mobilize heaven and earth in its composition, along with bodies and souls, property and law, gods and ancestors, powers and beliefs, beasts and fictional beings. Such is the anthropological matrix, the one we have never left behind. (107)

And he later adds: "It is this exploration of a transcendence without a contrary that makes our world so unmodern, with all those nuncios, mediators, delegates, fetishes, machines, figurines, instruments, representatives, angels, lieutenants, spokespersons and cherubim" (129). While I will not enter into the debate whether we indeed are not (or have never been) modern, I find the connection Latour draws between "a transcendence without a contrary" and the lists of hybridities we allow in our midst quite striking. It points, if nothing else, to the fact that the hyperbole, or the scandal of Derrida's formulation, actually does not lie in the fact that he includes these nonhuman realms—thus transcending the already radical, but still anthropocentric ethics of Levinas, as John Llewelyn has argued.[4] But where, then, does it lie? Does it lie in the political unfeasibility of his prescriptive urge to "say yes" to whoever or whatever turns up? Or in the assumption that this summons asks for more than what could legitimately be asked from a normal human being? Or might it not rather lie in the even more difficult suspicion that a normal being might indeed not be overtaxed by such a demand (the anthropological argument), and that heeding such a call might subvert the very political/national order that wants to retain the sovereignty to decide which nonhuman realms can and should be accommodated within its borders, and which should not? Is Derrida here offering transcendence via what could turn out to be a utopian scenario as well as a dystopian one? Or, as one colleague so succinctly put it when I presented this radical concept of hospitality in another context: "What if the animal that is admitted inside the walls of the polis turns out to be a Trojan Horse?" Or the dead body of a martyr that might instigate rebellion? What if the divine creature we allowed in proved to be a God of War? And what can all of that tell us about a possible "contrary" to transcendence?

Some of the objections mustered against such Derridean hyperbole certainly bear validity; they refer to the integrity of the state, which indeed might be threatened by the unconditional and indiscriminate welcoming of animal, divine, dead, or even living, and eventually heavily armed creatures. Two things have to be discerned here. The first is Derrida's inclusion of the Other, the Other as even nonhuman, as not-me, an inclusion before any prior identification or determination (another scandalous and hyperbolic aspect of his ethics). Such identification is what not only subjects the Other to a categorization that strips it off its otherness, but it also strips it off the very transcendence that this Otherness is—or could be. What enters with the Other is in fact transcendence proper, if we assume, with Luce Irigaray (2008a), that a transcendence projected from a subject position in fact never achieves a genuine form of transcendence. This is what I take her to mean when she writes:

> As soon as I recognize the otherness of the other as irreducible to me or to my own, the world itself becomes irreducible to a single world: there are always at least two worlds. The totality that I project is, at any moment, questioned by that of the other. The transcendence that the world represents is thus no longer one, no longer unique. And if the gesture of projecting the totality of a world can remain a gesture that has something to do with transcendence, to recognize the partial nature of such a transcendence is even more transcendental. (ix/x)

She adds that such a transcendence more transcendental than transcendence hitherto conceptualized will be, "at any moment, in-finite and in becoming" (ibid.). Any form of projection that grows out of a contingent, subjective, local perspective is still, and will always be, inhabited by the locality and particularity it has sprung from. Genuine transcendence thus would have to transcend transcendence as we have so far defined it.

Whether such a projection is a male phenomenon, growing, as Irigaray argues, out of a rejection of the transcendent other that is mother/woman, is something I will come back to, as well as to the question whether, in the face of what would seem a form of "limping dialectics," we can still retain the term *transcendence* (or, for that matter, the term *dialectics*). However, what I would like to point out here is that the identification of the Other as other—which is impossible, since to identify means to rob the other of both its otherness and its transcendence—and the identification of a transcendence out of a fixed subject position in fact both exclude transcendence, and thus are structurally analogous.

Secondly, what we consequently have to be aware of—and here I agree with Irigaray—is that transcendence, if it involves going beyond a subject position that identifies either other or transcendence (and thus annuls both), "genuine" transcendence has to be rethought as plural: transcendences. I am putting "genuine" in quotation marks because we are reaching the borderlines of what can be linguistically denominated, since the word "genuine" evokes aspects of both the "authentic" and the "real," both of which bind transcendence back to what it should be liberated from: its roots in the "is."[5] Transcendence has been defined as that which is both inside and outside the frame of reference, and what I am arguing for is that we have to reconceptualize the possibility that the transcendent is in fact that which is not inside the frame, nor stably outside of it—which, in the final instance, defi(n)es and thus makes transcendence the other/Other. According to Levinas (1969, 127), to whom I would like to come back here, not only does every single Other transcend me in innumerable ways, but there are also innumerable others who do so. Moreover, this transcending otherness—which also entails and points toward an "other" transcendence—is nothing that we could determine statically, as any stasis of transcendence implies a similarly static, Archimedian point that it derives from, since it is not only anchored in the "is," but also acquires this staticism from the very "is" that it is derived from.

It is from these three arguments—that transcendence has to be disentangled from 1) what is known, 2) what is statically arrested in time due to its rootedness in the "is," and 3) what exists as singular instance—that the admittedly rather unwieldy concept of transcend*ifferances*, to which I alluded in my title, takes its cue. It is not designed to ascribe a transcendent status to the Derridean "concept" of differance; it suggests, on the contrary, that transcendence has to be thought as differing from what "is," and that, by unhinging it from this relation, it also acquires, as in its Derridean variety, a processual, spatio-temporal quality. And that it has, by default, to be thought in the plural form.

Now, while Levinas's assumption that the Other transcends me in innumerable ways—and that there are innumerable others who do so— might seem to be just another, enlarged version of a liberal pluralism in vaguely moral-philosophical terms, Levinas's ethics is far from this. Indeed, I would argue that it offers, in its very hyperbole, an alternative and viable critique of liberalism. It is striking that an analysis of this aspect of his thought has, to my knowledge, not yet been attempted, nor will I be able to offer such an analysis within the frame of this essay. Once again, this alternative is cast in hyperbolic terms, and once again, it can be—and has been—refuted in "pragmatic," political terms.

If we take transcendence as transcendence of the Other—and thus as other transcendence(s)—seriously, we would have to acknowledge that not only the alleged *equality* between me and the Other is affected by this, but that we cannot even assume an *equivalence* of me and the Other. This radical—but I think perfectly logical—conclusion that Levinas (1997, 23) draws results in two hyperbolic claims: First of all, that I am, qua host, in fact hostage to the Other, as when he writes: "Subjectivity as such is primordially a hostage, responsible to the extent that it becomes the sacrifice for others"; second, that the aneconomics of sacrifice inscribed in such a scenario leads to the even more counterintuitive (and even more hyperbolic) question: "Do I have the right to be? By insisting on being, do I deprive others of their place, do I ultimately kill them?" (Levinas 1985, 121). Posing such a question not only seems to contradict common sense, but also the very evolutionary theory that challenged so much of the existing common sense of its times, namely Darwinism. Nevertheless, one can juxtapose the outrageousness of this putting into question my right to be to the fact that, strangely enough, national states have on innumerable occasions risked the lives of their citizens—and thus put the right of the state's existence above the right of the citizen's existence—in order to follow the same either-or logic. Nations have not only never been modern, but in interpreting Darwinism as survival of the body politic, they have also defied Darwinism on the level of the individual, and thus proven at least the legitimacy of Levinas's question.

Many objections have been voiced against this hyperbole of defining subjectivity as sacrifice to the Other who masters me. One is offered by Paul Ricoeur's (1992, 339) exhortation in *Oneself as Another*: "who will be able to distinguish the master from the executioner, the master who calls for a disciple from the master who requires a slave?"— a question echoing the question "what if the animal I welcome unconditionally turns out to be a Trojan Horse? " What Ricoeur, and even Derrida at points, try to do is to preserve a remnant of equivalence, while wishing to pertain to Levinas's notion of radical otherness.[6] This is to say that especially Ricoeur wants to retain the ontological and logical implications of otherness, while dispensing with the axiological implications of the other's transcendence, which manifest themselves in Levinas's hyperbolic uneconomy of irreciprocity. That such an ethics of sacrifice is not exactly politically feasible, especially for minorities who have felt and been—and still feel—sacrificed, is something that I have analyzed in depth in my book *Aesthetics & Ethics*. What I would like to point out, however, is that, far from being an idealistic projection, it has become clear—even if the political practices that result from this are yet far from unequivocal—that we will have to sacrifice in order to save the planet and to avoid the political unrest that will ensue if the economic stratification (or downturn) of the global market continues as is. The sheer principle of sacrifice as such is, then, not as far-fetched and scandalous as it would appear. Nor is there a doubt that this sacrifice will have to be managed structurally and politically, one way or another, and that this sacrifice will affect mainly the Western industrialized nations.

IV

Pheng Cheah (2003), in his brilliant analysis of the "spectral nationality" that inhabits, if not haunts, cosmopolitical claims to transcend the national, argues that this spectrality deconstructs, and thus discredits, any claims to transcendence, as the latter in fact not only depends on, but also is actually logically and temporally preceded, and even contaminated, by the very structures it claims to "move beyond." Cosmopolitanism can never really "transcend" the structures of the national that it tries to supersede and leave behind. Cheah thus argues against the claims, or residues, of transcendence as he discerns them in, for example, Habermas's thought. What he proposes in *Inhuman Conditions*, instead, is an "alternative understanding of normativity in a globalizing world that is not based on transcendence" (Cheah 2006, 47), since, as he concludes with a view on Horkheimer and Adorno's critique of instrumental reason,

> one cannot transcend this field of instrumentality because humanity itself is produced by the technologies of bio-power. The power of transcendence proper to humanity can be understood in terms of human capacities and needs and the will to express them in the juridical form of rights, or in terms of self-cultivation, *Bildung*, and even critical reason. The processes that generate this power, however, are part of the subjectifying or humanizing aspect of bio-power. This is why the humanizing moment is necessarily circumscribed. . . . the subjectifying process cannot be applied globally or uniformly to every person. (263)

While this insight is certainly pertinent, I would like to challenge it on two accounts: First of all, can it be claimed that subjectivization can and should be regarded exclusively as an effect and product of the technologies of biopower? Only then would the conclusion apply that transcendence has to be dispensed with. To insist on the state, its institutions, and its laws as the exclusive arena in which the forms of rights, self-cultivation, *Bildung*, and even critical reason are acknowledged and transmitted is to focus exclusively on what Levinas has called the Third, the realm of justice that grows out of, supplements, and runs the danger to blot out the ethical realm of the face-to-face. Furthermore, are self-cultivation, education, and critical reason thinkable without a realm of the other? I would definitely endorse Cheah's insistence that "the subjectifying process cannot be applied globally or uniformly to every person"; moreover, I would also underwrite his plea to take into account the "given" culture of every nation as something that might be both different from, and thus not subsumable under, the very forms of transcendence that the concept of culture has developed in Europe, and especially in German philosophy. What I have problems to see, however, are what claims to normativity can be upheld that do not subscribe to, and grow out of, an assumed or posited transcendence. To understand human rights and their "unconditional but contaminated normativity as arising from the alterity within the inhuman force field of global capital and learn how to track how this inhuman field induces effects of humanity" (Cheah 2006, 266) might be crucial to effectively negotiate the sometimes unwanted and unintended side effects of human rights' goodwill that he so convincingly unveils, but on what basis, in turn, is such a normative claim to rethink normativity founded? Either this argument involves a certain degree of tautology (comparable to that of Lyotard), or it is itself haunted by a specter it does not fully acknowledge.

Moreover, what status can the "alterity within the inhuman force field of global capital" that he refers to claim? It seems that Cheah ascribes to it a subalter(n) position, while the subjectifying processes of biopower indeed are conceded a more or less transcendent status. This state of affairs is a result of a redefinition of the very concept of culture that I referred to above, that Cheah's (2006) reading radically revises:

> Culture is supposed to be the realm of human freedom from the given. But because human beings are finite natural creatures, the becoming-objective of culture as the realm of human purposiveness and freedom depends on forces which are radically other and beyond human control. Culture is given out of these forces. Thus, at the same time that cultural activity embodies and performs human freedom from the given, it is also merely given because its power over nature is premised on this gift of the radically other. (100)

This passage resonates richly with many of the things I have addressed so far. The construction of simultaneity—"at the same time"—in which this paradox is inscribed does not, in my view, fully support the hierarchization between a totalized biopower and a normativity of human rights that seems utterly dependent on it, as Cheah introduces it later. What catches our attention is the connection between two othernesses and two correlating gifts: the first one being the forces "radically other and beyond human control" (the technologies of biopower), which "give" culture-become-objective; the second one being nature, also conceived as both radically other and gift. These two othernesses designate two different versions of the sublime: These one could call the technological sublime—*techne* as biopower beyond our control that nonetheless enables something like *Bildung*—and nature as non-sublime nature, as nature overcome and dominated, rather euphemistically clad in the rhetorics of gift. What is missing in this picture, however, is another sublime—the sublime Other.

It is in this instant that another hyperbole—if it could be called that—comes in: It comes into play when Derrida suggests, in a rather matter-of-fact way and almost in passing:

> Hospitality is culture itself and not simply one ethic amongst others. Insofar as it has to do with the ethos, that is, residence, one's home, the familiar place of dwelling, inasmuch as it is a manner of being there, the manner in which we relate to ourselves and to others, to others as our own and foreigners, ethics is hospitality; ethics is so thoroughly coextensive with the experience of hospitality. (2001a, 16–17)

What almost gets lost in this virtual equation of hospitality and ethics is an even more momentous one: "Hospitality is culture"—and, by extension, culture, then, is also ethics. Culture is an ethics of hospitality offered to both the familiar and the foreign, a hospitality to the other neither by expressed fiat, nor by state ideology, but structurally inhabited—or spectrally haunted—by what is other. Culture is, and always has been, a negotiation with the other, whether forced—as in the case of German culture, out of which the cosmopolitan/nationalist amalgamate that Cheah starts his analysis from emerges—or simply "given." Given as the gift not of *techne* or biopower, not of nature, but of the sublime other. What the sublime other shares with what is excluded from nature as a gift, as dominated, is that this other has not been invited to provide us with that gift. The gift—understood radically in the tradition of Blanchot and Derrida—is sheer aneconomy. Culture as a gift not only conceived as freedom from nature, and as given or provided for by the state, but also as a gift that only *a posteriori* comes to be seen and regarded as such, puts the other as guest in the role of the useless—as "useless" as sublime nature that cannot be controlled or exploited—and, at times as threatening or traumatizing due to this quality. This purposelessness in pecuniary terms threatens to undermine the economic foundations of a capitalist market society. As Anne Dufourmantelle so poignantly remarks:

> In another way, this is to denounce the subtle forms through which ethics ends up serving other ends than its own. It is as if nowadays throwing together the inessential and the essential in a jumble were an intolerable threat for our society, democratic as it might be. Everything ought to be justifiable at least by an ethical system. As though, for a society doomed to the quantification of what is useful and efficient, the supreme danger lay in the useless, the purposeless, the

absolutely gratuitous, and that in the refusal to justify gratuitousness, what is "for nothing," the whole edifice of efficient values was shown up. (Derrida and Dufourmantelle 2000, 62–64)

Thus, the concepts of what is "proper" and what is property—and thus, what "belongs" to me, and what is thus the (imperative) property I need in order to offer "proper" hospitality (cf. Cheah's essay in this volume) collides with what might be the "appropriate" thing to do, and maybe another imperative—to offer hospitality independent of whether I know who or what that guest I receive is, and whether he/she/it might have anything to offer in return; a radical imperative that eventually ends in my "a-propriation." The concept of the other as sublime in the sense of purposeless, useless—which strangely enough, aligns it both with Kant's maxim (as "not exclusively a means") and a sublime nature that is without purpose—contradicts and escapes the instrumental reason of bio-power, as does Levinas's ethics as a whole, in Slavoj Žižek's view.[7] What Dufourmantelle points out is exactly what Cheah's study proves: that society—and even more so the force field of a global capitalism—indeed tries to subjugate everything under its axiom of efficiency, and that even morally motivated interventions, say, in support of Philippine female domestic workers in Singapore, have to be clad in the rhetorics of profit, not that of human rights.[8]

It might be interesting, at this point, to look once again at Kant's maxim—which, by the way, reads that we should treat a human being not (only) as means but at the same time [*zugleich auch*] as an end (which actually admits for some simultaneity, and not the exclusion of the former by the latter).[9] Its demand not to instrumentalize a human being on the one hand, and what he in the *Critique of Judgment* defines as the "monstrosity" of a sublime nature perceived as sheer purposelessness and traumatizing threat on the other,[10] merge not only in the cases of terribly abused maids that Cheah analyzes; they do so also in Žižek's (2005, 158) objection that what Levinas's ethics excludes is the possibility that the neighbor's face might hide his or her sheer monstrosity. In his essay "Neighbors and Other Monsters: A Plea for Ethical Violence," Žižek's argument, though based on Lacanian psychoanalysis and philosophy, is quite similar to Cheah's in that he, like the latter, points to the "paradox that every normative determination of the 'human' is only possible against an impenetrable ground of 'inhuman,' of something which remains opaque and resists inclusion into any narrative reconstitution of what counts as 'human.'"

While Žižek's Real (as big Other) echoes Cheah's conjecture of the state's biopower as a sublime, uncanny, and incontrollable force, what he criticizes in Levinas is that the facial "sur-face," on which Levinas's ethics of the face-to-face is grounded, might indeed be nothing but a mask that hides a yawning, groundless threat, an abysmal otherness—the Trojan Horse par excellence; "the neighbor is not displayed through a face; it is, as we have seen, in his or her fundamental dimension a faceless monster" (185). This claim, in turn, leads him to conclude that it is not the Other's face that a universal ethics proper can or should be based upon, but the Third. This Third, if I am not mistaken, is coextensive with what he calls the big Other, which, however, begs the question whether this big Other, as it manifests itself in the regulatory (bio-)power of its *techne*, is not as faceless and monstrous as any neighbor might turn out to be. Žižek might be right in pointing out that "the limitation of our capacity to relate to Other's faces is the mark of our finitude" (184); this holds true, however, also as concerns the sublime big Other that Kafka—whom Žižek also interprets in this essay—has so brilliantly dramatized in his stories and novels. Just why the faceless monstrosity of the Real or the nation-state's biopower politics should be preferable to the presumably faceless monstrosity of the neighbor is not quite clear, nor why the neighbor, as Other, should not also offer some enabling gifts that enrich the subject's *Bildung*, enrich it, moreover, in ways that escape the state's monitoring and structures.[11] What is clear is that Žižek accords transcendence to the Third, but not to the Other; what remains unclear is in how far the exposure, to which Žižek refers to his in critique of Judith Butler's concept of Ethical Violence, should differ in both cases.[12]

This leads us, finally, back to the troubled relationship between politics and philosophy, (maybe) enlarged by the concept of culture as a third category to be reckoned with. What is interesting in Žižek's argument is that he shows in how far Levinas's ethics—similarly to what Cheah uncovers in the case of the cosmopolitanism of the German idealist philosophers—is spectrally haunted by a veiled form of nationalism (cf. Žižek 2005, 158), which is as much as to say that a form of politics inhabits his philosophy, undermining his alleged radical separation between ethics and politics. Levinas's (1997, 160) appalling utterances about "those underdeveloped Afro-Asiatic masses who are strangers to the Sacred History that forms the heart of the Judaic-Christian world," and his remarks about the chosenness of the state of Israel would seem to prove that much. I would, however, still argue that the contrary is true as well: that, in Levinas's view, ethics, if spectrally, inhabits politics as justice. Spectrally, since all attempts to narratively comprise (as in Lyotard) or dialectically sublate (as in Ricoeur) the inherent difference between them blots out the radicality of Levinas's ethics, as I've shown elsewhere.[13]

Monstrosity might not lie in the fact that it hides under my neighbor's face, but that, even if this were the case, I would still have to acknowledge my debt to him. If monstrosity resides in between the categories of human, animal, and divine creatures, between the living and the dead, all of whom Derrida's injunction to say yes to comprises, his or her monstrosity lies, as Žižek admits, in their very "unidentifiableness," before any identification and determination, as Derrida puts it.[14] My transcendence might be someone else's monstrosity; to deduce from this that we should shy away from monstrosity—to throw us in the arms of a potentially equally faceless, monstrous, but still enabling biopower machine and its technologies of control and identification—and sacrifice any alternative transcendence, might be self-defeating. Culture, I would argue, is more than the gift and given of this ominous machine, and if we accept this Danaean gift (Gift, by the way, means "poison" in German, and in Norwegian, it means both that and "married"), we might as well accept and welcome the monstrosity of the Other and his/her/its Gift/gift.

V

One of the other contributions to the collection *The Neighbor*—Kenneth Reinhard's (2005) "Toward a Political Theology of the Neighbor"—ties in neatly with some of the points I have made so far. Also arguing from within a Lacanian framework, Reinhard tries to sketch the possibility for what Derrida (2006, 123), in *The Politics of Friendship*, has called "the *philein* beyond the political or another politics of loving"; a political theology of the neighbor that would constitute an exception to the state of exception that, in Giorgio Agamben's view, the sovereign enjoys, since he or she (or, as Leviathan, it) is—as originator of, and (sometimes) subject to, the law— both inside and outside of it.[15] From a Lacanian point of view, this state of transcendence—since being both inside and outside of the frame is exactly what defines transcendence—is structurally analogous to that of the phallus in the process of sexation. Taking his start from the biblical injunction in Leviticus 19:18, "thou shalt love thy neighbor as thyself," which both Freud and Lacan (1992, 46) have commented upon extensively, Reinhard refers, as does Žižek, to the latter's claim that "*das Ding* [the Thing] is the true secret." It is this "thingness" that escapes our projection upon the neighbor as cohuman, and thus our faculty for empathy, which, as I have argued elsewhere, is dependent on the assumption of sameness (cf. Claviez 2008, 108–11). The encounter with this Thing that the *Nebenmensch* also is creates, according to Reinhard (2005, 34), "a state of emergency [*état d'urgence de la vie*, in Lacan's terms], through which the subject arises as a self-sovereign." Contrary to Žižek, however, for Reinhard this unknowable thingness of the neighbor should not and cannot be reduced to sheer monstrosity, as it also constitutes "the kernel of jouissance that is both foreign, strange and unrecognizable in the other and intimate to me" (46). That is, even though Lacan (1992, 184) argues that "we cannot avoid the formula that jouissance is evil," this evil is not a result of its alleged "monstrosity," but of its designation as such by (the law of) the father.

It is this law, then, to which an alternative has to be found in order to stand a chance to reach an alternative—or, in Latour's words, a "contrary"—to transcendence. This is because the law of the phallus is another instance—indeed, the defining instance, according to Lacan—of transcendence as such, since it is both men and women that are, in Lacan's view, subjected to it. What this means, however, is that, while all women are subjected to the law of the phallus, in the case of men there is one instance—the primal father—who is exempt from this rule, as he is the originator (like for Schmitt or Agamben) of the rule, which urges for the sublimation of jouissance. Quite rightly, however, Reinhard (2005, 57) asks: "Why shouldn't there be, as for the man, an 'exception that proves the rule,' a Great Mother who escapes castration?"

Lacan (1999, 73) answers this riddle as follows: "There is no such thing as Woman, Woman with a capital W indicating the universal. . . . There is no such thing as woman because in her essence . . . she is not whole." Woman thus not only has no essence, she defies the very concept, based, as it is, on sameness, wholeness, and singularity. By deconstructing essence, she consequently also deconstructs transcendence, as the latter cannot be thought without at least one foot in essence. (Here's some food for thought about limping Oedipus!) Woman, according to Lacan, can "only be written with a bar through it" (72)—what a strikingly allusive metaphor! This means, however, that she cannot partake in, cannot be conceptualized by, political discourse, since there is, as Reinhard (2005) points out,

> no common denominator for subjects who locate themselves as women, no way of characterizing "women in general," contrary to popular misconceptions about feminine essence and unlike the case for men, who are determined by the assumption that there is a totality of the set Man. . . . There is no figure of the sovereign woman who might adjudicate the claims of individual women to participate in feminine sexuality and determine the boundaries of the set. (58)

As far as politics as we know it—based on the phallic transcendence of the political theology of sovereignty—is concerned, this does not exactly bode well, since, as Reinhard concedes, an alternative political theology of the neighbor that avoids such an essentialization can only be thought as the "decompletion of the political theology of sovereignty, the supplement that both supplies something that was lacking and inserts something heteronomous into political economy" (60; emphasis Reinhard's).

Such a supplementary (ana)logics, by default, also escapes the dialectics that the work of Irigaray is intent on preserving. It is, if any, an Oedipal dialectics, where the supplement "limps" along that which it is supplemented to, although it might, in due time, create a counterweight, an otherness, a drag that might make the sovereign begin to hobble as well. It is quite striking that, in order to pursue an outline of a political theology of the neighbor, Reinhard refers to Alain Badiou's work on love, which, as he sees it, offers a way out of the "threeness" that not only denotes the Christian notion of love (plus a child), but also, I would argue, the very Third that, arguing from a Christian-ethics point of view, Žižek recommends us to return to. Badiou, on the contrary, defines love not only as the "condition of sexual difference" (Reinhard 2005, 68)—thus turning endeared romantic notions on their head—but defines the twoness of love as alternative to both the "hegemony of the one" (the sovereign or primal father) and "the inclusion of the three" (which can be thought of as both the biopolitical legitimation of twoness—the child—or the Third in the Levinasian sense). Strangely enough, Badiou (2003) presents this "two" also as "limping":

> love is the only available experience of a Two counted from itself, of an immanent Two. Each singular love has this of the universal—that, were it ignored, by everyone, it contributed on its part, while limping along as long as it could, to establish that the Two can be thought in its place, a place supported partially by the hegemony of the One as well as the inclusion of the Three. (48)

VI

If a political theology of the neighbor, based on the immanence of twoness that love both characterizes and is constituted by, can only "limp along" (as it is exposed to the force fields of) both the One and the Three, it is still moving. And there is no doubt that this constitutes a hyperbolic and radical ethics—an ethics, as Levinas has put it, that can only be exposed, flash-like, in the Saying, as it is chained, shackled, betrayed by the Said that it needs in order to manifest itself. There can be no doubt that such an ethics, from which a political theology of the neighbor takes its start, starts limping once its attempts to gain the status of a politics (and here the bar is in the right place), of neighborhood, of hospitality. Mireille Rosello's (2001, 173) study *Postcolonial Hospitality* makes clear that to transfer such a hyperbolic, radical, transcend*ifferance* of hospitality and neighborly love becomes entangled with the vagaries of both the cultural and the political; her remarkable analyses and readings show, if anything, that hospitality can work as gift as well as poison. That, consequently, "a completely harmonious and pacified level of interaction may not be the best test of successful hospitable gestures," and that "the very precondition of hospitality may require that, in some ways, both the host and the guest accept, in different ways, the uncomfortable and sometimes painful possibility of being changed by the other" (176). And she concludes:

> Perhaps, then, it is the paradoxical nature of conditional and unconditional hospitality alike to be a practice that cannot tolerate perfection, that is inherently perverse, always and eminently corruptible. It constantly tests the host's and the guest's threshold of fears, and their willingness to live with that fear, and with their malaise. (ibid.)

Or, for that matter, with a limp . . .

What makes "limping" such a seductive metaphor and binds it back to the alternative form of concept that I have—rather "limpingly"—called transcend*ifferance*, is that it can serve multiple functions: It reminds us that unconditional hospitality toward the neighbor can indeed leave us wounded; there is not, and there cannot be, any guarantee that the neighbor does not turn out to be a Trojan Horse that, if not worse, will kick us in the shin. In its Oedipal resonances (including, for that matter, those of castration), it can make us aware that the self-assured (male) stride, which we preferably conceive human history to display, is in urgent need of revision, as this process has surely left others (limping) behind. History as dialectics might be heavily limping as such, in as much as the teleological sublation (into transcendence) of the same and the other always comes at a price—mostly for the latter. Consequently, we might be called upon—and here I would like to come back to Irigaray once more—to actually leave both dialectics and transcendence behind, as an alternative transcendence—or transcend*ifferance*—puts into question not only transcendence, but a dialectics of two transcendences, as Irigaray envisages them. My encounter with the neighbor cannot be captured exclusively in terms of sexuated identities. Or, to put it a little more polemically: I may try to love my neighbor like myself, but if I start loving his wife, I'll probably get into trouble.

If the figure of two legs moving alternately and equally toward some *telos* adequately captures the teleological movement of dialectical sublation, limping toward a radical concept of hospitality that dispenses with a dialectical economy of reciprocity connotes the fact that we acknowledge multiple transcen*dances* moving and tearing left and right, veering us off a fixed track, and maybe making us go in circles—even in our own homes.

Toward a Mutual Hospitality

LUCE IRIGARAY

In some cultures, hospitality does not raise any problem. In these cultures, which are generally feminine ones, the world is open, as is life itself. All, men and women, are children of a mother, in particular of the mother as nature. Thus peace governs, and also hospitality.

But cultures of masculine origin have imposed other codes and perspectives, another logic with respect to a natural economy, a living economy. Human children have become separated by artificial boundaries that all, men and women, did not share, did not even understand. Women, the guardians of the ancient laws of hospitality, have been divided and enclosed, according to diverse modalities, in residences belonging to various owners, various countries, various cultures. They have been subjected to specific laws unfamiliar to the universal law of love, of desire, of generation, of life.

First, gender became confused with genealogy, without a sufficient regard for sexuate belonging as a differentiated identity, and, later, with race to the detriment of genealogy itself.[1] We find traces of this notably in the evolution of languages, in Greek for example, and also in the evolution of representations of the divine and conceptions of the other. What was sharing between all the children of the mother, in particular as Earth, has become welcome, tinged with moralism and paternalism, a welcome of the strange or the foreign, the one, he or she, with whom it is difficult to share, and who is considered to be more or less inferior to oneself.

It is impossible for us to merely return to the time in which we lived as being all, men and women, the children of the mother, yet a return to our natural origin is necessary. It is also impossible to practice a universal coexistence in a culture constructed without respect for our natural belonging. We are thus obliged to build a new culture in order to be capable of practicing hospitality as coexistence and not as a more or less imposed integration of the other into our culture, considered to be the only horizon within which it is possible to live.

Spaces Provided by Our Natural Belonging

The first gesture to be accomplished is to lay out space so that a spatial architecture will allow for the existence of each one and the meeting between each one. This is no easy task in a culture in which we are presumed to occupy a place already defined, as is already defined the manner of meeting one another. Most of our cultures resemble chessboards in whose frames we apparently can move, but without our movements being really free, nor with a still-virgin space remaining in which we can meet outside of our respective chessboards, assuming that we can go beyond them.

In order to practice hospitality, in the sense of a coexistence with the other, each of us needs a place of our own to which we remain faithful. This place cannot amount to a space already assigned to us by a logic proper to a particular culture, because such a place does not permit us to respect the place proper to the one who belongs to another culture. Then we can only lay out, within the architecture of our own space, a place within which we propose to the other to become integrated. This, no doubt, permits the other to recover himself or herself, but does not imply that some exchange with them exists. Now, the ancient laws of hospitality presupposed a reciprocal right to obtain housing and protection from one another (cf. the definition of the word *hospitality* in the Robert dictionary), which means a sort of mutual hospitality. Moreover, the word 'host' has a meaning that is in some way reversible in many languages—but not in English, which distinguishes between "host" and "guest"—alluding both to the one who welcomes and the one who is welcomed, something that bears witness to a time when hospitality referred to an exchange implying reciprocity.

Such a conception of hospitality would better suit our multicultural era. But a practice corresponding to a unilateral and condescending gesture toward one more destitute than oneself has little by little been substituted for it. Hospitality has gradually come to be considered as a sort of charity toward someone who is in want. Nothing, then, testifies to a real relation between people other than a quantitative and hierarchical assessment of the one with respect to the other—which evokes, at best, a parental link.

This kind of hospitality is not the one that can solve the problems arising from the interlacing of peoples and cultures with which we are confronted today. But we no longer have at our disposal the space(s) provided to us by our natural belonging to a gender and to genealogy. A space—or spaces—both proper to each one and universal, and where it is possible to open free spaces to meet the other in his or her difference—of nation, of culture, of race, and so forth—especially thanks to the connection and crossroads between a vertical belonging to genealogy and a horizontal belonging to gender.

All humans are born from a mother and more precisely from a couple—the effect of the two parents on human identity not yet being well valued—and all humans also have a gender. Faithfulness to this lot, which all of them share, allows them to coexist without superior or inferior position, and without one having the real possibility of assuming the place of the other. Each has at one's disposal a place in which one must live while respecting the place of the other. Safeguarding and cultivating the place that naturally corresponds to each, man or woman, favors the development of a civilization shareable by all, men and women, a civilization that does not exclude difference or differences but in which difference(s) serve(s) to weave links—especially of mutual hospitality—between humans. This is fostered if gender, the most universal belonging, transcends the verticality and the particularity of genealogy.[2]

Unfortunately, our cultures have developed in opposition to our belonging to a natural identity and place. Identity and place have been constructed in large part to overcome our natural origin and through structuring the real in ways that are not the same in all cases. If a culture claims to be universal it is because it disregards the real. This may seem suitable in a single cultural horizon, but proves itself to be inadequate today given the discovery of a multiplicity of civilizations and traditions, unless one prefers the imperialism of one culture rather than a sharing between cultures—a choice that cannot correspond to a gesture of hospitality.[3]

Nature itself provides us with some teachings about what hospitality could be in our time. For example, if a woman can give birth to a child, and even to a child of another gender, this is possible because, thanks to the two, a place in her is produced—one could say in Greek *gignestai*—that does not belong to the one or to the other, but permits their coexistence: the placenta. Neither the woman nor the fetus could survive without this organ that secures both the existence of each and the relation between the two. Likewise, yet differently, sexuate belonging cannot assert itself or be kept and cultivated without a third, especially a spatial third, which does not belong to one gender or the other but happens through the between two, without it being possible for this third to be appropriated by or to one or the other gender.

Our culture has not recognized the necessity of these third organs and places that are provided by nature itself. Thus, it has imagined that the relationship between the mother and the child was too close and that it was essential for the father to lay down his law in order to separate the child from the mother. Now it is the masculine discourse, a discourse parallel to nature, that has compared all humans to so-called neuter or neutral individuals, who are both impersonal and lacking in difference(s), thus leading us to regress with respect to our individualization. Nature acts in a more intelligent way than a culture that has intended to dominate nature while really doing worse for human life and coexistence. By being unaware of the mediating part of the placenta, our tradition misjudged, and even destroyed, the role of the third organ that allowed a sharing of life with mutual respect. Similarly, by reducing sexuate belonging to a reproductive and parental function, this tradition has abolished in the one of the child—or of the family unit—the insuperable space existing between the two sexuate identities, a space that is necessary to guarantee their existence and coexistence in difference. Man and woman, then, would have no other aim than reproducing, as is the case for most living organisms, and all possible means to reach that aim would be acceptable. But reproducing is not specifically human, unlike the aptitude for transforming sexual attraction from instinctive attraction, including procreative instinct, into desire and love respectful of our difference(s) and into cultural creation thanks to such difference(s).

What nature prepared as a place for a possible and fruitful coexistence in respect of difference(s) has been annulled by a culture that is, in fact, parallel to the living world, and that has hindered our sharing with respect for our difference(s). Such a culture has prevented us from practicing hospitality in a way that is essential in our times, given the multicultural context in which we live.

The Vital Rebuilding of a Spatial Architecture

Without turning back to a merely natural order, we have to reopen the differentiated places prepared by nature itself in order to resume a cultivation of our natural belonging that takes into account the difference(s) between us at the vertical level of genealogy and, above all, at the horizontal level of difference between the genders.

The first gesture consists in not assimilating the other to or into our culture as well as not aspiring to a unique and universal culture before having learned how to take into account the difference(s) between us. What matters first is to attempt to give back to each one, man or woman, the place that has been taken away from them by a culture that has aimed at mastering nature through a language and a logic parallel to it.

In our tradition, the spacing between words and their organization into a discourse has been substituted for the space between things, in particular between living organisms, in this way hindering their growth and relations in respect for life. This is especially the case with regard to humans. The grid of language or discourse takes place between the real and us, and thus prevents us from growing and entering into relations in faithfulness to who we are. Henceforth, we can communicate only through this grid, which does not permit us to be in relation in the present as living beings. Moreover, this culturally constructed grid is not necessarily the same as the one with which another culture has provided itself. This is already the case between the genders, and indeed between the generations, even if such a difference is not recognized, and does not exactly meet the same needs as those that are at stake for cultures.

How, then, could we welcome the other as other without being able to prepare a place outside our own world for him or her? The other stays beyond our own horizon. To offer him or her hospitality would mean that we are capable of perceiving the limits of our own world and of opening it to make room for a beyond. A beyond that is not defined with respect to our present, indeed our terrestrial life—as our tradition has taught us—but a beyond with respect to the place where we live here and now, the only place to which we are accustomed, and to which we belong more often than not unconsciously. Hospitality requires that we first become aware of the limits of this place and be able to leave it, without giving up on it, in order to become ready to welcome another place that will never become our own. Giving the other hospitality compels us to realize the spatial a prioris in which we came into the world, grew, and acquired culture, and to modify them. Welcoming the other asks us for awareness of the relative aspect of all that was familiar to us, including its frame and organization, and acceptance of the fact that what is familiar to us is not shared by the other, is not universal. This is especially essential with regard to the absolute—the Absolute—that has secured the closure of the horizon of our culture and its coherence. Indeed, this absolute—or Absolute—is often different from that of the other and, without being able to suspend, to practice an *epoché* regarding our relations to this absolute, or Absolute, we cannot meet the other. No doubt we can show charity toward him or her, give material, even parental, hospitality to them, but this does not amount to proposing a sharing between two different human adults. We go no further than a sort of paternalistic or maternalistic behavior toward the one whom we consider to be inferior, poorer, more childlike, more lacking in a natural or spiritual family than we are. Although this is not nothing, it does not correspond to the cultural evolution that is needed from us today.

To reopen the circle of the horizon within which we stay is thus the first gesture to carry out in order to approach the question of alterity as it presents itself to us today.

Because we cannot share the same discourse, the same beliefs, the same customs and habits, it is a gesture that must show the other that we are ready to welcome him or her. Such a gesture does not consist in opening to them the space of the house, including the political or cultural house, in which we live. Rather, it is a question of succeeding in crossing the threshold of this house, and of staying in a space, which in a way is virginal, where we are prepared to welcome the difference(s) between our guest and ourselves. Nature itself could be this space, but it is often already appropriated for or by one culture, so that it is no longer indifferent with respect to some other culture. Thus, a decision from us is needed to prepare a place beyond the space defined by any culture.

It is also important that we restore an environment to the body that each, man or woman, is—an environment in which this body can live, grow, and express itself according to the relational world proper to it. We are not allowed to integrate the other in a spatial, political, or cultural architecture that, warm though it is, prevents this other from living according to what or who he or she is. To approach the other, we must preserve a space where we can welcome them without exiling them from the surroundings that suit them. Without being necessarily neutral or neuter, it is crucial that the place of hospitality permit each one to feel free. On the condition that it not be adapted to a particular culture, nature could be an ideal place for coexistence, if the climatic contingencies would allow it, but this is not always the case. A space for life, not yet organized according to certain criteria, has to be kept around the bodies that want to welcome, to meet one another.

Bodies ought to approach one another in a naked way, that is to say, without being already submitted or compared to customs that might thwart or mask their natural belonging through cultural difference(s) that would render them irreducibly unfamiliar to one another.

Nevertheless, these differences are part of the habits and ways of life of each one. Ignoring them can make our manner of welcoming incomprehensible, even unacceptable. For example, if in our cultures we generally shake the other's hand in greeting, this corporal touching would be unacceptable to guests who are accustomed to greeting from a distance, a greeting that we rather reserve for God. In certain traditions, on the other hand, it is quite common to kiss one another in greeting, which does not correspond to our customs. These are only modest examples regarding the attention that we must pay to the alterity of the other. Such attention must also be turned toward the way of dressing, of behaving, of eating, of arranging the place for hospitality, and so forth. The body has been trained according to certain cultural norms that cannot be modified from one moment to the next, whatever tolerance and goodwill there may be on both sides. Having the same human genetic inheritance—with some sexuate difference, it is true—does not mean that we are accustomed to the same dishes, the same sounds, the same smells. Most political discourses on coexistence forget such aspects and amount to idealistic and sententious words that do nothing but render a real hospitality impossible. They also generally neglect the fact that hospitality ought to be potentially reciprocal. All of this can be explained by a construction of our culture(s) that had little regard for the body and sensibility. Moreover, today we are asked even more to give up these dimensions of our identity, whereas it is a return to universal natural belongings that can lead us to discover the path toward a world coexistence.

Words to Favor Welcoming

We have to both return to the origin of our culture and elaborate a new culture. Our habitual language, our mother tongue, cannot meet such an undertaking. No doubt, it can help us to think about the task that we have to carry out, but it does not yet correspond to the discourse that we ought to direct to the other, to a language we can share with him or her.

To render this sharing possible, a space for silence needs to be prepared—as it was necessary to preserve a space that is virgin with respect to the one and the other in order to render a meeting possible. The first word that has to be said to each other by way of welcome is our capacity for remaining silent. This sign of welcome shows that each one accepts to leave the circle of one's own discourse—or usual house of language—in order to listen to what the other wants to say, wants to address to him or her, from a horizon of language that is unknown to them. This undertaking is not simple! Once again, it is a gesture—a more strictly linguistic gesture—that can favor communication between people belonging to different cultures. Such an utterance can seem paradoxical. But, in the verbal exchange, some ways of saying amount to gestures more than others. This is already the case at the level of words themselves.

Generally, the verb can better express a current process—one could say, can be equivalent to a gesture—than the noun, which refers to a denomination that took place before meeting. Moreover, the verb ensures the structure of the message, and the choice of the verb can favor or thwart the communication with the other. Thus "to speak of" does not amount to "speaking with" in relating to or with the other, and the second choice must be preferred to the first. The verbs that establish an indirect relation between two subjects are more conducive to creating a framework for welcoming the other than are transitive verbs, which respect poorly the distance or the difference between subjects, and even the subjective status of the one who acts as object. Thus, before feeding or sheltering the other, it is important to ask him or her what they expect from us. Language itself has to prepare the meeting, to build the space necessary for an exchange to be possible.

The logic that determines the wording of the messages ought not be governed by a concern about fixing a univocal meaning, as has too often been the case in our tradition, but by a concern about allowing for a mutual exchange. Then, as organizing patterns for a verbal exchange, the forms: "we talk to one another," "we question each other," "we respect each other," "we love each other," "we give to one another" must be preferred to the forms: "I say to you what that is," "I inform you about something," and even "I love you," "I offer you hospitality," all of which do not imply an equivalence of status, dignity, or maturity between "I" and "you." It is essential that this equivalence be ensured by the syntactic structures themselves and not only by the content of a discourse that expresses good intentions or moralizing dictates without any measure allowing them to be put into practice. The way we talk, with and to one another, reflects or develops a manner of being in relation with oneself, with the world, with the other or others, to which we must pay attention if we want to make hospitality that respects difference(s) between us possible. We have to become aware of this in our own language and also, as much as possible, in the language of the one, he or she, to whom we offer hospitality, for this hospitality to truly be human; that is to say, for this hospitality to correspond to a culture of the between-us that, while it takes into account our natural belonging, permits us to live this belonging without being submitted to our instincts. To succeed in this, we must always prefer the "to" of an indirect relation, the "with" or the "between" of a relation of two subjects, to the direct transitivity of one subject upon an other, transformed into an object of our action, or to a collective "together" that risks canceling the spacing that preserves the difference between subjects. We must favor the gestures in words, the gesturing words corresponding to certain verbs—for example: "to greet," "to thank," "to ask," "to question," "to praise"—that presuppose the existence of two subjects and the participation of the two in the action with a possible reciprocity.[4]

Underlying all these utterances that imply a relation between two subjects, we have to keep in mind and effective the question: Who are you, you who will never be me or mine, you whom I will never exhaustively know, and for whom I will never substitute myself? A question that holds open the horizon of my world and prevents confinement within the familiarity of a single world from happening, so that I would not really be able to give the other a truly human hospitality. A question that must first be put between each masculine and feminine subject because the most basic, universal, and irreducible difference lies between them.

It is also important not to let a distribution between the active and the passive poles be established, as has too often been the case between man and woman—but also between parents and children, teachers and students, and in some way between the rich and the poor, the powerful and the weak, ourselves and foreigners, and so forth—in our tradition. Each subject alternately ought to occupy or assume the two poles so that hospitality can be potentially reciprocal and not reduced to a bipolar relationship between dominant-dominated, acting-acted, superior-inferior, but also nature-culture, body-spirit. To restore the equilibrium between the active and the passive in each subject and between subjects means entering a new stage of our evolution, a stage that we really need in order to reach the maturity that a human relationship with respect for difference(s) requires. This new mode of exchanging between us will liberate us from the vestiges of dependence on our parents that are still too effective in our cultures, and consequently will restructure the relationships between sexuate identities, notably by modifying the economy of the connections between animality and spirituality, body and soul, sensibility and thought, external and internal perceptions, the visible and the invisible, desire and culture, and even the human and the divine. The contribution of the divine dimension to our horizontal exchanges, especially our sexuate exchanges, and to our everyday becoming, is necessary if we want to have access to a mutual hospitality between cultures and traditions because these have been constructed according to different absolutes—Absolutes—which render them incompatible and keep them in conflict with one another, and not in harmony.

A hospitality that cares about welcoming the other with respect for the difference or differences between us also requires that we not confine ourselves to the past, to our individual or collective history, but pay attention above all to the present of our meeting and the future that we can build together. In general, the past has divided us rather than gathering us together. Attempting to build a common world, even if only for the time of a meeting, cannot be carried out by favoring our respective histories but by transcending them, without disowning them, toward a human becoming still to come and that we have to create through respectful exchanges between us. Our epoch must no longer devote itself solely to ethnology, to the observation of other peoples and other civilizations, or to a more or less scientific cultural tourism, but instead to the construction of a human world culture that gathers together, and goes beyond, all the various ways of becoming humans and the diverse cultures that have been elaborated up until now.

All these gestures, including these linguistic gestures, with a view toward a mutual hospitality, cannot obey a logic defined by one or the other already existing civilizations. They must be invented by each one, in particular during the time of meeting. And, in order to be both cultured gestures and faithful to our universal nature, they need to resort to an artistic expression that better suits language for conveying a total approach between those who are meeting one another. Of course, it is not a question of interposing between us art works, in the classical sense of the word, but of transforming ourselves into works of art, through which we unify all that we are—body, sensibility and sensory perceptions, feelings and thoughts, and so forth—and express them to the other with restraint, a welcoming capable of both proximity and distance, with a meeting and a cultural fecundity between us in mind.

The Basic and Universal Home

The gesture of hospitality that we direct to the other cannot be inspired by mere moral obligation. This would amount to acting like a superior with respect to the other and, moreover, to retaining an abstractly ideal attitude that does not allow a comprehensive exchange between two different subjects. Now, this kind of exchange is essential for us to meet the one, him or her, who does not share our culture. In order for such a meeting to happen, each one must be capable of being and remaining oneself, of staying in oneself. It is not through becoming one—or One—with the other that I can offer a real hospitality. We must remain two. And this two must correspond to two comprehensive identities and not to two parts of a single unity—as was too often the case in our culture built upon pairs of complementarities or opposites: for example, man and woman, or the masculine and the feminine.

To give hospitality to someone of another culture—and, first, of another gender, or another generation—I must be able to open my own horizon while remaining capable of turning back within it, even if it will be modified by the meeting with the other. It is essential to remain two, and two who are different. But this difference cannot merely be constructed; otherwise, I could not, especially not only by myself and from one minute to the next, go beyond the horizon of this construction. In our multicultural era, the more we must deal with what or who is unfamiliar to us, and distant from us, the more we must discover what is really proper to us. Opening one's world, opening oneself, calls for the capacity to return home. Henceforth, however, this home cannot be merely a country, an area, a family house, not even a culture or a language. It is necessary for us to return to a more original home, to a home that we have lost and forgotten in the elaboration of customs, laws, political and cultural orders that are not in continuity with our real identity.

It is to this identity that we have to return because it is shared by the whole of humanity, because it is universal, apart from the fact that this universal is two: man and/or woman. Humanity is differentiated in itself and it is such a difference that makes possible a world culture of hospitality without any fusion or confusion, complementarity, domination, or subjection of one with respect to the other. Such a world culture of coexistence with one another cannot develop without us cultivating both our own identity and the relation with the other in respect for our difference(s), beginning with the one that differentiates each gender from the other. This asks us to discover, and in part rediscover, a relation of intimacy with ourselves that allows us to stay in ourselves when relating with the other.

Such a relation to and with ourselves can be called self-affection, provided that we do not mistake self-affection for auto-eroticism.[5] Self-affection designates a more comprehensive affect than auto-eroticism, and refers more to an ability to remain in oneself as in a home than to a more localized and specific excitement and expense of energy. Self-affection ought to evoke a state of gathering with oneself and of meditative quietness without concentration on a precise theme, an attitude that is practiced in certain cultures, more than a Western auto-eroticism or a gesture of religious nature in connection with a divinity defined as external in relation to us.

It seems that our culture has known such states, but that it has gradually moved away from them because of a tendency of the Western masculine subject to favor activity, domination of nature, subject-object relation, and also looking-at rather than touching, activity of the mind rather than a more comprehensive experience. Signs of this progressive remoteness, indeed forgetting, of self-affection, can be observed in the passage from Ancient to classical Greek culture, especially through the evolution of language. From Ancient Greek language, dual cases have vanished little by little, cases that were used to express a relation between two different elements that can form a whole thanks to their difference: the hands, the eyes, the lips, but also the two sexes or the two genders. Some grammatical forms have also vanished, such as the middle voice that served to convey a total relation, including a corporal one, of oneself with oneself, that is neither a mere activity nor a mere passivity—nor the later reflexive form, which bears witness to a sort of scission between oneself as a subject and oneself as an object of the action of the subject—and, sometimes, a relation of reciprocity between two subjects. At the same time, the sexuate and dual sense of the word *genos* vanished in favor of the genealogical sense, and even the racial sense referring to different genealogical groups.

These are only a few symptomatic examples of an evolution that has accompanied the cultural domination, both human and divine, of one gender and one genealogy over the other. Now this culture is a masculine one and it was imposed to the detriment of a culture of natural identity, and to the detriment of those who generally are its guardians: the mothers, the women. All those who once formed the great human family as children of the mother, of nature, have been divided into various family groups no longer organized according to the universal law of nature but according to cultural systems fitting the different ways through which man has attempted to substitute his order for it to differentiate himself. In such a diversity of human families or tribes, differences of geographic environments, of traditions linked to religious beliefs, of races, of generations, and even of rhythms of economic development have been mixed up. These differences are heterogeneous and impossible to treat in the same way because they are more or less natural or constructed, and they do not belong to the same era of human evolution, to the same forms of exchange, and so forth. What is implicitly common to them is that they are based on a quantitative and hierarchical assessment that prevents horizontal coexistence in difference from happening. The members of different groups can relate with one another only through integration into or submission to groups or members considered superior, thanks to paternalistic condescension, by means of war to bring victory to an order that is presumed better, or by the imposition of an abstract and so-called neuter or neutral and universal model. It seems that the monetary exchange system today is closely related to such a model, but it is also what endangers humanity itself without having solved the problems, especially the economic ones, that arise from quantitative differences between the various human groups.

The dilemma we have to resolve today is that of choosing between the respect for life and the submission of all humanity to artificial models that endanger life. If we want to preserve a future, it seems that a return to a universal natural identity and the elaboration of a culture faithful to this identity are essential.

To Conclude

To build a universal culture, we need irreducible, and not quantitative, difference(s). In other words, we need difference(s) that open(s) our horizon to a beyond, to a transcendence in comparison with the state and being in which we already are—a transcendence respectful toward our self-affection and shareable by the whole of humanity, without any hierarchy, domination, or subjection between humans. Such a difference exists in nature itself: the difference between the genders, provided that we consider our sexuate identities in a human way, that is to say, not only as a natural but as a cultural belonging, still to be developed in a suitable manner. It is not the exchange of women between various groups of men that can contribute to a democratic world civilization, but rather the cultivation of a sharing in difference(s) between all the humans, as brothers and sisters, who inhabit our earth. Such a culture allows us to take care of life, to enrich it with the energy that the difference between the genders brings, to develop our self-affection while keeping opened up the horizon of our own world thanks to the relation to and with the other as transcendent to us.

The difference between the genders is a place that requires us to be both faithful to ourselves and welcoming to the other in his or her difference. This place is shared by all humans, and within it can be woven, continuously and at various levels, ties of mutual hospitality between all, men and women, whatever their tradition, their local belonging, their race, or their age. Thanks to such a place and the global weaving of ties respectful of our difference(s), a History can be built that meets the requirements we have to face in our time, while trying to harmonize our presents, and even ideally our pasts, with a view to the construction of a still-possible future for humanity.[6]

The Politics of Hospitality

To Open
Hospitality and Alienation

PHENG CHEAH

Hospitality has emerged as a key concept in our contemporary era of global migration. The *Oxford English Dictionary* defines hospitality as "the act or practice of being hospitable; the reception and entertainment of guests, visitors, or strangers, with liberality and goodwill." The host (from the Latin, *hospes*), the individual agent who practices or gives hospitality, is "a man who lodges and entertains another in his house."[1] Whether it is an ethical, political, or juridical concept, a matter of philanthropy or a matter of right, the central gesture of hospitality is that of opening, more precisely, to open oneself up to an other or foreigner. When we speak of hospitality in the context of globalization, it is synonymous with being part of a world that is increasingly becoming borderless. The imperative "to open (up) to" thus arises from the fact that the world itself has opened up and become open such that it can and should receive every single human being.

But what does the gesture of opening involve? The characterization of hospitality as a right can be misleading because it emphasizes a duty that a subject owes to another, or at least a response in the face of a demand or claim from the other. This obscures the fact that hospitality is primarily a demonstration of the power of the host. Hospitality is always inseparable from power because it is an ability, capacity, or strength to receive and give shelter to a stranger, foreigner, or other. In the case of ethics or philanthropy, this power is coupled with the intention to exercise the capacity for hospitality in a generous or liberal spirit. In the case of law or politics, we see the juridical codification of this capacity into a right that the other can expect and demand. There are at least two other dimensions to the power of hospitality. First, there must be some basis of commonality before hospitality can be given. However different he or she may be, the other must be recognizable as another human subject to whom hospitality can be given or who can claim a right to hospitality. Hence, hospitality involves a power of calculation and homogenization that establishes the basic ties of human commonality through which concrete subjects of hospitality are determined. Second, and more important, the power to give hospitality presupposes both a prior power to make and maintain a world in which channels of hospitality exist and an imperative to exercise this power.

What is so radical about Jacques Derrida's idea of hospitality, what makes it so difficult to understand in practical terms (since the practice of hospitality and, indeed, any practice always implies strength) is his insistence that a radical vulnerability or weakness is always structural to hospitality. Moreover, in his view, hospitality is not merely an openness to every member of humanity. A true hospitality, Derrida suggests, must be radically inhuman in the sense that it is an opening to a nonhuman other in a manner that radically dislocates the power of humanity. Accordingly, he has described hospitality as a figure of "unconditionality without sovereignty" (Derrida 2005a, 149), and indeed, as "a name or an example of deconstruction" (Derrida 2002a, 364). "Hospitality," Derrida writes, "is the deconstruction of the at-home; deconstruction is hospitality to the other, to the other than oneself, the other than 'its other,' to an other who is beyond any 'its other'" (ibid.).

What new perspective can Derrida's idea of hospitality bring to our understanding of the urgent social, ethical, and political problems posed by the intensifying flows of people in contemporary globalization? This chapter examines the distinctive features of deconstructive hospitality by situating it in relation to two earlier modern discourses of hospitality that directly confronted the upheaval and destruction brought about by the globalization of capital accumulation: those of Karl Marx and Hannah Arendt. These discourses of hospitality can be called proper discourses of hospitality because they are concerned with the power of making a hospitable world that is proper to humanity. I explore the ways in which Derrida's deconstruction of the at-home unsettles this human power of worldmaking by pointing to a constitutive vulnerability to the other as *arrivant*, a curious figure of migration under erasure. The essay concludes with a consideration of the limits of understanding hospitality through the figure of migration within the larger frame of globalization's impact on the postcolonial South.

Proper Hospitalities, Economic and Political (Marx and Arendt)

Discussions of hospitality customarily refer to Kant's great essay on perpetual peace because it names hospitality as the sole cosmopolitan right (cf. Benhabib 2004). But Kant could only grasp hospitality as something that occurs across established borders because his account remains within the geopolitical framework of the post-Westphalian system of sovereign territorial states. In contradistinction, both Marx and Arendt envisioned a borderless hospitality. This proposition may seem strange because the concept of hospitality is seldom associated with Arendt and never with Marx. But hospitality implies the existence of a world that can welcome, be open to, and receive every human being. Moreover, to be received is not merely a passive stance. Once it takes the form of a right, it implies the power of a claim or demand. But for this demand to be satisfied, there must also be an ability or capacity to create, make, or bring into being a world that is open. Marx and Arendt were fundamentally concerned with hospitality in this active sense: the making and opening of a world that can be hospitable.

For Marx, creative labor or labor that creates useful things necessary for human subsistence is a process that transforms nature or the earth into a world, a home for the epigenesis of humanity. There are three moments to labor as a world-making process. First, labor is purposive action that

> mediates, regulates and controls the metabolism [*Stoffwechsel*] between himself [man] and nature. He confronts the materials of nature as a force of nature. He sets in motion the natural forces which belong to his own corporeality [*Leiblichkeit*] . . . in order to appropriate the materials of nature in a form adapted to his own needs *[in einer für sein eignes Leben brauchbaren Form anzueignen]*. Through this movement he acts upon external nature and changes it, and in this way he simultaneously changes his own nature. He develops the potentialities slumbering within nature, and subjects the play of its forces to his own sovereign power [*Botmäßigkeit*]. (Marx 1973a, 162; 1976b, 283)[2]

It is a process of objectification (*Vergegenständlichung*) that involves the idealization of the exterior world through the imposition of a purposive form so that it can be made fit for or appropriate to specific human needs. Second, this transformation of the material or natural world is simultaneously the process of the subject's self-formation (*Bildung*). In recognizing himself in this other, man affirms his sovereign power over nature and augments and transforms himself in the same movement. Third, the inherently cooperative nature of labor means that a fundamental sociality is immanent to productive activity.[3] Human life is constitutively social. Human beings are always already produced as social beings by virtue of the social character of productive activity, what Marx called "the social production" of human existence. Hence, production creates, and is coextensive with, a social existence, that is, a world. As Marx indicates by referring to architecture as a paradigmatic example, the human capacity for appropriation makes a world that is habitable for humanity.

> What distinguishes the worst architect from the best of bees is that the architect builds the cell in his head [*in seinem Kopf*] before he constructs it in wax. At the end of every labour process, a result emerges which had already been conceived by the worker at the beginning, hence already present ideally [*ideel vorhanden war*]. Man not only effects a change in form in the materials of nature; he also actualizes [*verwirklicht*] his own end [*Zweck*] in those materials. And this is an end he is conscious of, it determines his mode of activity with the rigidity of a law, and he must subordinate his will to it. (ibid., 162; 284)

The centrality of hospitality to Marx's thought is more clearly indicated by his materialist reinscription of the Aristotelian-Hegelian motif of idealization. For Hegel, idealization is the power of the concept to exteriorize itself by taking on a corporeal or objective shape while remaining at home with itself. Spirit is that which stays at home even as it becomes something foreign to itself. The paradigm for Hegel's characterization of spirit is paradoxically the animal. The animal's possession of a nervous system and its ability to have sensation enables it to distinguish between itself and the external world. Hence, the animal does not lose itself in its contact with the outside. It can assimilate the external world because it can limit or check its relation to the other. Animal subjectivity "consists in preserving itself in its corporeality and in its contact with an outer world and, as the universal, remaining at home with itself [*bei sich selbst zu bleiben*]" (Hegel 1970a, 430; 1970c, 352).[4] In the assimilative process, the animal's appetite opens and directs it to the outside, but it does so only to idealize objectivity, to purge external material of its foreignness so that it can be used to remedy a lack within the animal.

> The animal is thus, in the negative, at the same time positively at home with itself [*bei sich*]; and this, too, is the privilege of higher natures, to exist as this contradiction [*Widerspruch*]. But equally, too, the animal restores its lost harmony and finds satisfaction within itself. Animal appetite is the idealism of objectivity [*Gegenständlich-*

keit], so that the latter is no longer something alien to the animal. (ibid., 472; 387–88)

Spiritual activity is therefore the movement of a certain hospitality: spirit opens itself up to an other that is not itself and relates to this other in such a way that it always returns back to itself from this otherness and so endures and contains alterity as a contradiction within itself. Spirit is being that can make a home, be positively at home in its other. At the level of social and political life (what Hegel calls objective spirit), this ontological topos of being at home in otherness takes the concrete shape of relations between the individual and civil society, and subsequently, those of the citizen to the state. In the individual's relation to civil society, being at home with oneself in the other is manifested in the process of formative maturation whereby the individual overcomes the revolutionary ardor he felt as a restless youth and his sense of alienation from the larger social world and its values. He learns to be a productive member who is at home in civil society (qua ethical substrate or *Sittlichkeit*) through his immersion in a profession.

> With his entry now into practical life, the man may well be vexed and morose about the state of the world and lose hope of any improvement in it; but in spite of this he finds his place in the world of objective relationships and becomes habituated to it and to his work [*lebt in der Gewohnheit an dieselben und an seine Geschäfte*]. . . . [T]he longer the man is active in his work, the more does this universal rise into prominence out of the welters of particulars. In this way he gets to be completely at home in his profession [*in seinem Fache völlig zu Hause zu sein*] and grows thoroughly accustomed to his lot. (Hegel 1970b, 85; 1971, 63)

Marx, on the other hand, derives a fundamental right to hospitality from the power of material labor to make a world. The most visible impact of the constant revolutionizing of production under modern industrial capitalism is the thorough transformation of the physical landscape of the world into an interconnected and borderless global system of exchange and production—the world market—that should satisfy all human needs.

> [The bourgeoisie] has been the first to show what man's activity can bring about. It has accomplished wonders far surpassing Egyptian pyramids, Roman aqueducts, and Gothic cathedrals; it has conducted expeditions that put in the shade all former exoduses of nations [*Völkerwanderungen*] and crusades. (Marx/Engels 1932a, 528; 1976a, 70)

> The bourgeoisie, by the rapid improvement of all instruments of production, by the infinite [*unendlich*] facilitated means of communication, draws all, even the most barbarian, nations into civilization. The cheap prices of its commodities are the heavy artillery with which it batters down all Chinese walls, with which it forces the barbarians' intensely obstinate hatred of foreigners to capitulate. It compels all nations, on pain of extinction, to adopt the bourgeois mode of production; it compels them to introduce what it calls civilization into their midst, i.e. to become bourgeois themselves. In one word, it creates a world after its own image [*Bilde*]. (ibid., 529–30; 71; translation slightly modified)
>
> The bourgeoisie, during its rule of scarce one hundred years, has created more massive and more colossal productive forces than have all preceding generations together. Subjection of nature's forces to man, machinery, application of chemistry to industry and agriculture, steam navigation, railways, electric telegraphs, clearing of whole continents for cultivation, canalization of rivers, whole populations conjured out of the ground—what earlier century had even a presentiment that such productive forces slumbered in the lap of social labour? (ibid., 530; 72)

In principle, this world created in the image of bourgeois industrial capitalism should be a world of the greatest possible hospitality, a home that can receive every single member of humanity. Capitalism not only remakes the lived environment so that it is habitable by new and rapidly growing populations and so that it can satisfy the needs of these populations. It also breaks down cultural and political borders that obstruct human material intercourse (*Verkehr*), the paradigm of which is commercial exchange and the flow of goods. The primary claim of Marx's theory of alienation, however, is precisely that although capitalism creates a connected world, this world is radically inhospitable because capitalism renders homeless the worker who makes up the mass of the world's population. The worker can never be at home in bourgeois civil society or its political superstructure, the state, because by alienating the products of his life activity from him, capitalism brings about the worker's alienation from social life and, indeed, from his own humanity.

Alienation is a perversion of the affirmative opening to the outside world that characterizes objectification. Because the worker's products are the property of another (the capitalist), they become an alien and hostile second nature that dominates their producer like a monstrous power. Hence, labor is no longer a form of *Bildung* that adds greater meaning to his life. It becomes a heteronomous activity, a mere means of subsistence that deforms his inner being and depletes the worker's humanity. In Marx's (1973b, 366; 1975, 325) poignant words, "the more values he creates, the more worthless he becomes; the more his product is shaped [*geformter*], the more misshapen [*mißförmiger*] the worker; the more civilized his object, the more barbarous the worker." Capitalism undermines the human ability of being at home with oneself in the world. The world it creates is inhospitable because it diverts, stifles, and even destroys the human power to make the external world a social substrate that can receive the human individual and allow the full development of his personality as a member of humanity. Hence, the worker "does not confirm [*bejaht*] himself in his work.... Hence ... [he] feels himself only when he is not working.... He is at home [*zu Hause*] when he is not working, and not at home when he is working.... [His labor] is therefore not the satisfaction of a need but a mere means to satisfy needs outside itself" (ibid., 367; 326). He loses his humanity because he can no longer recognize humanity in his life activity or see any common human connection in his relations with others because all relations have been reduced to quantified commodity relations. Alienation is the opposite of hospitality. Instead of creating a world that can be a place of welcome for the human being, a home where he can fully develop himself through universal human cooperation or sociality, he is subject to an expropriation, a pernicious opening that takes away what is proper to humankind. Alienation propels us into a hostile, foreign world.

In Marx's view, alienation can only be overcome by the reappropriation of the totality of productive forces by socialized labor. The revolutionary act of appropriation (*Aneignung*) is the reaffirmation of the human capacity to be at home with itself in the external world. It will create a world that is truly hospitable in two senses. First, the total character of the appropriation means that the world it generates is truly universal.[5] Second, this world will also be borderless because the global spread of the capitalist mode of production has made material intercourse cosmopolitan. Even in its bourgeois form, (civil) society already transcends the borders of the territorial nation-state. It has opened up world history (ibid., 25–26; 57). Accordingly, the return of the global totality of productive forces to their true producers will create a borderless society. Although Marx did not discuss the free global mass migration of workers, he clearly envisioned a universal and borderless hospitality. Because socialized labor will annihilate everything external to it, the body of the host will extend throughout the world. Henceforth, the world will be a home open to all workers. Indeed, for Marx, humanity can only be actualized in a condition of borderless hospitality in which all territorial borders are eradicated. We find a similar vision of borderless hospitality in Michael Hardt and Antonio Negri's (2000, 400) political demand for global citizenship, their exhortation that "the existent fact of capitalist production be recognized juridically and that all workers be given the full rights of citizenship."

The philosophical topoi of alienation and appropriation in Marx's account of hospitality are part of a discourse of the proper, a discourse concerning the characteristics or attributes (properties) that define the essence of something or someone, what is one's own (appropriateness), that which can be owned, etc. This means that the opening to otherness is always controlled and limited by recourse to values of the proper. A proper discourse of hospitality has two key features. First, it is always a discourse about alienation and its overcoming, in which the other is always figured as a part of the self that has been made alien through autonomization. The overcoming of alienation involves the return or restoration of this other to the proper self through appropriation. In Marx's account, socialized human labor consolidates itself by integrating the foreign other (products that are also forces of production) within it as a contradiction that can be sublated. Marxian hospitality is limitless precisely because the entire world has been made part of the process of humanity's self-actualization. Second, the opening to the other is always conditioned by the determination of a proper community, a community that is present to itself in its self-possession. The hospitality Marx envisions may be universal and unlimited insofar as it pertains to all workers irrespective of national or cultural ties; it is nevertheless limited and conditional because the world created is a world of workers or producers, where work is what is proper to humankind, its defining characteristic or essence and, therefore, the proper of mankind.

Despite its different philosophical underpinnings, we see similar features in Hannah Arendt's (1968) political understanding of the right to hospitality. In the well-known chapter of *The Origins of Totalitarianism* entitled "The Decline of the Nation-State and the End of the Rights of Man," she explains the lack of hospitality shown toward the displaced populations created by the two world wars in terms of their loss of a world.

> The fundamental deprivation of human rights is manifested first and above all in the deprivation of a place in the world which makes opinions significant and actions effective. Something much more fundamental than freedom and justice, which are rights of citizens, is at stake when belonging to the community into which one is born is no longer a matter of course and not belonging no longer a matter of choice, or when one is placed in a situation where . . . his treatment by others does not depend on what he does or does not do. This

extremity, and nothing else, is the situation of people deprived of human rights. They are deprived, not of the right of freedom, but of the right to action; not of the right to think whatever they please, but of the right of opinion. Privileges in some cases, injustices in most, blessings and doom are meted out to them according to accident and without any relation whatsoever to what they do, did, or may do. (296)

In Arendt's view, the world is coextensive with a certain publicness because it is created through speech and action instead of material labor. What she calls the human right to have rights is first and foremost a right to hospitality, a right to be part of a home or organized political community understood as a field where one exchanges words and deeds with others. A person's entitlement to specific rights such as freedom and justice springs from being part of a community with others. But this community is not based on kinship, blood, or even material labor. Its relations or ties are established through words and deeds. Through such exchanges, one announces one's belonging in that community and has one's status acknowledged by others, thereby acceding to the privileges, rights, and duties that membership to the community brings. The human right to hospitality is therefore a right to be received by others coupled with a fundamental duty to receive others. It captures the fact that humanity and belonging to a world are mutually defining terms.

Arendt argues that in the past the coextensiveness of humanity and worldliness was obscured because of the limited scope of communities, which corresponded to territorially bounded sovereign units that had no formal institutional connection to each other. Hence, the loss of a home or a state did not mean that someone was deprived of humanity outside one's former community. However, in the twentieth century, treaties of reciprocity and international agreements organize humanity into a community of legitimate nation-states according to principles of mutual recognition. Hence, a person deprived of a polity was also cast out of humanity (294–97). Seen as illegitimate or without political status in the eyes of all countries, the stateless person is also deprived of access to juridical instruments that can protect his inalienable human rights. In Arendt's poignant words, "the prolongation of [the lives of the rightless] is due to charity and not to right, for no law exists which could force nations to feed them; their freedom of movement . . . gives them no right to residence which even the jailed criminal enjoys as a matter of course; and their freedom of opinion is a fool's freedom, for nothing they think matters anyhow" (296).

The right to hospitality has its ontological basis in the fact that human beings only exist amidst plurality.[6] Our being is always a being-with-others, always a being within a world. Worldhood is the fundamental condition of human as opposed to merely biological existence because it is a web of relations that has permanence and durability beyond the relentless cycle of merely natural life and its processes of consumption. The world's persistent endurance is precisely what makes it a place of hospitality, a place that is open to and can receive each and every individual human life. The world marks out an individual's mortal life span and gives his life significance beyond mere living.

> Birth and death presuppose a world which is not in constant movement, but whose durability and relative permanence makes appearance and disappearance possible, which existed before any one individual appeared into it and will survive his eventual departure. Without a world into which men are born and from which they die, there would be nothing but changeless eternal recurrence, the deathless everlastingness of the human as of all other animal species.... The chief characteristic of this specifically human life, whose appearance and disappearance constitutes worldly events, is that it is itself always full of events which ultimately can be told as a story, establish a biography; it is of this life, *bios* as distinguished from mere *zoe*, that Aristotle said that it "somehow is a kind of praxis." For action and speech . . . are indeed the two activities whose end result will always be a story with enough coherence to be told, no matter how accidental or haphazard the single events and their causation may appear to be. (Arendt 1958, 97)

The world makes human life possible because it is the milieu in which human life can be received, sustained, and endowed with a meaningful permanence in its very finitude. At the same time, however, the world is repeatedly constituted through human endeavor. In the first instance, it is a world of objects created for use by human work (as opposed to labor, which only creates things for consumption). The repeated use of objects gives rise to an enduring web of relations. Pointing to the double meaning of use as utility and habitual intimacy, Arendt suggests that through the repeated use of objects, "we become used and accustomed. As such, they give rise to the familiarity of the world, its customs and habits of intercourse between men and things as well as between men and men" (94). But more significantly, what has even greater permanence than object-directed intercourse, Arendt argues, are the ties created by action and speech as processes that disclose agents. Although objects of use are more durable than the "products" of action and speech by virtue of their tangibility, the fact that they are made for use deprives them of meaningful permanence. Their existence depends on their continuing usefulness and their exchangeability. Since these are relative or conditional matters, determined by the subject of use or by the market, they cannot give rise to standards and universal rules required to establish the permanence of a world. In contradistinction, speech and action create intrinsically meaningful "phenomena" that transcend biological life and mere instrumentality. Indeed, Arendt argues that the world of words and deeds is a priori to, more fundamental than, the objective world of things because there cannot be any activity of fabrication without the disclosure of human beings to each other as subjects and the establishment of relations between them. The primary purpose of words and deeds is to disclose subjects and form an intersubjective world. "Since this disclosure of the subject is an integral part of all, even the most 'objective' intercourse, the physical, worldly in-between along with its interests is overlaid and, as it were, overgrown with an altogether different in-between which consists of deeds and words and owes its origin exclusively to men's acting and speaking directly to one another" (ibid., 182–83). This subjective in-between has a fundamental reality despite its nontangibility, for it is nothing other than the entire web of human relations.[7] Its reality is a human reality, the strange phenomenality of human beings for each other in the purely intersubjective intercourse that necessarily accompanies all making as the latter's precondition.

For Arendt, the world opened up by speech and action has its ontological ground in natality, the original opening by which we come into the world. The constitution of such a world is a second birth by which we commemorate and freely confirm our first coming.

> With word and deed we insert ourselves into the human world, and this insertion is like a second birth, in which we confirm and take upon ourselves the naked fact of our original physical appearance. . . . [I]ts impulse springs from the beginning which came into the world when we were born and to which we respond by beginning something new on our own initiative. To act, in its most general sense, means to take an initiative, to begin . . . to set something into motion. . . . Because they are initium, newcomers and beginners by virtue of birth, men take initiative, are prompted into action. (Arendt 1958, 176–77)

We therefore have to understand the power of opening a world that cobelongs with human life as a power of self-opening and self-becoming, a practical affirmation of the opening and coming-to-be that is the human being.

This power is, however, undermined in the modern era, which Arendt (1958, 253) characterizes as the age of world alienation. Property, she argues, is what initially gives someone a place or location in the world. It is an indication of what is proper to man, namely, being part of a world. To own property "indicates the privately owned share of a common world and therefore is the most elementary political condition for man's worldliness." In contradistinction, expropriation, the process necessary for the accumulation of wealth, is a process of world alienation because by taking away the property of some it is "the deprivation for certain groups of their place in the world and their naked exposure to the exigencies of life" (254–55). In the past, expropriation did not lead to complete alienation because it always led to the creation of new property. Modern capitalist expropriation, however, is world destroying because it does not create new property. The relentless process of the transformation of wealth into capital means that any wealth generated by expropriation is "fed back into the process to generate further expropriations, greater productivity, and more appropriation," and this endless process of productivity brings about world alienation (Arendt 1958, 253–55).

> The process can continue only provided that no worldly durability or stability is permitted to interfere, only as long as all worldly things, all end products of the production processes, are fed back into it at an ever-increasing speed. In other words, the process of wealth accumulation, as we know it, stimulated by the life process and in turn stimulating human life, is possible only if the world and the very worldliness of man are sacrificed. (ibid., 256)

The modern age presents the following paradox: on the one hand, the interconnectedness brought about by globalization has made the unity of humanity a phenomenon that actually exists, "an inescapable fact" instead of a mere ideal.[8] On the other hand, the erosion of a common public world undermines the achievement of a borderless hospitality. The loss of the right to hospitality experienced by stateless peoples is merely a synecdoche of this general condition of homelessness and world alienation. Indeed, the situation is so dire that Arendt (1968, 298) is doubtful about the feasibility of a supranational juridical solution even if a world government could be established. "The right to have rights, or the right of every individual to belong to humanity," she writes, "should be guaranteed by humanity itself." But the problem with the extant organization of humanity is that its utilitarian logic not only expels certain peoples from humanity but also makes everyone worldless.[9] Arendt's (1968) solution to the radical inhospitality of modernity is to reaffirm the human powers that make a meaningful world. We can reopen the world through action, she suggests, because it is an opening that recollects the original opening of human existence.

> The miracle that saves the world, the realm of human affairs, from its normal, "natural" ruin is ultimately the fact of natality, in which the faculty of action is ontologically rooted. It is, in other words, the birth of new men and the new beginning, the action they are capable of by virtue of being born. Only the full experience of this capacity can bestow upon human affairs faith and hope. (247)

The full significance of Arendt's grounding of the right to hospitality in the human power of opening a world is succinctly captured in the opposition between the political figure of the stateless refugee and the ontological figure of the newcomer. The newcomer is the power of welcome itself. It opens a world that is radically open to all human beings. It follows that Arendt's account of hospitality is also a discourse of the proper. First, the right to hospitality arises from capacities that are proper to humanity—the powers that create a world, give it meaning, and make it capable of innovation. The proper here involves a return, but unlike the Marxist-Hegelian topos of "being at home with oneself in otherness," it is not a return to a collective self that is immanent to human existence. Instead, the proper is that which projects us into the world. It is the movement of relating to others, an opening onto others, because it is only in the copresence of others, in human plurality, that we achieve what is proper to our humanity, namely, our worldliness. Second, the reopening of the world in the face of its alienation involves yet another return. To reaffirm our capacity for work and action is to recall the original opening that is our proper/makes us proper: the fact that only human beings are born and come into the world as something new, and therefore have a proper life, an existence with a proper beginning and end.

For both Marx and Arendt, therefore, hospitality is synonymous with the proper. To be hospitable and to be received hospitably means to receive others and to be received by others as part of this circle of the proper, to integrate all human beings within this circle of the proper either through the socialization of production or through work, action, and thought. Hence, there is a certain economy at work in hospitality, a return to an origin that is also a perpetual movement of origination. This has two implications. First, the right to hospitality is at heart a manifestation of humanity's power and capability, the power to be proper, the capacity to return to its proper. Second, the opening of hospitality, the opening that is hospitality, however borderless it may be, is always limited and conditioned by this proper.

Improper or Aneconomic Hospitality (Derrida)

The theory and practice of hospitality in our era of global migration is governed by an economy of the proper. The home or site of hospitality must always be strong and secure enough to be opened to a stranger. Moreover, the host must be sufficiently powerful and secure in itself, in the sense of having enough confidence and being at home with itself, to welcome and endure the other's entry and to relate to the other (with respect, appreciation, etc.) in such a way that, regardless of the alterations or transformations in its constitution that may result from being with the other, its core integrity will remain intact. It must always remain proper to itself. One should open up to the other and allow the other to find a home in oneself, but this other must always be made part of the circle of the proper. Hence, there are always calculations about the nature of opening. If we take the paradigmatic case of the relation between a country or territorial entity or even a continental formation such as Europe and the immigrant or refugee, they can be cost-benefit calculations concerning the economic advantages of migrant workers or the economic drain of refugees. Or, in the case of public discourse on the transformation of European national or continental identity or U.S. cultural identity by global migration, the calculations are cultural. What is at stake in these cultural debates is precisely this ability of the proper, this "I can" of the host region or country to maintain and conserve itself as an ongoing project in the face of the challenges of global migration by multiculturalizing itself in a salutary way while still remaining European or American. Conversely, the erosion of this power of the proper will lead to alienation and anomie in both the migrant and native sectors of host societies.

The continuing significance of Marx's and Arendt's discourses of hospitality lies in their rejection of the capitalist determination of the proper in terms of the calculative reason of accumulation and exchange (and in Arendt's case, instrumentality) on the grounds that it can only lead to inhospitality. Accordingly, they redefine the proper in terms of the human capacity to make and to open a world that can receive humanity. Because this human power is more original or fundamental than the capitalist processes that alienate and make us homeless, it can overcome these processes of inhospitality. What makes the deconstructive idea of hospitality so radical is that it breaks away from this schema of the proper and envisions an improper hospitality where the opening is that of the human host's structural vulnerability to a nonhuman other instead of a power that cobelongs with humanity. This structural vulnerability is not simple or measurable. It is an opening to an other that is so radical that it brings about the nondeterminability of both host and other.

In the first place, Derrida suggests that the paradoxical nature of true hospitality—what he calls absolute or unconditional hospitality—is such that the host can neither be prepared nor intend to welcome the other.

> One must not only not be ready nor prepared to welcome [*accuellir*], nor well disposed to welcome—for if the welcome is the simple manifestation of a natural or acquired disposition, of a generous character or of a hospitable habitus, there is no merit in it, no welcome of the other as other. But . . . it is also true that if I welcome the other out of mere duty, unwillingly, against my natural inclination, and therefore without smiling, I am not welcoming him either: One must [*il faut*] therefore welcome without "one must" [*sans "il faut"*]. . . . If, in hospitality, one must say yes, welcome the coming [*accuellir la venue*]. Say the "welcome"; one must say yes, there where one does not wait, yes, there where one does not expect, nor await oneself to, the other [*là où l'on ne s'attend pas soi-même à l'autre*], to let oneself be swept by the coming of the wholly other, the absolutely unforeseeable [*inanticipable*] stranger, the uninvited visitor, the unexpected visitation beyond welcoming apparatuses. If I welcome only what I welcome, what I am ready to welcome, and that I recognize in advance because I expect the coming of the *hôte* as invited, there is no hospitality. (Derrida 2002a, 361–62)

True hospitality cannot be generous or gracious in the Western tradition of grace (*gratia, kharis*) because the intention to welcome generously, like the intention to give, makes the opening to the other conditional.[10] It limits the opening according to the host's good nature and to what he wills in relation to an other that he can determine in advance. A generous hospitality is conditional because it remains within the host's power and control. It is an opening where the host is in total self-control. He remains in power, remains sovereign, because he is confident in and knows fully his own power. Second, true hospitality also requires that the other I welcome not be recognizable, determinable, anticipatable, or foreseeable. If I decide to be hospitable to this or that kind of other, hospitality once again becomes conditional because I am limiting the opening to certain known or imaginable categories of others that I determine according to my calculations, for instance, refugees, asylum seekers, some kinds of economic migrants, etc.

The same argument applies to Marx's and Arendt's accounts of borderless hospitality where the world's hospitality to every single person is not merely a matter of the host's kindness or generosity but a matter of right that cobelongs with humanity. What is at issue here is the power of the "I can" who posits the right and makes the claim to hospitality on the basis of knowing that it is human and can therefore expect hospitality within the world just as it is expected to render hospitality to other members of humanity because both the right and duty are grounded in the human capacity of making a world. The opening remains conditional on and limited by membership in the human community even if membership is defined not by a human essence but by the capacity for performance and action. This is why Derrida insists that absolute hospitality can neither be a matter of charity or philanthropy, nor of right: "the law of absolute hospitality commands a break with hospitality by right, with law or justice as rights. Just hospitality breaks with hospitality by right" (Derrida and Dufourmantelle 2000, 25; 55–57). The pact of membership implied by any right is necessarily accompanied by violence because it involves exclusion and, therefore, policing and monitoring.

What then is the precise nature of the opening that characterizes absolute hospitality? Whereas the opening of the world in Marx's and Arendt's accounts of hospitality is a self-opening, an opening that is a power of the human subject, absolute hospitality is an exposure that renders any power completely vulnerable to the other. Derrida argues that this vulnerability is a priori, always already at work in the constitution of any power. Power is a temporal category, a phenomenon that takes place in time. But time itself, which cannot be anything temporal, can only be thought as the coming of the pure event, the coming of the absolute other beyond presence as such. Hence, any form of being, any power, must remain open to this coming of the other. This exposure to the other from which time comes is therefore constitutive. But since the other is not of the order of presence, its coming makes power impossible even as it makes it possible. As a quasi-transcendental weakness that constitutes the strength of the strong, this exposure is the inerasable trace of power's compromise and undoing.

We can isolate at least four salient features of absolute hospitality. First, absolute hospitality is fundamentally inhuman. It is not a power that issues from and cobelongs with humanity. The force of this opening is not something that is within human power. It is the structural exposure of any finite being or thing—mineral, vegetable, animal, or human and, indeed, any form of presence—to the coming of time as the pure event. This force is the coming of an other who cannot be determined in advance as a presence, much less another human being. Second, although this openness is marked by unconditionality, its urgency or exigency is not the unconditional force of universal human reason, that is to say, an imperative of reason that transcends particularistic self-interest, whether this takes the form of morality or juridico-political right. In Derrida's view, rational imperatives are not truly unconditional because processes of reason are themselves conditioned by and grounded in an opening to the absolutely other from which time comes. Hence, it is this opening that is genuinely unconditional. By definition, we cannot know if and when there will be a pure event. Hence, the exposure to the other is something that cannot be determined in advance. It exceeds any conditions that reason lays down, even the condition that the opening is to all human beings, that is, the human other in general. It is in this spirit that Derrida (2003, 128–29) describes absolute hospitality as a hospitality of visitation rather than invitation: "pure and unconditional hospitality . . . opens or is in advance open to someone who is neither expected nor invited, to whomever arrives as an absolutely foreign visitor, as a new arrival, nonidentifiable and unforeseeable, in short, wholly other."

Third, unlike the proper hospitalities envisioned by Marx and Arendt, absolute hospitality implies the radical alienation of the host instead of the overcoming of alienation. For Derrida, the *hospes* is nothing other than the constitutive trace of the foreign within the proper home of humanity. The alien is therefore not something that can be contained by being integrated, reappropriated into, or returned to the circle of the proper. What may perhaps come is the wholly other, and this is not the newcomer in Arendt's sense. The latter is merely the second coming of the human self in its movement of self-opening. Absolute hospitality is therefore a constitutive movement of expropriation, a movement that is prior to the proper that makes the proper proper in the first place, what Derrida calls ex-appropriation.

Fourth, because it renders impossible the self's ipseity or power, absolute hospitality is, strictly speaking, impracticable. Any rational practice or action, indeed, existence as such, necessarily presupposes a power that is sovereign or present to itself in its sameness. It therefore presupposes the closure or self-return of the proper. All discourses of making the world and human self-making, all discourses of conditional hospitality, are discourses of the proper. This self-return of the proper is precisely what the defenselessness of absolute hospitality undermines. At the same time, however, absolute hospitality exists in an aporetic embrace with conditional hospitality insofar as they both destabilize and require each other. Without the sheer vulnerability of an unconditional opening to the other, there would not be any world, place, or home, no host that can offer hospitality, nor any relation or being with the other at all. This openness to the coming of the other is necessary because without it, there would not be time. We would not be and therefore would not be able to make anything, much less the world or ourselves. Hence, no conditional hospitality would be possible. As Derrida (2003) puts it,

> An unconditional hospitality is, to be sure, practically impossible to live; one cannot in any case, and by definition, organize it. Whatever happens, happens, whoever comes, comes (*ce qui arrive arrive*), and that, in the end is the only event worthy of this name. . . . [T]his concept of pure hospitality can have no legal or political status. No state can write it into its laws. But without at least the thought of this pure and unconditional hospitality, of hospitality itself, we would have no concept of hospitality in general and would not even be able to determine any rules for conditional hospitality (with its rituals, legal status, its norms, its national or international conventions). Without this thought of pure hospitality . . . we would not even have an idea of the other, of the alterity of the other, that is, of someone who enters into our lives without having been invited. We would not even have the idea of love or of "living together (*vivre ensemble*)" with the other in a way that is not a part of some totality or "*ensemble*." Unconditional hospitality, which is neither juridical nor political, is nonetheless the condition of the political and the juridical. (129)

This is undoubtedly why Derrida has always insisted that systems of thought that close themselves to the coming of the event are in solidarity with totalitarian institutions and practices (cf. Derrida 2002b, 182). They are death-dealing, they have no *à-venir*, no to-come, because they claim and wish to be immune to time. But conversely, conditional hospitality, which violates absolute hospitality by limiting the opening to the other, is also necessary so that absolute hospitality can be practicable or effective and offer something concrete to the other.

Derrida's idea of absolute hospitality grounds the human right of hospitality in a more fundamental opening of the world that is not a matter of the will or capacity of human reason. The world is not, in the first instance, something that human beings create by virtue of their powers or capabilities. It is opened up by the coming of the wholly other, and this opening is something that cannot be predicted or calculated in advance by human reason. Hence, we cannot control how we open up to the other or determine in advance the kind of other to whom we open ourselves. Derrida's thought of the constitutive opening to the nonhuman other must be rigorously distinguished from the more widespread socio-discursive constructionist argument that the human subject is constituted through the deployment of socio-discursive norms that repress and exclude as nonhuman a variety of minority subjects and other peoples.[11] This popular theoretical schema for understanding oppression suggests that the hegemonic social or political subject is formed by a foundational negation, namely, a forceful act of exception or exclusion that is then repeated. In contradistinction, the constitutive opening that Derrida has in mind is a nonnegative relation in which the human subject is ushered in or inaugurated by a structural vulnerability to the nonhuman other, a receptiveness to and affirmation of the other that dislocates and suspends the human subject in all its vitality, power, and possibility. The constitutive opening to the other is therefore not a simple negation of the subject by an outside that has been formed by exclusion. It is instead the weak force of an internal, structural principle of contamination and ruination.

The advantage of Derrida's thought of absolute hospitality in comparison with the proper hospitalities of Marx and Arendt is as follows: Because Marx and Arendt located the power of opening a world in the human being, they viewed the inhospitality of capitalist accumulation as a consequence of the alienation that befalls humanity, corrupts and degrades it and obscures its true power. Accordingly, overcoming inhospitality involves transcending the calculative and instrumental "logic" of capitalist accumulation through activities that affirm and recuperate this original human power. In our current global conjuncture, where the transcendence of capitalism is not in sight, neither the account of alienation nor the recuperation of pure human activity is plausible. Instead of relying on these onto-theological figures of human redemption, Derrida's argument that the world is opened up by the coming of the nonhuman other points to a force of destabilization that necessarily constitutes the "logic" of global capitalism. But this destabilizing force equally accompanies all the shapes of human power that claim to be the solution to capitalist accumulation. It is, in short, the inerasable trace of a principle of change. This trace cannot be effaced or destroyed by human calculation precisely because it cannot be determined by, reduced to, or exhausted in human power.

In the more concrete context of a nation-state as host, absolute hospitality is not a simple rejection of existing practices of conditional hospitality. The opening to the coming of the other is the exigency of an interminable pressure that can loosen the borders and boundaries of the host as this is expressed and determined by conditional hospitality. Absolute hospitality can persistently unsettle and undermine the limitations of existing determinations and calculations of how we open to others and which others we open ourselves to. It is precisely the movement that gives the host an *à-venir*, the force of its living on or surviving in the rapidly changing world of globalization. At the same time, absolute hospitality can also be life-threatening since it requires the suspension of the immunity that protects the host from the other. Hence, the opening must always be limited again. This aporetic transaction or shuttling between absolute and conditional hospitality is an endlessly shifting ground for the renewal and transformation of existing practices of juridical and political hospitality, and, indeed, for the inventing of new practices that can revitalize the host.

Migration as the Privileged Figure of Hospitality: Some Limits

In the spirit of Derrida's acknowledgment of the dangers of absolute hospitality, I will conclude by questioning the exigency of opening itself. Hospitality is, I have argued, a matter of opening or making a world that is hospitable. Humanities scholarship on globalization has quite appropriately focused on flows of people and culture instead of economic flows. In an age of global migration, the intuitive ethical appeal of the concept of hospitality is due to the fact that it pertains to flows of people who should have the right to free movement and refuge, especially those others who are weak. Hence, barriers to this free movement have historically been associated with xenophobia, racism, and other forms of discrimination. Despite his critique of the determination of the other as human, Derrida's account of hospitality curiously maintains this focus on migration. In his view, true hospitality is offered to what he calls an absolute *arrivant*, who is defined through a negative relation to the sociological, anthropological, or political figure of the approaching foreigner. The *arrivant* is

> whatever, whoever, in arriving, does not cross a threshold separating two identifiable places, the proper and the foreign, the proper of the one and the proper of the other, as one would say of the citizen of a given identifiable country across the border of another country as a traveler, an emigré or a political exile, a refugee or someone who has been deported, an immigrant worker, a student or a researcher, a diplomat or a tourist. Those are all, of course, arrivants, but in a country that is already defined and in which the inhabitants know or think they are at home. . . . No, I am talking about the absolute *arrivant*, who is not even a guest. He surprises the host—who is not yet a host or an inviting power—enough to call into question, to the point of annihilating or rendering indeterminate, all the distinctive signs of a prior identity, beginning with the very border that delineated a legitimate home and assured lineage, names and language, nations, families and genealogies. The absolute *arrivant* does not yet have a name or an identity. It is not an invader or an occupier, nor is it a

colonizer, even if it can also become one. This is why I call it simply the *arrivant*, and not someone or something that arrives, a subject, a person, an individual, or a living thing, even less one of the migrants I just mentioned. It is not even a foreigner identified as a member of a foreign, determined community. Since the *arrivant* does not have any identity yet, its place of arrival is also de-identified: one does not yet know or one no longer knows which is the country, the place, the nation, the family, the language, and the home in general that welcomes the absolute *arrivant*. (Derrida 1993, 33–34)

We can read the opening to Derrida's curiously emptied-out figure of the migrant, the migrant *sous rature*, in two ways. On the one hand, we can understand it in terms of the limits of the intersubjective or interpersonal figure of the migrant as the main reference point of hospitality. If we take this relation as the paradigmatic relation of hospitality, it can prevent a fuller engagement with how globalization is making the world today in ways that make absolute hospitality decidedly dangerous. Today, the world is primarily fabricated by economic flows of money and commodities from the North to the South and back again within the framework of an unequal international division of labor: outsourcing, international subcontracting, the setting up of export-oriented production zones, etc., all in the name of the development of the postcolonial South. Marx's and Arendt's diagnoses about their times apply equally today: These processes of world-making are at the same time world-destroying and world-alienating. The world has indeed become more borderless but it is not thereby more hospitable. Marx could at least envision a practical way out of this bind through global revolution. The prognosis for our times is less encouraging. In the uneven world of capitalist globalization, it seems that the only way for countries in the postcolonial South to be more hospitable to their citizens, that is to say, to offer better welfare and honor their right to employment so that they are not compelled to migrate out of economic necessity, is to play the game of attracting global capital so that they can gradually increase their power and ascend the hierarchy of the international division of labor. In this context, the desirability of an opening without defense becomes more questionable.

Significantly, openness is also a paramount value of bourgeois economic discourse. In the writings of Adam Smith (1976, 514–19), for example, the topos of an open port or a market without artificial monopolistic barriers linked the free movement of goods not only to the prosperity of all nations but also to the advantageous development of humanity. Such free movement, Smith argued, accords with "the common sense of mankind." I cite only two among the many instances of this topos in *The Wealth of Nations*: "Trade which, without force or constraint, is naturally and regularly carried on between any two places, is always advantageous," and "Commerce . . . ought naturally to be, among nations, as among individuals, a bond of union and friendship." We see a similar connection between commerce and cosmopolitan sociability not only in Kant, but also in neoliberal ideology.

But hospitality without defense to foreign flows of finance capital can be devastating, as illustrated by the Asian financial crises of the late 1990s, the series of linked events set off by the assault on the Thai baht by currency speculators on May 14–15, 1997.[12] The falling currency triggered investor panic, leading to a crashing stock market and falling property prices. As the result of a "contagion" or "domino effect," the pattern was repeated with some variations in countries throughout the region, some of which were generally perceived to have much stronger economic fundamentals than Thailand, for instance, Malaysia and South Korea. The reversal of short-term capital inflows led to a severe liquidity crunch that caused the collapse of local corporations and massive unemployment even as inflation grew as a result of the devalued local currencies. The combined effect was a drastic deterioration of living standards, especially for the millions of poor people, and this suffering escalated into social and political upheaval, riots, destruction, and death. This is an ironic allegory of the dangers of absolute hospitality. On the one hand, the exposure to global capital flows is constitutive because it is crucial to the prodigious growth and development of these Asian nation-states. At the same time, the opening of the nation-state to free market structures implies an a priori vulnerability to the speculative disequilibria and retrogression associated with international capital markets. The conditions of possibility of the strength and power of these countries are at one and the same time a structure that makes them radically vulnerable. Hence, some countries saw the need to introduce capital controls—the economic version of conditional hospitality—in opposition to the IMF and the World Bank's agenda of market liberalization.

Indeed, such flows of global capital are part of the material conditions of migrant flows from the South to the North. I mention only two obvious examples of this structural connection between the two types of opening in the South and North: export-oriented production zones (EPZs) and international tourism. First, the practice of outsourcing or the relocation of production to EPZs in the South establishes strong channels for the entry of migrant workers seeking to escape the extreme poverty of the peripheries. As Saskia Sassen (1998, 119–20) has observed, "the strong presence of foreign firms facilitates access to information and a sense of familiarity with the potential destination." This removes the deterrence of distance by giving the "promised land" in the North a more imaginable, sensuous presence. Second, the promotion of countries in the South such as Thailand as exotic destinations for international tourism opens up avenues for the transnational migration of sex workers. The rapid industrialization of a capital city such as Bangkok at the expense of rural regions leads to the migration of young girls in search of work for the alleviation of rural poverty. This increases the supply of potential sex workers, since failure to find adequate income from nonsex work such as factory or service work can lead girls to prostitution. Sex tourism is an important but unacknowledged part of international tourism and the city in question becomes a gateway for the overseas migration of sex workers, trafficked or otherwise.[13] Ironically, sex work often goes under the euphemism, "the hospitality industry."

What we see in these cases are two distinct but structurally related scenes of hospitality: an opening to economic flows in the South followed by the need of the North to open up to different kinds of foreigners. The first scene of hospitality, the primal scene, if you will, is always to capital flows and the second scene is always to people. The first scene is a material condition of contemporary Northern multicultural migrancy and the pluralization of Northern cultures, and the important debates on these topics. We therefore need to understand hospitality in a way that takes us beyond the customary focus on flows of people. We need to situate this scene of hospitality and, indeed, the very emergence of hospitality as a key ethical or political concept in our current conjuncture within their material conditions: the hospitality to capital flows that are making our world. To critically engage with these flows requires rational determinations and calculations of conditional hospitality at different levels or orders of the proper: how to open and to what, since opening is a necessity; what is the degree of opening and how can it be controlled and limited? Whether they are progressive or reactionary, such decisions and determinations are, in the final instance, continuous with capitalist globalization because they are cases of the proper economy of calculative reason whether this takes the form of instrumental or critical reason. There does not appear to be a way out of the necessity of calculative reason because any power of making the world requires some closure to the coming of the other.

But by the same token, we can also read Derrida's figure of the migrant under erasure by stressing the erasure of the subject or person and noting his emphasis on the fact that the coming is that of the inhuman other, namely, a force that cannot be contained by or reduced to the flows of capitalist globalization. In other words, in this immanent global plane, what Derrida's idea of absolute hospitality enables us to think is the pure randomness that disrupts and unsettles from within the sovereign power of human reason and its calculations that experience of pure chance that opens up the world to the nonhuman, wholly other. Absolute hospitality is the chance that reopens the possibility that we might again remake the world against capitalist globalization in the hope that it may yet become more universally hospitable.

Frictions of Hospitality and the Promise of Cosmopolitanism

THOMAS HYLLAND ERIKSEN

I

In an original analysis of food consumption and exchange in the everyday life of a small hamlet on the southern seaboard of Norway, Runar Døving (2001; 2003) develops some subtle insights into the dynamics of hospitality. Describing the conventions of social visits in the community, he asks what the reactions would be if a guest insisted on not being served anything but a glass of water. Convention dictates that coffee be served on these visits, usually accompanied by a slice of cake or some biscuits.

In Norway, "a glass of water" usually refers to tap water, which is, in effect, understood as being tantamount to nothing. "Water," Døving (2003, 30) notes, "is something one tends to think of as free. It is categorized as an unlimited good." Referring to the Biblical myth in which Jesus transformed water into wine, Døving adds that water was not seen as fit for wedding guests in ancient Galilee, either.

By refusing to imbibe anything but water, the guest refuses to accept the host's offer of reciprocity. In effect, he or she rejects an offer of engaging in a relationship of mutual moral commitment. This is why the host has a culturally sanctioned right to feel offended.

My friend Eduardo Archetti, an Argentine anthropologist who lived in Norway from the early 1970s until his death in 2005, commented upon the inclination toward balanced reciprocity characteristic of civil society in Norway. If he bought a colleague a cup of coffee in the canteen, he said, the colleague would immediately pay him for the coffee. Rather than entering

81

into a long-term relationship of small gift exchanges, the colleague would "settle his debt" here and now. This fear of intimacy prevented, in Archetti's interpretation, the glue of civil society from thickening. Anthropologists distinguish between balanced and generalized reciprocity, where the former refers to businesslike transactions with no promise of further involvement. The eagerness to pay back immediately that Archetti commented upon could actually be interpreted as a reluctance to enter into a long-term exchange relationship with no exact calculations of gains and losses on either side (generalized reciprocity). Only the latter kind of relationship can be seen as a form of gift exchange; the former is a mere transaction.

By refusing to accept a gift, one effectively says: I reject your offer of friendship. In Marcel Mauss's ([1925] 1990) seminal treatment of the gift, the institution of gift exchange (which can be material or immaterial) consists of three elements: the obligation to give, the obligation to receive, and the obligation to offer a return gift. The fulfillment of these three elements ensures that respect is confirmed and trust can develop.

One can be a disgraceful guest by demanding too much or too little of the host. But one can also be a disgraceful host by not showing any interest in one's guests. A host can serve the most sumptuous dishes, but little is gained if he fails to listen to the guest's conversation or accept an offer of a return visit. In such a situation, the guest is left humiliated.

Many refugees and immigrants in rich countries feel this way about their relationship to the host society. The refugees have been offered shelter and food, for which they are grateful, and they now wish to reciprocate by doing something in return. They are, however, often denied the right to do so. Right-wing populists of every political shade sometimes argue the need to "place demands on immigrants." This kind of formulation turns the problem on its head and reveals a poor understanding of the dynamics of reciprocity. In fact, there is nothing immigrants want more than being "placed demands upon," which would indicate that they are needed, that someone out there asks for their contribution to society. I have met asylum seekers at detention centers who have spent months waiting for a decision. They are grateful to Norwegian society for having given them protection, but they have one big wish: to be allowed to do something useful.

King Carl XIV Johan of Sweden and Norway (1763–1844) was an immigrant from France. Born Jean-Baptiste Bernadotte, he never learned to speak Swedish, but his motto is telling of the aspirations of many immigrants: "The love of the people—my reward" (*Folkets kärlek, min belöning*). Carl Johan struggled hard to gain the love of his people, and succeeded well enough in the Norwegian part of the kingdom for the main avenue of Christiania (now Oslo) to be named for him after his death.

Immigration policies in Europe tend to be based on suspicion and indifference. A truly hospitable attitude would encourage a situation where minorities are able to gain just such love of the people. This demands of the majority that they do not insist on "just a glass of water" when offered something from the minorities. A lack of interest in one's guests may in fact be a more serious impediment to integration than is commonly assumed. This attitude is a recipe for the development of asymmetrical relationships where humiliation replaces gratitude, and pity turns into contempt.

Add to this the situation in Afghanistan, where—it is reported—foreign soldiers do not even buy fruit in the market. Instructed to take their precautions, troops from the rich countries bring their own food. One is reminded of the apocryphal story about Bill Clinton who, when visiting Bangladesh during his presidency, is said to have brought everything, down to his bathing water, from home. Being a disgraceful guest is as little conducive to establishing mutual trust and respect as being a disgraceful host.

Hospitality, in other words, relies on the observance of the simple rules of reciprocity, which, when followed, engender trust and respect. Yet, giving and receiving in a mutually bonding fashion, so crucial both in social and intercultural relationships, presuppose a social ontology where difference is not seen as a threat, and where the world is acknowledged to be a complex web of interlocking cultural worlds. To this issue I now turn—the problem of cosmopolitanism, its pernicious cousin, identity politics, and its opposite, imperialism.

II

Asked, doubtless by an adoring disciple, about the nature of truth, the German polymath and iconoclast Rudolf Steiner reacted by asking a counterquestion: "What is the truth about a mountain?" Responding to his own question, the great man said that one could approach the mountain from the north, from the south, from the east, and from the west—and, indeed, from above—and one would see different things. And, one might add: One could approach the mountain with the mind of a mountaineer, a geologist, a skier, or a landscape painter. So what is truth? One of the most significant contributions of European thought to world culture is perhaps the insight that all these views of the mountain are equally true, and that we need a world where all the perspectives are accorded a rightful place. As Goethe so famously put it in *On Art and Antiquity*: "He who does not know foreign languages does not know anything about his own." This openness is a prerequisite for a cosmopolitan attitude seeing the world's inhabitants as equals, not as either friends or enemies.

Tzvetan Todorov (2000), in his memoir from the twentieth century, describes three dangers facing the post-totalitarian world. One is instrumentalization of social relations—typically expressed as unfettered market liberalism, or rather, a loss of the social principles of solidarity and decency, which prevented markets from expanding outside the economy strictly speaking, and which also curtailed the power of state bureaucracies in liberal societies. In passing, it may be mentioned that these anxieties are neither uncommon nor new. Similar concerns with bureaucracies were expressed by the inventor of the theory of modern bureaucracy, Max Weber, and worries about market expansion were voiced by Jürgen Habermas in the 1960s, Georg Lukacs in the 1920s, and Karl Marx in the 1850s. The second danger is moral correctness—sanctimonious and authoritarian conformism, in European countries typically expressed through the recently implemented bans on smoking in public places. The third danger identified by Todorov is the main topic to be explored here: fragmenting identity politics, where universal values are bracketed in the name of group self-determination, where commitment to shared societal projects is weakened, and where open conflict between identity-based groups may easily flare up—not so much because they are culturally different, but because they have few interests in common. This is a vision of a classic plural society without a colonial ruling class.

I share all his anxieties; in fact, I might have added one or two myself. Yet there is no easy way out. The only credible responses to the challenges facing humanity have to be ambivalent, doubtful, cautious, with instincts favoring pluralism and a multiplicity of voices rather than universal recipes for happiness. It is, in other words, the open-mindedness of the Renaissance and the optimistic view of human nature of the Enlightenment we should carry with us in this new, old world. It is an ironic fact—given that neither the United States of the Bush II era (2001–2008) nor its adversaries, real as well as imagined, are easily given to ambivalence—that two of the perhaps most influential ideological thinkers of the American right, Francis Fukuyama and Samuel Huntington, are both partly correct, although they are wrong in crucial respects. Both are authors of widely distributed books about the "new world order," and both are keenly listened to in circles close to the White House. However, they seem to be saying opposite things.

Francis Fukuyama (1992) has argued that Western democracy is the only game in town worthy of the name, and that global politics nowadays simply consists in attempts, by the less unfortunate nations, to achieve the same levels of consumption and liberal rights as those enjoyed by Americans. In this context, he also argues that the quest for recognition is fundamental and accounts for various forms of identity politics. The late Samuel Huntington (1996), on the other hand, has argued that current and future conflicts will take place not between ideologies, but between "civilizations," that is, related clusters of cultures, such as the West, Islam, Hinduism, and Eastern Christianity. Both Fukuyama and Huntington have been severely criticized by academics and other intellectuals, but this is not the place to repeat all the criticisms. On the contrary, I would argue that they are both partly right. Fukuyama is right to assume that recognition by others is a notoriously scarce resource in the contemporary world, but he is wrong in believing that recognition can only be achieved through the successful adoption of Western values and ways of life. Huntington is correct in saying that cultural differences are important, but he is hopelessly off the mark when he tries to map out those differences—his concept of civilizations is theoretically inconsistent and empirically misleading; furthermore, there is no reason to assume that such differences necessarily lead to conflict. In fact, it has been argued that none of the armed conflicts of the 1990s were in line with Huntington's predictions (Fox 2000).

We must nonetheless concede that these conservative American thinkers correctly claim that recognition and respect are important, and that cultural differences matter in politics. But if we do, where does this lead us? Well, it seems to lead us in the general direction of postcolonial theory. According to writers like Frantz Fanon, Ngugi wa Thiong'o, and Edward Said, the most difficult form of decolonization consists in purging the mind of imperial categories and prejudices (Ngugi 1986)—in developing a self, an identity, and a self-consciousness that are not confined to the frame of mind imposed by the colonizers. In giving the people of the world the choice of being either with the United States or with the terrorists, Bush II refused to acknowledge any position growing out of concerns other than the U.S.–al-Qaeda axis. This attitude is the opposite of a cosmopolitan vision based on trust and the laws of gift exchange, and this way of thinking has had repercussions in many parts of our societies, from the idiotic and humiliating security checks in airports to earnest debates about the possible incompatibility of Islam and democracy. The postcolonial view, by contrast, insists on equality and mutual respect across differences.

III

In the context of the twenty-first-century global-security crisis involving U.S. global military hegemony and violent reactions often based on identity politics (a situation which has deep structural dimensions and will therefore not end following the election of Obama in 2008), this starting-point implies certain preliminary conclusions: Effective human rights activism requires at least a minimal knowledge about local contexts and, particularly, about local conflicts. For poor countries to give wholehearted support to notions of the inalienable rights of the individual, more is required than decisions to cut aid to countries that are not yet committed to a free press and multi-party parliamentary democracy. What is needed are social reforms which give people increased control over their own existence—land reforms, job opportunities, accountable state institutions, and so on, in order to be able to engage in symmetrical relationships with others in situations of work as well as play. By implication, a global policy is needed where both big power (state, geopolitics) and small power (family, community) are more equitably distributed. This struggle, moreover, is as much about the means of communication as about the means of production. As the Algerian author Rachid Mimouni (1992, 156) put it, what ought to be required of the Europeans is "an attempt to understand rather than material aid. What can democracy mean in a country like Ethiopia, where dozens die of starvation every day?"

There are, in other words, serious problems which cannot be solved by a formulaic introduction of human rights, and there are people, who for perfectly understandable reasons, consider any talk about the freedom of expression as diverting from the real issues. One may by all means argue that Muslim men should offer their wives the same rights and opportunities as, say, Scandinavian women have, but it would be silly to assume that they think the same way as we do. If one does so—promoting human rights with the subtlety of a bulldozer—one implicitly says, as missionaries and foreign-aid aristocrats have done for years, that the experiences of others have no value, and that the others had better become like ourselves before we bother to listen to them. They are obliged to accept our gift, but there is no reciprocal obligation that would apply to us. In effect, one says that they have no legitimate rights until they have become more similar to us. Respecting other life-worlds is, it must be emphasized, not the same as ethical relativism but, on the contrary, a recognition of the need for a dialogue to go both ways since the alternative is monologue or silence.

The very conceptual pair "the West" and "Islam" is deeply problematic. "The West" is a vague, relational, pseudogeographic term, which includes the European Union, the United States, and their richest satellites (Canada, Norway, etc.), as well as two of the easternmost countries in the world, Australia and New Zealand. "Islam" is a universalistic religion with adherents in every country, including all the Western ones. Could "the West and the East" have been used instead, as a more consistent dichotomy, or perhaps "Christianity and Islam," as in the old days? Hardly. All such dichotomies are Trojan horses concealing the hidden agenda of overstating the importance of one particular boundary at the expense of all the others.

There is little to indicate that religion as such can be a source of conflict. A Christian fundamentalist has more in common with a Muslim fundamentalist, at the level of basic values, than each of them has with nonreligious persons. The forms of religiosity and the expressions of respect for *al-Lah* (or God, as we say in English) are similar in both cases. Some European Muslims have discovered this and have joined Christian Democratic parties. Moreover, there are important ecumenical dialogues taking place across "religious divides" in many places, including a major Islamic conference in Cairo in 1995, where central Muslim leaders condemned all forms of terrorism on Islamic grounds, calling for an extensive dialogue with the other monotheistic religions from West Asia (i.e., Christianity and Judaism). At a more everyday level, it is easy to see that folk religions on either side of the Mediterranean, for example, share many facets—saints, prayers, beliefs in the evil eye, and so on, which indicates the existence of broad commonalities across religious boundaries. Following the attacks of September 11, one should also keep in mind that all Muslim heads of state—except Saddam Hussein and the Taliban—condemned the mass murder. On the same evening that the towers collapsed, the *Tehran Times* stated that Islam forbids suicide and that a murder of an innocent, according to the Koran, is tantamount to a murder of all humanity.

Malaysia's Prime Minister Mahathir offered to negotiate between the United States and its adversaries in the autumn of 2001, and this might have been a fruitful move: Malaysia is an overwhelmingly Muslim country, but it is also committed to Western notions of modernity. The United States did not take the offer up, and during a visit a month after the bombing had begun, I heard of no Malays who defended the terrorist attacks, but a lot of them seemed to admire Osama for his courage.

If Malaysia's "moderate Islam" had been granted its place in the sun, fewer Malays would have looked up to Osama bin Laden, and more Westerners would have discovered the similarities between the three great West Asian religions. Seen from a Hindu or East Asian point of view, the three religions appear as virtually identical. Even from the inside, the parallels are striking. The Muslims who have joined Christian Democratic parties in European countries have done so because Christians and Muslims have shared interests in fighting phenomena such as religious slackness, secularization, birth control, and divorces. During another Cairo conference, in the autumn of 1994, the Catholic Church and Muslim clerics joined forces to make a joint statement condemning abortion. Moreover, anthropologists, journalists, and others have relentlessly emphasized the absurdity of lumping together Indonesian rice farmers with Turkish merchants under the umbrella of "Islam," just as intellectuals in Muslim countries are perfectly well aware that "the West" contains something close to a billion individuals with a large variety of values, societies, and ways of life.

IV

The current trend is nonetheless one of growing polarization and a weakening of gifting relationships. The relationship between the West and Islam, as it has developed since the Gulf War, is beginning to resemble the armaments race between the United States and the Soviet Union. At the end of the latter, both superpowers had enough nuclear weapons to annihilate humanity many times over. These days, self-proclaimed representatives of both Islam and the West compete in a similar way—not over the number of warheads, but over the souls of unattached individuals—in rhetorical attacks on each other. In research on ethnic relations, this kind of mechanism is sometimes called dichotomization, which designates the mutual definition of the other as the opposite of oneself, as that which one does not want to be—an efficient antidote to attempts at building relations of reciprocity. Enemy images always depend on this kind of simplistic, stereotypical depiction of the other. Realistic, nuanced descriptions contain too many shades of gray and too much complexity to be of ideological use in creating hatred and implacability. Seen from the North/West, Muslims or "Islam" may thus appear as undemocratic, sexist, illiberal, underdeveloped, brutal, and culturally stagnant. The enemy image, incidentally, is adjusted as relationships change historically. While the generalized Muslim woman today is depicted as an oppressed, intimidated, and powerless person, in Victorian times it was common to depict her as a profoundly erotic, mystical, and seductive character—both of which, needless to say, are stereotypically reductive.

Seen from the South/East, the Europeans, or the people of the West, may be depicted as cold individualists, lacking norms, who are immoral, arrogant, brutal, decadent, and insensitive. These dichotomizations owe little to objective differences between Islam and Christianity but to power relations feeding into assumptions about cultural differences. Roughly the same stereotypes that are now commonly used about Muslims have been used variously to describe South Europeans, North Norwegians, blacks, and "Hindoos" in the past. They are responses to a need to reduce others to stereotypes that usually tell us more about those who create them than those they are applied to.

Muslim stereotypes of "the West" would themselves have been worthy of a book-length treatment; suffice it here to say that they are no less simplistic and no less antithetical to openness and dialogue than Western images of Islam and the Muslims. For a recent example, it has been shown how the Pakistani press, in the months following the attacks, contributed to strengthening mutual stereotyping through portraying the "clash of civilizations" perspective as the only Western view on the matter.

Beyond cultural stereotypes lies the language of undiluted bigotry and chauvinism, as evinced in certain forms of war reporting. During the Gulf War, the Western press wrote about the U.S.-led forces as "lionhearted, professional, heroic, daring, loyal, resolute, brave," while Iraqi soldiers were described as "brainwashed, paper tigers, cowardly, desperate, bastards from Baghdad, mad dogs, unscrupulous, fanatical." Some years later, Bush II notoriously spoke of the suicide pilots of September 11 as "cowards." As Susan Sontag pointed out shortly afterwards, many strong words may be used to describe these madmen (such as, for example, brainwashed or psychotic), but cowards they were definitely not (cf. Eriksen [2001] for a full analysis). Similarly, it is difficult to defend the view that the U.S. pilots, who dropped their cluster bombs on Afghanistan from a comfortable height before returning for breakfast, were exceptionally courageous.

In Gregory Bateson's (1972) original model of schismogenesis, elaborated in his seminal *Steps to an Ecology of Mind*, the only way self-reinforcing circuits can be changed is through the interference of a third agent (or network node) leading to a new framing of the issue. Translated into poststructuralist language, the discursive hegemony pitting "the West" against "Islam" in a deadly embrace can only be broken through the intrusion of one or several counterdiscourses framing the world in different terms. These counterdiscourses have been abundantly available both before and after September 11.

However, politicians and a majority of influential media commentators seem to accept that the conflict has something to do with the West and Islam, even if they usually concede that Islam is complex and that most Muslims are peaceful. In the Muslim part of the world, where the media are less liberal and the political leadership by and large less attuned to the population, the situation has been different. While political leaders have supported the Western powers in their so-called war on terrorism against the Taliban and al-Qaeda, the media have generally not offered a very nuanced picture of the West, portraying the "clash of civilizations" view as representative of "Westerners."

In spite of important cracks spreading in the mutual-enemy images, there are clear indications that they have been strengthened in the years following the events of 9/11. The anti-immigrant new right in several European countries experienced a healthy growth after the attacks, and in countries like the Netherlands and Denmark, they currently enjoy considerable political power. Public debates about minorities in several European countries have shifted from a dominant focus on discrimination and labor-market issues to a less charitable focus on enforced marriages, sexual mutilation, and, most recently, *hijabs* (headscarves worn by some Muslim women on religious grounds). Condoleezza Rice is on record as having explained to a concerned citizen that the reason "they" hate "us" so much is that "we elect our leaders" and that "you and I [meaning women] are allowed to work." Traveling in Muslim countries in the months following the attacks, the French Islam scholar Gilles Kepel (2002) met religious leaders who were concerned that the attacks had led to a deep setback in the ongoing, and in many ways productive, intellectual dialogue between Muslims and Westerners.

There are some exceptions, however. A few influential commentators and politicians saw the terrorist attacks and the retaliation of the United States in the same light. In an address to the summit of the Organization of Islamic Countries in February 2002, Malaysia's then Prime Minister Mahathir defined a terrorist as "someone who attacks civilians," thereby putting the 9/11 suicide pilots and the U.S. Air Force over Afghanistan into the same category.

V

At this point, some personal reflections of a general character may be appropriate, which have nothing to do with the current impasse in global communication as such, but which concern the role of "the West," or the North Atlantic, and particularly the United States, in world society. Europeans and North Americans of predominantly European origin have now dominated the world for more than five hundred years. It may perhaps be about time that this long hegemony comes to an end, whether it happens indirectly through migration, violently through self-destructive entrenchment against a foe that is generated from within (terrorism), or simply through shifts in the dynamics of the global economy.

One may only hope that, if this happens in the new century, the new hegemons will continue to absorb, renew, and develop the valuable contributions of the European and North American history of ideas to global civilization, such as the respect (at least in principle) for human life and integrity, impartial bureaucracy, and, especially, the capacity for skepticism and ambivalence, which has been a trademark quality of European culture (if not of European power politics) since the Renaissance; in this respect, the new American president quite clearly takes a position very different from his predecessor. It may also be hoped that the new hegemons are able to learn the right lessons from the mistakes of Europe and the West: the fanatical technological optimism, the lack of community and solidarity, the class divisions and indifference, the fundamentalist arrogance in relation to others, the stressful way of life under careerist regimes of work, the growing street crime, the racism and discrimination, the lack of consideration for the environment . . .

Looking back on the last centuries—let us say the period that began with Columbus's landing on October 12, 1492, and the subsequent expulsion of Muslims and Jews from Spain a few weeks later—chances are good that the networked, decentralized world, which may now be emerging, might turn out to be more humane than five hundred years of European hegemony have been. It will not happen with the help of Osama bin Laden and Taliban-like networks, but it will not happen with the help of American bomber planes either. One has to be blind and deaf in order to believe that this is the "best of all possible worlds," a world where every person has the same value(s) and where opportunities are equally distributed. The currencies of the global society are dollars and bombs, and this society speaks business English with an American accent. Nobody ought to be surprised if some of those who are overwhelmed, or overrun, by this power react the same way as greenhouse plants allegedly do to heavy metal rock: by rolling up into small, hard balls.

No matter where power and dominance may be concentrated—now and in twenty years' time—this period, in which the world is probably about to be remolded, is a good period for a review (if not a renewal) of worldviews. The old, dominant worldview was characterized by a hierarchical world composed of peoples, civilizations, and nations that were clearly delineated in relation to each other, geographically and culturally speaking; they had their own history, their own values, and their own customs, as it were. Europe and the West, according to this view, represented reason and progress, even if others had also contributed bits and pieces. This image is now about to be replaced by a world characterized by exile, flows, intensified contacts, creolization, hybridization, and all forms of mixing; a world in which no boundaries are absolute, all attempts at building ever taller walls notwithstanding; a world, however, where people continue to have different experiences because they live under varying circumstances. Territorial power is faltering and is being challenged from all sides—Microsoft to al-Qaeda—by the more flexible power of networks. If the demands for justice, respect, and recognition from Muslims and others are not met by responses other than condescending arrogance, this world will almost certainly catch fire. In the old world, injustice and rage could be "contained"—not so in the network world.

This is a world of impurities, fuzzy frontier zones, uncertainties, and ambiguities, where the belief in progress is being replaced by ambivalence, where self-confidence is being replaced by anxiety, where trust is threatened by suspicion, and where the ability to listen has become a more important faculty than ever before in history.

VI

Yet, a mere plea for dialogue and mutual understanding will not do. Nor will it be sufficient, even if it is necessary, to follow Amin Maalouf (2001) and many other subtle and wise intellectuals in their attempt to show that each of us has many potential identities, and that it is our duty to resist attempts to classify ourselves as incumbents of only one—be it national, as in Norway, or religious, as among many Jews and Muslims, or ethnic, as in many parts of Africa. In order to break out of the vicious circle of identity politics, we need to build structures that immunize politics against being taken over by the latter. It is a human right to belong, to feel the security of group membership and the intimate warmth of cultural familiarity—and, of course, to leave that group or to invent one's own hybrid identity. Making ironic comments about neotribalism, as Western liberals routinely do, fails to take into account the need for security and belonging, and it also underestimates the very real and perfectly understandable feeling of humiliation that constitutes the basis of mobilization for various forms of identity politics.

Instead, impersonal structures must be put into place that prevent legitimate personal and collective identities from degenerating into political mass movements. Few have anything to gain in the long run from the politicization of religious and ethnic categories. The complaints from the non–North Atlantic world are legitimate, but once they end up crystallizing in sectarian religious or ethnic movements, this might serve as an indicator that these grievances have been sent to the wrong address. It is necessary to gain an understanding about how this can happen, and it may often be equally necessary to engage in earnest dialogue with identity politicians, but at the same time, it is also indispensable to insist that, in order to make the human world come to terms with itself in this century (which has had such a bad start), it takes not only economic redistribution and a global dialogic democracy, but also universal values and a proper separation of culture, including religion, from politics. But, as I have tried to argue, the universalism of the twenty-first century has to be more accommodating and wide-angled than former, unilateral universalisms; it has to make some detours and acknowledge that the universal is always particular as well. It has to approach the proverbial mountain from all four sides, morning, afternoon, and evening.

In a review of Kwame Anthony Appiah's (2006) *Cosmopolitanism: Ethics in a World of Strangers*, John Gray (2006) states that "[a]s a position in ethical theory, cosmopolitanism is distinct from relativism and universalism. It affirms the possibility of mutual understanding between adherents to different moralities but without holding out the promise of any ultimate consensus." In other words, fervent missionary activity is not, according to this view, compatible with cosmopolitanism, nor is an ethical position that assumes there is but one good life. The question asked by liberals is why they should tolerate intolerance; the answer is that they do not have to. They are only asked to coexist with and collaborate with people of different persuasions when the need arises.

Most conflicts involving immigrants in Oslo, where I live, are of a practical nature: Why do the parents of immigrant children active in sports so rarely take part in the community work—organizing flea markets, selling hot dogs on match days, and so on—which is essential to raise money for the children? Why do immigrant parents let their children play noisily outside late in the evening? Why do Norwegians never invite their immigrant neighbors for a cup of tea? It is those kinds of everyday problems that create coldness and distance between natives and newcomers; I have yet to hear of a single conflict between ethnic Norwegians and immigrants that directly involved differences in religious beliefs. Everyday cosmopolitanism, as well as everyday friction, is usually expressed through shared or colliding practices, not through discussion. Where I live, we do not really care which political party our neighbors votes for, and we do not know if they have any religious beliefs similar to ours or if they love European classical music as much as we do, nor do we care, as long as they take their turn shoveling snow in our common courtyard during the winter months.

Cosmopolitanism may degenerate into missionary liberalism, but it may also degenerate into indifference. As long as there are practical tasks at hand, which need to be handled collectively, this is not a danger. If anything, it is the lack of such tasks that prevents cosmopolitanism in North Atlantic societies, not the lack of things to disagree or agree about in the media. This brings us back to the topic with which I began this essay: the obligation to give, the obligation to receive, and the obligation to offer a return gift. It is as simple as that. And as difficult.

Proximity and Paradox
Law and Politics in the New Europe

BONNIE HONIG

> If then a not-yet is inscribed over all redemptive unison, there can only ensue that the end is for the time being represented by the just present moment, the universal and highest by the approximately proximate . . . to begin with the neighbor and ever more only the neighbor, the well-nigh nighest. . . . Where . . . someone or something has become neighbor to a soul, there a piece of the world has become something which it was not previously: soul.
>
> —Franz Rosenzweig, *The Star of Redemption*

In *Another Cosmopolitanism*, Seyla Benhabib promotes the idea that recent developments in international institutionalism evidence the growth of what she calls cosmopolitan norms.[1] She turns to an emergency to set the stage. Genocide serves as her synecdoche for several new legislative and normative trends in human rights, especially in Europe. Noting the lack of appropriate institutions with which to try Adolf Eichmann in 1961, Benhabib presses upon her readers the need to support international tribunals now. But the lens and mood set by Eichmann and genocide set us up to relate in a certain way—in a mode of dependence and felt need of rescue—to the project of interstate law and cosmopolitan norms that Benhabib here seeks to promote. It is problematic in a way that recalls the question posed by Bernard Shaw to Mike Dukakis in the 1988 American presidential election campaign, (something like) "What would you want done to the perpetrator, if your wife was raped and murdered?"[2] Dukakis's dispassionate response, in which he said he would want the perpetrator to be tried, underscored for the electorate what was seen as his passionless bureaucratic character. But the problem was with the question, not the answer. Facing the specters of genocide, rape, and murder, one is thrust into extremes of (il)legality: passionate vendetta or sober, fair judicial process.

Benhabib begins and ends *Another Cosmopolitanism* with the concern about genocide and the need for institutional accountability for it. That may be because she senses greater consensus on that particular issue than on some of the more intractable issues of multicultural politics that she discusses in the pages in between. She hopes the divisions of multicultural politics may become less intractable if they are adjudicated by way of the universal norms that condemn genocide and to which, on Benhabib's account, the new International Criminal Court gives expression. In short, Benhabib's intention is to enable widespread acceptance of new developments in EU law that she sees as expressing moral condemnation of intolerance from genocide to multicultural politics. But, although universal outrage against genocide may seem a promising ground for a new cosmopolitanism, Benhabib's universal norms also insulate us from the urgencies of contingency and contiguity out of which solidaristic progressive politics often arise. If we focus on the fact that those who happen to be here have no more claim on us than those far away, or if their being here can only "count" once it has passed a test of universalizability, then the impulse to act in concert with them simply because they are here is attenuated and indeed delegitimated. The same goes for those who are distant, physically, but with whom we might feel neighborly in the sense of sharing a common cause. Here, Franz Rosenzweig's (2005, 252) idea that "the just present moment, the universal and highest [is represented] by the approximately proximate" is potentially very powerful, as I will suggest below.

I turn now to look at recent developments in Europe focused on by Benhabib. Benhabib works her views out by way of Kant's idea of a right to hospitality. I begin with Derrida's own reading of that right, for it motivates an alternative to Benhabib's neo-Kantian cosmopolitanism. That alternative is often termed cosmopolitics and, as I argue here, it is better served by Rosenzweig's idea of neighborliness than by neo-Kantian universals over which the neighbor, as such, famously has little claim.[3]

Hospitality and Rights

As with many of the concepts he deconstructs, including the gift, justice, forgiveness, and democracy, Derrida (2005a, 145) casts hospitality as belonging to two discontinuous and radically heterogeneous orders, conditional and unconditional, whose conflict and asymmetrical necessity render ethical-political life (im)possible. There is no question of a choice that must be made between one order and the other, between the conditional and the unconditional. Nor is there a fundamental compatibility between the two such that, for example, one is legal and one is moral or one is specific and the other generic, in which case the latter could subsume the former and make sense of it or complete it. Rather, the two orders or concepts coexist in "paradoxical or aporetic relations . . . that are at once heterogeneous and inseparable."[4]

Unconditional hospitality postulates a giving without limit to the other, an infinite openness that both enables and jeopardizes one's capacity to host another (Derrida 1999a, 47; Derrida 2000, 25–27). Conditional hospitality, by contrast, postulates a finite set of resources and calculable claims. It is "the only one . . . that belongs to the order of laws, rules, and norms—whether ethical, juridical, or political—at a national or international level" (Derrida 2005a, 173n12). In this second order of hospitality, distinctions must be made and limits set, lest hospitality be extended to or demanded by everyone and encompass everything to a point at which the would-be host would be dispossessed of the very property and scope that enable him or her to offer hospitality to the dispossessed other.[5]

Kant delimited hospitality (to the right of those washed ashore to be permitted visitation or offered refuge) precisely in order to avert this risk of dispossession and thereby secure, by limiting it, the duty of (conditional) hospitality. Derrida, by contrast, insists we see what the averted risk itself intimates, that against which we cannot inoculate ourselves: That those who claim a right to hospitality are positioned inevitably in an ambiguous and undecidable terrain marked by both hospitality and hostility.[6] The undecidability of host/hostility and its ethico-political implications are erased, not expressed, by an analysis like Benhabib's that identifies hostility with one singular principle—ethnos, republican self-determination, or state nationalism—and hospitality with another that is distinct and apart—Enlightenment universalism. The division of host/hostility into two binarily opposed options cleanses hospitality of its fundamental undecidability and misleadingly casts the threat to universal hospitality as something that always comes to it from some distinct and unrelated outside source.[7] The mutual implication of host/hostility, by contrast, illustrates the persistent trace even in our own most cherished ideals of that which we seek to overcome.[8]

Any right to hospitality is caught in the aporia signaled by the two orders, each heterogeneous to the other, and yet in some way necessary to it. And, as Derrida (2005a, 172n12) points out, although "unconditional hospitality [is] impossible . . . heterogeneous to the political, the juridical, and even the ethical . . . the impossible is not nothing. It is even that which happens, which comes, by definition." One way to think (part of) this thought might be as follows: Any particular right to hospitality takes its motivation, its energy, and its animation not just from a finite economy of right, a moral law, universal human right, or a particularist ethics, but also and problematically from the infinitude of the unconditional hospitality that is both expressed and betrayed by any proclaimed table of values or by any enacted right to or gift of hospitality as such.

The distinction between the unconditional and the conditional might illuminate from a new angle Arendt's (1968, 296) famous call for the right to have rights. This is a call in the name of an unconditional order of rights, something that is quite distinct, as she herself makes clear in her reading of *Billy Budd* and elsewhere, from such tables of rights as universal human rights, the Rights of Man, or EU charters (Arendt 1963, 82–87). The right to have rights is itself a double gesture: It is a reproach to any particular order of rights (albeit certainly to some more than others) and a demand that everyone should belong to one such order.[9] A double gesture is necessary because, paradoxically, we need rights because we cannot trust the political communities to which we belong to treat us with dignity and respect; however, we depend for our rights upon those very same political communities.[10] Are we helped out of the paradox by locating the ground of rights in a different, higher order of belonging, such as international institutions? Yes and no. Having another instance to appeal to when you lose in one venue is a good thing. But being able to do so still presupposes a belonging whose fragility those very same rights are supposed to protect us against. In the international arena, no less than in the national, rights still presuppose belonging, now not only to states but (as in Benhabib's depiction) also to a legal, bureaucratic, and administrative order like the EU.

The unconditional—such as Arendt's right to have rights—is a way of marking the fact that no venue and no armory of rights, no matter how broad or developed or secure, can represent the subject's absolute value in economies of rights-adjudication that are at once contingent, communal, legal, judicial, bureaucratic, moral, administrative, governmental, and discretionary. And there is no way out of the paradox of rights, though awareness of it can inflect our politics in useful ways. Indeed, Arendt's right to have rights—a polemical, political call—directs our attention repeatedly to the need for a politics whereby to express and address the paradox as it is experienced by the minorities, the stateless, the powerless, and the hapless.

Benhabib, too, wants to endorse a politics in response to a paradox that she wants not to resolve but to ease. For this she turns to what she calls "democratic iterations": particular culturally or politically inflected enactments of universal or cosmopolitan norms. One way to assess the differences between her approach and mine is by comparing our distinct diagnoses of the current situation and the different paradoxes on which we focus. From a vantage point shaped by awareness of the conditional/unconditional and modeled on Arendt's call for the right to have rights, things look more ambiguous than on Benhabib's account.

For example, although Benhabib is right to point out the great promise for democratic citizens in the development of Europe's newly porous borders, in new recognitions of extracitizen human rights and alien (but still membership-based) suffrage, and in extrastate fora to which state-based injustices can be appealed, it is also the case that a focus on these developments is misleading, as is the casting of these developments as signs of an increasingly capacious normative universalism.[11] In recent years, the new porousness of territorial borders between EU countries has been accompanied by the erection of new, non-permeable borders around the EU. The hosts are by no means only welcoming; they are also hostile.

And this is no accident. In France, for example, as postcolonial immigrants exercise their option in recent years of French citizenship or legal residency, those who do not fit the profile of the proper citizen are subjected by formal and informal state agents to police or administrative control and informal intimidation. When policed, postcolonial subjects, only some of them *sans papiers*, are constantly asked for their papers; this renders fraught and fragile the place of all postcolonial immigrants, residents, and ethnic minorities on the territory to which some of them now belong in some sense under French and EU law. Is it not significant that at a time of new economic pressures a new class of workers is created, an always already criminalized population unable to access resources of law and rights that are at the same time being expanded by the EU? Criminalized populations are often quiescent. But they sometimes take the risk (riskier for them than most) of politics, as the *sans papiers* movement has demonstrated. What that movement also demonstrated is that in practice if not in law, French residents are now repartitioned not along the formal juridical line—undocumented or documented—but along racial lines. Many are moved by the situation to joke cynically that their *cartes d'identité* are their faces, their skin/color. Etienne Balibar names the new racialized political order "apartheid in Europe."[12]

In this Europe, formal law lives side by side with, but is also both aided and undercut by, an administrative police state apparatus and a xenophobic public that legalists disavow at their peril. (These points may ring familiar to readers of Arendt's insightful analysis of the situation in inter-war Europe.[13]) Benhabib (2006, 60), however, in the second lecture of *Another Cosmopolitanism*, "Democratic Iterations: The Local, the National, and the

Global," focuses for the most part on formal law-state and regional powers, commissions' rulings and Court decisions.[14] She has a formalist's understanding of law as independent of and prior to politics: "The law provides the framework within which the work of culture and politics go on. The laws, as the ancients knew, are the walls of the city, but the art and passions of politics occur within those walls and very often politics leads to the breaking down of those barriers or at least to assuring their permeability (ibid.)."

Although Benhabib's call to break down the barriers between law and politics by way of politics seems to attenuate law's autonomy, it does the opposite. It posits a chronology in which law is, first, prior to politics and capable therefore of providing a framework for it; then, second, law is corrupted by politics; and finally law is brought into the political arena in order to wrest from law (in its limited democratic or republican form) payment on its universal (context-transcendent, that is, extrapolitical) promise: "It is only when new groups claim that they belong within the circle of addressees of a right from which they have been excluded in its initial articulation that we come to understand the fundamental limitedness of every rights claim within a constitutional tradition as well as its context-transcending validity" (ibid.).

A view of rights as always pointing beyond themselves is deeply attractive. But what do they point to? Benhabib assesses new rights in terms of their fit with molds and models already in place, incomplete, but definitive in their contours. Notwithstanding her commitments to reflexivity and revisability written about in detail elsewhere, what changes in Benhabib's practices of democratic iteration is the subject's relation to universalistic categories, not the categories themselves: the universal stays universal, the particular stays particular. Benhabib (2006, 61) notes: "It is clear that all future struggles with respect to the rights of Muslim and other immigrants will be fought within the framework created by the universalistic principles of Europe's commitments to human rights, on the one hand, and the exigencies of democratic self-determination, on the other."[15] Although she treats the universal and the particular as two moments in a dialectic, the two are not equal. One overcomes the other: Universality represents a principle, democratic self-determination an exigency.

With Europe's commitments cast as universalistic (in theory if not in practice, Benhabib might concede; but then something in her theory prevents the practice—racial stratification, police-state style policing, and so on—from being seen as significant evidence regarding the theory), there is little room to take seriously the sort of concern aired by Derrida in *Of Hospitality*: "The foreigner who, inept at speaking the language, always risks being without defense before the law of the country [or region] that welcomes or expels him; the foreigner is first of all foreign to the legal language in which the duty of hospitality is formulated, the right to asylum, its limits, norms, policing, etc." (Derrida and Dufourmantelle 2000, 15). Here we find ourselves in the paradox of politics, the chicken-and-egg conundrum of democratic life as such: "He has to ask for hospitality in a language which by definition is not his own" (ibid.).[16] For that request to be heard, for it to be audible, the hospitality in question has to always already be extended to the speaker. It has to be given before it is asked for, and in spite of the fact that (indeed precisely because) the request for hospitality is incomprehensible or dangerous. This is hospitality's unconditionality. It is risky. That is why it is always partnered with its conditional, risk-assessing partner: conditional hospitality.

The unconditional makes no promise about our future, and it inspires and haunts every conditional order of rights. From its vantage point, we wager that every political-legal settlement generates remainders, no matter how progressive or expansive that settlement aims to be. This is in no way to suggest that all orders are equal from this perspective, but only to suggest that even those that are better than others still depend upon the supplement of a politics different from Benhabib's dialectically iterative politics. From the vantage point of the unconditional—but not from that of Benhabib's universal—even a full realization of universal human rights on earth would necessitate further political work, generating new claims, each of which would make its own universal appeal, perhaps on behalf of the remainders of the conditional order of universal human rights.[17] Benhabib by contrast would see such further claims as coming from a particularity in need of education or adjustment, one in want of appreciation for that full achievement of universality.

The Double Gesture's Paradox

Benhabib's idea of democratic iterations is her response to paradoxes that afflict her cosmopolitanism. The paradox of democratic legitimation, which Benhabib and I have written about in detail elsewhere (what happens when the majority whose will legitimates a democracy itself favors undemocratic actions?), reappears in her later work on cosmopolitanism, but it shifts.[18] The paradox of democratic legitimacy slips into the paradox of bounded communities when Benhabib (2006, 17) says the paradox of democratic legitimacy is "the necessary and inevitable limitation of democratic forms of representation and accountability in terms of the formal distinction between members and nonmembers."[19] In fact there are two paradoxes, or, as Benhabib puts it in her first lecture, "The Philosophical Foundations of Cosmopolitan Norms": "On close examination, we are dealing with a dual paradoxical structure" (35). She restates the paradox of democratic legitimacy, thus highlighting again the troublesomeness of mere majoritarianism (as opposed to a more normative variety) by demanding "that the republican sovereign should undertake to bind its will by a series of precommitments to a set of formal and substantive norms, usually referred to as 'human rights'" (ibid.). This is a paradox between liberalism (universal human rights) and democracy (republican sovereign). The problem of membership is now cast as a different distinct problem, not between democracy and its others but rather "internal to democracy, namely that democracies cannot choose the boundaries of their own membership democratically" (ibid.). This "paradox of bounded communities" is, in her view, an "anxiety that must be faced by any serious deliberative democrat" (18).[20]

The paradox of bounded communities is actually a product of the deliberativist commitment to a certain universalism, though Benhabib would not put it that way:

> Because the discourse theory of ethics articulates a universalist moral standpoint, it cannot limit the scope of the moral conversation only to those who reside within nationally recognized boundaries; it views the moral conversation as potentially including all of humanity. (ibid.; original emphasis)

Boundaries themselves require moral justification, since "membership norms impact those who are not members precisely by distinguishing insiders from outsiders, citizens from noncitizens" (ibid., 19). The problem is that

> either a discourse theory is simply irrelevant to membership practices in bounded communities in that it cannot articulate any justifiable criteria of exclusion, or it simply accepts existing practices of exclusions as morally neutral historical contingencies that require no further validation. (ibid.; original emphasis)

The second paradox captures a somewhat different problem than the first. The first worried that a majority could betray its legitimacy by willing the wrong thing, that democracy could be immoral by failing to will only universalizable legislation. In the second, the concern is that those defined as the majority by the happenstance of boundaries are arbitrarily relevant from a moral point of view. The focus here is not on what is decided but rather on who is doing the deciding. This shift in focus is welcome because it calls upon us to consider the politics of membership and solidarity more centrally than did the paradox of democratic legitimation. It also calls attention to a problem with universalism. In the first paradox, universalism solves the problem (or tries to) by insisting that the people's will must be universalizable. In this second (version of the) paradox, universalism is causing the problem: It is from the perspective of universalism that proximity, community, territory, and boundary are morally irrelevant. So a world in which these contingencies still define life chances, as indeed they do in ours, is subject to the paradox of bounded communities if we take a universalist perspective: How can a people morally constrained to will universalizably premise that willing on nonuniversalizable contingencies of membership? The answer, Benhabib says, is that the conflict between particularity and universality, between membership and cosmopolitan norms, must be mediated by democratic iterations and by international and national law with the aim, she says, not of exiting the paradox but rather of relaxing it. As sovereign states adopt increasingly cosmopolitan constitutions, and citizens internalize cosmopolitan norms, the paradox will, she wagers, be further eased.[21]

I favor a different, two-pronged strategy that does not draw for its solution on the very thing—universalism—that is causing the problem. First, a democratic politics should be committed to diminishing international inequalities so that it would matter less from a moral and material point of view where one was born. Such a response highlights the power relations that govern the international sphere and subject some nations and nationals to the will of others. But since this first strategy can never be entirely successful and there will always be differences of power and privilege associated with different locations, a second strategy is needed to respond to that inevitability. The second strategy seeks not to ease but rather to embrace the paradox of bounded communities by supporting action on behalf of those contingent neighbors who just happen to be here for no good universalizable reason (though they are often "here" for known reasons of political history—as the slogan goes: They came here because we went there). At the same time, of course, we must realize that proximity and neighborliness are no longer dictated alone by spatial nearness. We have global neighbors as well. Democratic activists enter into coalition with those near and far. Some become our neighbors as a result of the way pollution, consumerism, and capital cross borders. Shared challenges make neighbors out of us, putting us into common cause with those who might otherwise have been distant. I have noted elsewhere how before the American revolution the colonists and revolutionaries cannily expanded the distance between themselves and the king by pretending never to have received sovereign instructions sent from England.[22] Here, too, we see that distance is not a fact, as it were. It can, conversely, be shortened by way of political work as well.

It matters whether we relate to those near or distant under the sign of universality or under the sign of the neighbor. Indeed, I suggest, those who resort to universalizable norms in order to ground a sense of moral connection and obligation may find that the promise of contingent connections of geography or common cause are undone, not solidified, by a universalist morality and politics. Universalism attenuates such connections and insulates us from the call of the other. Universalism may seek to ground human rights, but human rights also postulate the very memberships and proximities with which universalism is ill at ease, as Hannah Arendt knew.[23] Thus my preferred two-pronged strategy points to the need for a "double gesture" that both affirms the values of universal human rights (the equal dignity of persons) while calling for forms of action that may seem to violate that universality at the same time, as when we act on the basis of geographic or political proximity in solidarity with those who are near just for that reason—because they are near.

Such double gestures are necessary because, in any case, rights are not enough. When Benhabib points out that over time second-class members of democratic regimes, like women and African Americans, have been brought into full possession of formal rights, she does not note that these subjects have never come to bear those rights in the same way as their original bearers. Her optimism is supplemented by her assumption of a progressive, evolutionary time, in which supposed systems of rights are "tapped" (to borrow Jürgen Habermas's [2001] term) as liberal democracies take the protections and privileges first only granted to propertied white males and spread them outward to encompass all classes, races, and genders. Thus, the human-rights side of the democratic legitimation paradox seems to win. But we are not yet at the end of the story, nor can we ever be, and thus we will never know who or what wins in the end.

In Benhabib's (2006, 67) text, the constitutive tension central to her argument is a bit more past than present, with universality positioned toward a (cosmopolitan) future and particularity toward a (Westphalian) past. Discussing the French veiling controversy, for example, Benhabib says of the girls who stood up for their "cultural rights" that having learned to "talk back to the state," they will likely one day learn to "talk back to Islam" as well.[24] Here Benhabib's cosmopolitanism seems to both presuppose and "anticipate" citizens who do not yet exist. These citizens negotiate state and cultural powers on behalf of universal human rights, which are themselves (again) both the condition and the goal of liberal democratic statehood in a cosmopolitan setting. So far, so good. But Benhabib breaks the vicious circle, first by staging it as a conflict between universality and particularity (returning us to the paradox of democratic legitimation as she recasts it in *Another Cosmopolitanism*) rather than between or within democratic freedom and democratic (self-)sovereignty, and then by inserting the amended paradox into a time sequence: She wagers that these young women will likely talk back to Islam too one day and thereby show, in the course of historical time, that they have internalized democratic and cosmopolitan citizenship. The prediction of an Islam eventually overcoming itself confines the paradox of politics to a particular historical moment, to a present precosmopolitan moment, the eventual, promised overcoming of which is what underwrites our affirmation of their culturalism now.

Whether or not this wager is right (a great deal depends upon domestic and international political and economic developments in France, Europe, and the Middle East, not simply on the trajectory of rights) is less important than the work the wager does. The wager privileges the backward-looking gaze of a still future cosmopolitanism. We assess the present from the perspective of a posited future in which the particularities of the present are overcome. That temporality anchors what I have elsewhere called the chrono-logic of rights, the quasi-logical unfolding of rights in accordance with the sequencing demands of linear, normative progress, and it also occludes from view impositional and violent processes that help secure such developments when they do occur.[25] Benhabib is aware of current xenophobic policies, but she does not worry that any coming cosmopolitanism may be not only obstructed, but itself partly produced by them. She does not worry that cosmopolitanism might carry the traces of the beliefs and practices it is said to oppose. That is, she does not ask whether such policies might both violate and help produce the (post-)cultural cosmopolitanism she promotes.

Benhabib casts the history of democratic (trans-)statism as a history of expansion and increasing universalization. Its linear time trajectory occludes from view that which does not fit its narrative frame—for example, the history of disenfranchisement in the Jim Crow South, in which newly won juridical rights were rendered nugatory by local political intimidation and a failure to secure and enforce the political and material conditions of rights-taking. Another example: In the United States and Canada, resident-alien voting was once an uncontroversial practice, but it was ended by the xenophobia of the World War I era. Historically, it is worth noting, alien suffrage occurred without all the conditions that Benhabib sets up as necessitating it now: border attenuation, pressures on state sovereignty, and extranational institutions.[26] Faced with the prior practice of alien suffrage, it is hard to think of recent EU gains in alien suffrage as the latest in a line of serial expansions earned by our progressive tapping of the system of rights.[27]

Instead, from a perspective oriented to the politicality rather than universality of rights, is it not highly significant that the idea of alien suffrage appealed to the province of Schleswig-Holstein in 1989 when the aliens to be empowered to vote were all citizens of Northern European countries, while the new minorities putting the most pressure on traditional German conceptions of citizenship at the time were from Turkey? And is it not significant that recent debates in Europe about the social rights of aliens, specifically about whether "we" should share our social welfare with "them," have occurred in the last two decades at the very moment at which European social welfare rights have been downsized? Depictions of foreigners as those who want to come "here" to take "our" welfare have worked productively to reassure Western Europeans that they still have social welfare worth taking (which they may, by comparison with others, but which they do not, by comparison with themselves thirty years ago).[28] Benhabib (2006, 46) knows that at the very moment in which "the entitlement to rights is" expanded, "the condition of undocumented aliens, as well as of refugees and asylum seekers . . . remains in that murky domain between legality and illegality," but she does not read this remnant as a remainder produced in part by the conditional order of universal hospitality (as I myself have been suggesting, though other forces are at work, too). Instead, her language suggests, the problem is that some people have been left passively behind by an imperfect but still progressive cosmopolitan law, in which case appeals to human-rights commissions and exercises of cultural political interventions may correct the wrong, and result in a truer universalism. She subtly puts us onto a temporal register in which this limit is always already about to be overcome. From that register, we are in no position to ask whether these remainders are the direct products of the political project of Europe-formation—which is, we might note, not only a way to transcend national belonging, but also a way to resecure national belonging: In a time when claims to national belonging, say, in France, are being made by non-Europeans, the political (re)formation of Europe as a site of belonging is surely a way to resecure, and not just attenuate or transcend, national belonging. As Derrida (1992a, 48) points out in *The Other Heading*: "I am (we are) all the more national for being European, all the more European for being trans-European, and international."

The challenge, then, is to see the situation in all its ambiguity, and from that vantage point to intervene in ways that claim Europe for a different present, for different futures, for different constituencies, for a different politics. The challenge is to open up room for the much-needed double gesture: For example, one might oppose the constitutionalization of the EU in the name of an alternative locatable and accountable rule of law, to counter that future with another in the name of the very democratic and human rights that constitutionalization has historically claimed to entrench, and to do all this without being cast as a mere agonist or defender of national particularity, or as a member of the National Front, as if these were the only options (naysayer versus lawgiver, NF or EU).[29] Or one might argue in favor of such constitutionalization while seeking to embed in it countermeasures to its own gravitational pull toward centralized sovereignty, as some U.S. founders sought to do and assumed they did. We know, however, from the U.S. example, that no charter can deliver on its promises of stability and accountability without an activist politics that both risks and secures them.

The same challenge of the double gesture is incited by Benhabib's (2006, 47) treatment of sovereignty. Here the very same evidence that allows her to speculate hopefully but cautiously that "the conflict between sovereignty and hospitality has weakened in intensity" could also suggest that sovereignty is on the contrary in the process of being shored up, transformed into something altogether new. The new openness Benhabib endorses could just as well be a sign of sovereignty's adjustments, accommodations, and relocations. Arguably, the new Europe is constituted by a move from visible peripheral borders to less visible internal ones (city/suburbs, French/Algerian, Catholic/Muslim/Jewish/secular), from states to regions. Such adjustments may restore nationalist fervor or salvage it while perhaps also attenuating or redirecting it.[30] Just as the problem of refugees, to which Benhabib briefly alludes, may not be (just) a problem for state sovereignty but rather, or also, an occasion for the refinement and enhancement of state power, as Nevzat Soguk (1990) argues, so too the problem of refugeeism in Europe, testified to by the many refugee camps lined up on both sides of Europe's old and new borders, may serve as a sign of the new continental sovereignty of the EU.[31]

Postscript

In a response to my response to her Tanner Lectures, Benhabib (2006, 161) attributed to me an antistatist, governmentality-centered Foucauldianism: "For Honig, neither the state and its institutions nor the law and its apparatus can be sites of democratic iteration and emancipatory politics." Moreover, she considers me endorsing "movement politics" and manifesting "hostility toward institutions" (163). The charge of antistatism is also a charge of nonseriousness.[32] The latter charge is made explicit later—"political struggles which address the state and its institutions . . . mean getting serious about the political by engaging with it at all levels of state, law and civil society" (164). To ignore the state is perforce, to be lite, marginal. It goes to the heart of what we think we are doing as political theorists. Do we aspire to write constitutions for emerging democracies, influence sitting judges with amicus briefs, map out agendas, be part of the action, point the way forward? Or will we editorialize from the sidelines, write critiques, diagnose our being stuck, and call for double gestures to engage the complexities of the current situation?[33]

The precise phrasings in my original reply to Benhabib belie the charge of antistatism.[34] The state and its institutions are always our addressees. They would not have it any other way. But when they are our addressees, when they privilege themselves as our most important addressees, we are called—indeed interpellated—into and by their perspective, and we lose hold of our capacity to imagine politics otherwise. There is nothing "holier than thou" (Benhabib 2006, 164) about pointing this out, surely. It is one of the many double binds of political action in the contemporary world.

To use the term *interpellation* is risky; it is, Benhabib (163) says, "old Althusserian language." But for me, it continues to capture something no newer term does: the ways in which our entire being is swept up in the address of the state and its agents, even in anticipation of such address. Not just that of the police, though they are pretty good at it, but also that of immigration agents, passport controls, transportation safety employees, the Internal Revenue Service, health insurance agents, and so on. One of the things progressive democratic activists must do is join those swept up in the interpellations and help engage these institutions: elect different representatives, protest institutional injustices, educate members and aliens, demand accountability, strive for better legislation, and demand better court appointments.

Engaging the state is a feature but not the essence of democratic politics. The choice between social movements and a more juridical politics focused on state and transnational institutions is a false one. To focus on institutions of governance without a foot in movement politics and critique is perforce to perform juridical politics differently than would otherwise be the case, without the balancing perspective of a life lived otherwise. It is to be left vulnerable to the self-privileging perspective of statism and its formalisms.

Juridical politics is always in need of the support and orientation of life lived in political movement. In addition to engaging state and transnational institutions directly, democratic actors must also, and not as a secondary matter, in some ways begin living now as if we had already succeeded in that first endeavor. Otherwise we get locked into the eternal agon of small (or even large) institutional victories and never do what we want those institutional changes for and what can and must happen even in advance of those victories—live otherwise. Better to get on with the business of what Franz Rosenzweig might have called neighborliness and what Hannah Arendt called action in concert. In so doing, we do not ignore or sideline the state; we insist, however—and we remind it and ourselves—that it does not exhaust life.

By Hannah Arendt's (1963, 239) account, the American revolutionaries did the most revolutionary thing long before the revolution occurred. More important than their protests and challenges to the King, more weighty than any tea party, was the experiment in living they undertook alongside sovereigntist politics, an experiment whose reverberations moved from the margins to the center of an empire and succeeded in becoming an institutional revolution because the form of life it presupposed had somehow been magically brought into being through the daily work of life.[35] Some changes do need to be argued and fought for on judicial or formal institutional terrains; however, they also need to be lived. From a democratic theory perspective, neither tactic is more serious or central or important than the other, and both carry risks. The work of institution-building simply cannot succeed without the support and perspective of life lived otherwise. This means democratic actors and activists must enter into the paradox of politics and risk forms of democratic solidarity and action that may not yet license or be licensed by the always imperfect universal or cosmopolitan norms from which we also, necessarily, take our bearings.

Agonistic Cosmopolitics

Arendt's unconditional right to have rights is as good a motto as any for the project of an agonistic cosmopolitics, as long as we understand rights to imply a world-building that is not incompatible with the project of building juridical institutions. In the name of such a right to have rights, and motivated by the doubly gestured diagnoses developed here of (in)formal law and politics as they are operating in early twenty-first-century Europe, an agonistic cosmopolitics might call for the following: the enactment of underground railroads devoted to the remainders of the state system, such as refugees (cf. Rogin 1987); the designation of some spaces as cities of refuge (but not camps), such as Jacques Derrida called for (following the recovery of them by Emmanuel Levinas, who commented on the biblical injunction to establish six of these in Ancient Israel); or to stand up for *droits de cité*, a demand to extend full hospitality to refugees and other nonimmigrant border crossers simply because they are here (cf. Rogin; Derrida 2001a).

The phrase "simply because they are here" rejects the legitimationist demand that some justification be given for privileging those who are proximate. The Habermasian concern on this front is with "the paradox of bounded communities," which Benhabib says must be attended to by any "serious" deliberative democrat. The worry encapsulated in this paradox is that it is an arbitrary matter who is in and who is out of this particular community, which now has to hold itself responsible for universalizable legislation that will apply, however, only to this contingently bounded community. But there is in fact no problem of logic here, only a political problem introduced by the particular form of the demand for universality made by Habermas and his followers. Another way of thinking universality might be to view proximity not as a problem but as an opportunity, not as an artifact of the contingency of boundaries, but as a device for their attenuation. This or something like it is what Franz Rosenzweig is after when he thematizes neighbor-love, which he characterizes, in Eric Santner's (2006, 207; original emphasis) phrasing, as a process of "ensoulment" in which we "by acts of neighbor-love—small miracles, as it were, performed one by one[—]mov[e] from one neighbor to the next (rather than by way of a love directed immediately to all humankind)." Or, as Rosenzweig (2005, 252) richly puts the point: "the universal and the highest reality . . . begin[s] with, the neighbor [the well-nigh nighest] who is precisely there. . . . [W]here someone or something has become the neighbor of the soul, a part of the world becomes what it was not before: soul."

Here, the neighbor does not present a moral problem to be solved (Why him or her and not someone else? What justifies that?), but an ethical and political opportunity to be acted upon. Qua acts of neighbor-love, we can enact *droits de cité*—by taking people in, harboring them, offering them shelter, finding sympathetic agents of discretionary power who are willing to look the other way—while also risking the reauthorization of law's authoritative institutions by working through them to win papers or amnesty for those who are here "simply because they are here." Thus, the poor migrants and refugees living in that murky space mentioned by Benhabib will not be so dependent on law to position them with more clarity in its network.

In his remarks on neighbor-love quoted above, Rosenzweig took advantage of a pun in German in order to put proximity and urgency into connection. As Santner (2006, 207n19) points out: The German for neighbor, *der Nächste*, is shifted in the passage from Rosenzweig's *Star* to *das Nächste*, as in the well-nigh nighest, a term which connotes now not proximity but urgency. The pun is apt, not because urgency is never distant but because when it is proximate, we often find ways to render it less so, to reason our way out of action. The need is greater elsewhere; what justifies my actions here? Or: Their proximity to me here is illegitimate and illegal. Why should they gain from breaking the immigration queue when others wait legally? Or: We must work through the proper channels. These concerns are not wrong. These worries about consistency and principle are important. But they undo the compelling call of the neighbor. That is their troubling remainder.

For Arendt, the chief political virtues are worldliness and care for the world; these are in danger of being sidelined by versions of cosmopolitanism in which law, states, and state-like and interstate institutions are our principal addressees, guardians, ventriloquizers, impersonators, shapers and censors of our voices, our desires, our aspirations, our solidarities. Under the sign of worldliness, however, and in the name of neighborliness, potential commonalities might emerge between a normative cosmopolitanism like Benhabib's and an agonistic cosmopolitics. They may share a common motivation and a common cause: to combat the abundant forces of inequality in our world. But, committed to the view that all institutional settlements generate remainders, an agonistic cosmopolitics must remain always open and committed to the perpetual generation of new sites of action in concert on behalf of worlds not yet built or on behalf of those still emergent and in need of activist support and sustenance. This, surely, is one meaning of hospitality.

Conditions for Hospitality or Defence of Identity?
Writers in Need of Refuge—A Case of Denmark's "Muslim Relations"

ULRIK PRAM GAD

As one of the last decisions before it disassembled for the summer break in 2008, the Danish Parliament, *Folketinget*, passed two bills to facilitate the participation of Danish municipalities in the International Cities of Refuge Network (ICORN).[1] On the face of it, it might be good news that yet another country opens its borders to writers targeted with threats and persecution. As a condition for refuge in Denmark, however, any writer granted "refuge" under the umbrella of ICORN now has to sign a rather peculiar document—a "Declaration on recognition of the fundamental values of the Danish society" (cf. Appendix). The writer thereby declares to "understand and accept the fundamental values of Danish society"; to "protect Danish democratic principles" including nondiscrimination and the condemnation of terrorism; and finally to be aware that he or she is obliged to leave again within two years. My essay takes this puzzling document as its point of departure and relates it to the discursive situation in which it was produced. As a contribution to this collection, it is intended to serve as an analysis of the current strategic situation in relation to which any ethico-political action on behalf of hospitality must position itself.

As it were, the parliamentary debates and the detailed legal text framing this show of hospitality both reveal that Danish hospitality is far from being "unconditional." Still more worrying is the fact that the debate, the legal regulations, and the very problematic of freedom of expression in Denmark are placed squarely within a discourse on "Muslim relations"—which proves to be a troubling linguistic terrain. The analysis will proceed in three steps: First, it will focus on who the "good" and the "bad" guys are made to be when the Danish parliament discusses writers in need of refuge. Second, an answer is offered to the question of whose security is important. Thirdly, the intervention addresses the difficulties involved in making the Muslim an Other. I will conclude by briefly considering the strategic tasks which any proponents of hospitality toward Muslim strangers—in Denmark and beyond—will encounter.

Who Are the Good Guys—and Who Are the Bad?

In his initial presentation, the Minister of Culture stated that "this bill is presented to show that Denmark supports the struggle for freedom of expression and open, democratic societies which takes place outside the borders of our country." In their contribution to the committee reports on the bills, the government parties claimed that "Denmark, after facilitating this arrangement, will be in the forefront of spreading freedom of expression." Even if this assertion is debatable, it obviously defines Denmark as a nice place to live (and, conversely, places evil oppression somewhere outside Denmark); moreover, it presents Denmark as a benevolent agent capable of doing and furthering good deeds beyond its borders.

In many ways, there exists a general agreement in parliament about this picture of reality. Only a few minor problems (e.g., civil servants disagreeing with their political bosses, cf. MP Ammitzbøll, soc.lib, "Folketingets forhandlinger, 2008.04.15, 13:59) are mentioned: "Our freedom of expression is, on the whole, unlimited" (MP Kjær, con., 2008.04.15, 14:08). At the very least, everybody seems to concur that Denmark is a "country which has many a time been pioneering exactly when it comes to freedom of expression" (MP Mortensen, soc.dem., 2008.04.15, 14:02).

So Denmark is on the side of Enlightenment. At first sight, the opposing dark side consists of oppressive states, since "in many countries those in power want to control the opinion of the citizens of the country and how it is expressed" (MP Christensen, lib., 2008.04.15, 13:39), and hence, "certain writers . . . are persecuted for being critical towards the system ruling the country they are living in" (MP Kjær, con., 2008.04.15, 14:08).

The opponents of freedom of expression, however, need not be states. A critical attitude toward the state is not the only reason for persecution; another reason may be that "they write or in other ways express themselves about something that is not accepted where they live" (MP Kjær, con., 2008.04.15, 14:08). Moreover, "the dictatorship [which] many writers are fighting" (MP Christensen, lib., 2008.04.15, 13:39) need not be a state; it might be an ideology or another system of thought.

The Minister of Culture himself sets the context straight: "We have seen it here at home too, most recently the plots to kill cartoonist Kurt Westergaard [who drew the cartoon of an angry bearded man with the bomb in the turban in the *Jyllands-Posten* that provoked such an outcry among many Muslims, U.P.G.]. It is a shame, and terrible to think, that even in this society we find forces who might want to eliminate a cartoonist just for expressing opinions diverging from their own (2008.04.15, 14:27). Or, in the more radical formulation of a speaker for the Danish People's Party: "[T]he freedom of expression has within the last decades come under pressure in the Western World, especially from extremist Muslims" (MP Henriksen, DPP, 2008.05.23, 11:34).

The Discursive Context I: Danish-Muslim Relations and the Question of Security

With this framing of the Cities of Refuge debates as a sequel to the Cartoon Crisis, it is clear that the discussions are part of the ongoing struggle to define Denmark's "Muslim relations." Some opposition parties' speakers try to challenge this framing by distinguishing between good and bad manifestations of the freedom of expression: "This is about freedom of expression where it means something, where people have been fighting state power, and not just . . . trying to speak against people you dislike in a hateful way" (MP Ammitzbøll, soc.lib., 2008.04.15, 15:05). But as it was part of the government's platform to articulate "Muslim relations" with the nationalist Danish People's Party (DPP), these attempts to give the discussion a different turn proved rather unsuccessful.

The then-secretary general of the United Nations took the cartoon incidents as occasion to characterize Denmark as a "country which has recently acquired a significant Muslim population, and is not yet sure how to adjust to it" (Annan 2006).[2] It would, however, be more precise to say that "some in Denmark" are not yet sure how to deal with the new situation. The Danish government at the time consisted of a liberal and a conservative party, but relied on the right-wing DPP for its parliamentary majority. At least the latter seems quite sure about how Denmark should adjust to the new situation. Hints as to what this may look like can be found in the "Declaration on recognition of fundamental values of the Danish society," committee reports, and the records of the parliamentary debate. I will return to this in a moment.

The point to be made here is that—as Kofi Annan suggested—the rest of the Danish political actors were—and still are—rather unsure when it comes to the question of how to relate to the recent increase of the Muslim population. When in government, the liberal and conservative parties tried to keep their formulations sufficiently ambiguous in order not to estrange the DPP while insisting that their legal reforms are compatible with international standards and humanitarian norms. The rest of parliament, in turn, has oscillated between multiculturalism, varieties of liberal universalism, and some concessions to the right. Meanwhile, the DPP has moved in and filled the vacuum left by the equivocality of the center/right and the discordance of the center/left. They have set the conditions for the debate—the "conditions for hospitality." These mostly pertain to security: the security of the writers but, more importantly, the security of Danes—and by no means only the security of Danes in times of terror. What is at stake is the security of Danish identity in times of global migration.

The Danish Security and Intelligence Service (PET is the Danish acronym) plays a double role in the parliamentary debate on the writers in need of refuge. For the center/left parties, it is important to make sure that the intelligence service takes care of the security of writers who might need protection even in their Danish refuge—and that the state pays for their protection (e.g, MP Mortensen, soc.dem., 2008.04.15, 13:46).

The DPP, however, envisions another role for the intelligence service. As a condition for their support of the bill, they want to make sure that "the stranger in question is in advance security checked by the PET" and that "the stranger in question may be refused without further explanation if the PET finds that he constitutes a threat to Denmark." Furthermore, they insist that "the stranger in question is falling within provisions for expulsion . . . if [he] abuses the stay in Denmark . . . e.g., by engaging in criminal activities" (Committee report on the bill to amend the Literature Act, p. 3).

The Discursive Context II: The Violence of Islam(ists)

Both provisions make sense if your chosen danger is immediate and comes in the form of the violent Islamist: He or she might try to curb our freedom and way of life as an assassin killing a writer or as a terrorist blowing up a commuter train: "[W]e shall not just roll over and wait for others to take over our right to express ourselves and our democracy" (Minister of Culture, con., 2008.05.23, 11:20). Thus the government assures that the PET will cater to the security of the writers (Minister of Culture 2008.04.15, 14:41) and protect the Danes against potential violent attacks (Minister of Integration's answer to questions no. 8 & 9, reprinted in the report from Committee on Integration). When it comes to the duration of hospitality, however, the security of Danish cultural identity wins over the security of the individual writers. They are not allowed to stay and possibly compromise the homogeneity of Denmark.

Refuge for . . . Refugees?

The International Cities of Refuge Network (ICORN) has members in a number of countries. But one cannot help noticing that Norway houses a greater number of writers than any other country. In addition to the beauty of the landscape and the friendly locals, one reason might be that the hospitality Norway extends to the writers in need of refuge is more generous than that of other countries: If a writer is accepted as in need of refuge by ICORN and invited by a Norwegian city, he or she is granted asylum under Norwegian law. A number of center/left parties in the Danish parliament suggested that Denmark do the same (MP Krag, soc., 2008.04.15, 15:07; MP Ammitzbøll, soc.lib., s.d. 15:11; MP Clausen, red/green, s.d. 15:17). On this point, however, the center/right government—as well as, notably, the Social Democrats—chose to follow the DPP: Within two years, the new arrival should return home.

Actually, the nature of the stay offered in Denmark by no means resembles asylum: "Writers etc. have under existing regulation the same possibilities as other foreigners to apply for and possibly attain asylum in this country if they have had to flee from their homeland due to persecution, but a special option to do this should not be offered" (Government's remarks to bill no. L 131, p. 3). The stay of the writer will rather be like a stay allowing time to work or educate himself or herself. Moreover, the writer is not considered a refugee—he or she has "more features in common with . . . strangers coming to this country as workers or students and whose basis for residence is temporary and connected to a specific activity" (ibid.). In conclusion, a warning is expressed "against using the term 'persecution' and against using it too much and over-interpreting it. We are after all not talking about asylum here. . . . We are talking about that you are granted permission to stay according to a very airy criterion for very special reasons and when part of a very special group" (Minister of Integration, 2008.04.15, 15:22).

The Discursive Context III: Limiting the Influx of Muslims to Secure Homogeneity

In this case, Danish language comes to the aid of the government, since a "city of refuge," when translated, does not refer to "refugee." A refugee is a *flygtning* in Danish, someone fleeing—while a city of refuge is a *friby*, a "free city," connoting *frirum* (free space) and even *fritid* (spare time). In general, according to the government's terminology, the writers to whom hospitality is offered or granted are not "persecuted writers" but "writers whose freedom of expression is infringed upon in their homeland." Especially the minister for integration painstakingly avoids calling the writers "persecuted" (2008.04.15, 15:27)—an attribute too closely related to the language of international law on refugees. Thus the clash of concepts is not as acute—since rhetorically not as obvious—in Danish as it might be in English.

The point to be made here is that it is of utter importance for the government not to undermine the efforts made to "limit the influx of strangers," an influx considered to have been disproportionate under the aegis of earlier alien legislation and their permissiveness to grant asylum and allow for family reunification (especially in regard to the influx of Muslim strangers, as their assimilability is questioned by the DPP). They are represented as a threat to the identity of what the Danes perceive to be their uniquely homogenous nation-state (Sjørslev 2007, 144; cf. Haahr 2003, 27–29; Gullestad 2002a).

Hence, the final point of the declaration put in front of the writer at arrival urges the writer to confirm that

> I am aware that my stay in Denmark as part of the Cities of Refuge arrangement is temporary and that it is intended that I shall return to my homeland. The purpose of my stay is, hence, to allow me to practice my literary activities in Denmark for a period of time, while afterwards return [sic] to my homeland.[3]

The importance of making sure to get rid of the guest again warrants two considerations—one on the future, one on the past—together implying a narrative of defense. First of all, Norwegian anthropologist Marianne Gullestad (2002b, 100n57) notes that Derrida in *Of Hospitality* concentrates on the immediate reaction to a guest as he or she arrives. On the one hand, this is not entirely fair, taking into account the considerations on the necessity of having a law to distinguish guests from parasites (Derrida and Dufourmantelle 2000, 59). This implies that the quality and duration of the entire stay of the guest is condensed into the situation of the arrival. On the other hand, the Danish "show of hospitality" amply demonstrates that the shadow of the future sometimes entirely eclipses the moment of arrival—the moment of hospitality.

Second, the importance of making sure to get rid of the arriving stranger points to the rhetorical question put forth by Derrida: "Perhaps only the one who endures the experience of being deprived of a home can offer hospitality?" (Derrida and Dufourmantelle 2000, 56). Denmark often prides itself of a thousand-year history as a Kingdom. Its borders have moved—mainly to shrink the territory—but what today counts as Denmark has, in the eyes of many Danes, served as their homeland since time immemorial. So Denmark may simply not be suited to offer hospitality; it might only be suited to "*show* that [it] supports the struggle for freedom of expression" (emphasis mine) as the Minister of Culture put it when introducing the law. If so, the list of values in the declarations presented to the writers of refuge is not meant to be the precondition to hospitality (i.e., the minimal recognition given by the stranger in return for an open door). It might simply be designed to ward him off by misidentifying him, by Othering her.

Making Us Good by Listing Their Vices

If you see yourself as the main character in a heroic narrative, defending yourself against Muslim terrorists and against floods of Muslim migrants, then it is obviously important to whom you're offering hospitality. Derrida (2000, 26–30) insists that hospitality can manifest itself only as conditional; usually, you at least ask the stranger for his name before inviting him in. In Denmark, however, some more conditions have to be met.

Actually, the declaration that the writers are required to sign upon arrival is a caricature catalog of the vices of Muslims as they permeate Danish debates on integration. Denmark awards the immigrants permanent residence or citizenship on the condition that they give up *not*, as Derrida remarks apropos the case of Algeria, "what *they* thought of as their culture" (2000, 145; emphasis mine) but the cultural traits that *we* identify them by. Why would you want someone to declare that he does not hit his children, unless you expect him of having just such an inclination?

Thus, according to said declaration, Muslims can be expected to

- violate Danish laws
- undermine the Danish democratic principles in every respect
- disrespect the freedom and personal integrity of the individual
- disrespect and oppress women
- disrespect freedom of expression and religion
- discriminate on the grounds of race and skin color
- threaten and scorn other religious and sexually oriented groups
- disrespect and oppress children (especially girls) to make sure that they do not grow up to be capable of making their own decisions

- support acts of terrorism (or at least refrain from assisting the authorities in preventing them)
- harbor no commitment to Danish society or democracy.

Indeed, the list in the declaration that people seeking permanent residence in Denmark (after being granted family reunion) are confronted with is even more comprehensive. These Muslims are expected to

- commit or at least threaten violence against their spouses
- circumcise their daughters
- use force to marry their children against their wills
- hit their children.

From the reports of the parliamentary committees we can deduce that the DPP actually wanted to further expand the list of the declaration that refugee writers have to sign, as they might

- behave in a disorderly manner
- assume a brazen and disrespectful attitude toward Denmark and the Danes and, finally, (as one of the prominent problems connoted with Muslims) he (!) might
- bring along more than one wife.

Let us leave the question of polygamy aside and rather focus upon the DPP's demands for orderly manners, humility, and respect for Danes, which were not included in the final version of the declaration. This because, as the Minister of Culture remarks:

> [D]ictators hate art; they are afraid of it. . . . They believed that they could eliminate the nuances and make people uniform. . . . But it is so that art and culture and writing insist on nuance, insist on the existence of things not just black and white. They insist on complexity, on showing us the ugly and the provoking and the things in our minds and hearts where the dictators have no access. (Minister for Culture, con., 2008.04.15, 14:21)

A DPP member of the parliament Committee on Culture asked the minister "how to secure that the persecuted writer when in this country is primarily occupied with literary activities directed towards his/her homeland—where the literary freedom is infringed—and not towards entirely different countries, e.g. Denmark, the USA, or a third country?" (additional committee report dated 28 May 2008, app. 11, p. 4). The minister in his answer reassured him that "probably a persecuted writer invited to come to Denmark as a sanctuary with everything paid for will not feel occasioned to criticize his host country." And he added that,

> . . . since the aim of the Cities of Refuge arrangement is to promote freedom of expression, the writers must be able to speak and write freely, even if they might come up with criticizing conditions in Denmark or other third countries. To speak and write freely—even if the criticism hits ourselves—that is the essence; that is what freedom of expression is all about. (ibid.)

The Discursive Context IV: Othering the Muslims

For the Minister of Integration, however, things are a bit more complicated. Due to the complexities at hand, it is necessary to quote her at some length:

> [W]e cannot demand from our citizens that they must love the law or that they must love democracy—and had we been talking about asylum seekers . . . we could not have demanded this kind of declaration. Because in Denmark, you are allowed to be opposed to democracy. But here we are talking about a very specific, very airy and far-reaching basis for residence compared to the one we grant when dealing with refugees and family reunions et cetera. . . .
>
> [W]riters are people using the word as a weapon, and we might as well be honest and say: We are talking about a political agreement, and we are talking about not letting someone in who will use the word to break down the Danish society. . . .
>
> I have been eying through this declaration to make sure that there is no obligation to be a democrat, and we are not talking about that you have to love democracy—but you do have to respect and subject yourself to democracy when you are let in here on this far-reaching basis for residence. That is the reason why I can defend this and why I am of the opinion that it is right that we let the writer think for a moment if it is the right country he is coming to—and that we do not downright let in a fifth column who is after all not individually persecuted in the sense of the provisions for refugees under the Alien Act. (Minister of Integration, 2008.04.15, 15:22)

Consequently, the point of the list to be signed by the writer is not primarily to set the minimal conditions for hospitality; it is, rather and foremost, a defense against a fifth column entering to feed on the welfare state before finishing it off by turning it into a totalitarian sharia state. Not just parasites who feed on the host, as Derrida discussed (Derrida and Dufourmantelle 2000, 59), but parasitoids who will, in the last instance, kill the host.

However, will requiring that parasitoids sign such a declaration help keep them out? In an earlier debate, parliament discussed introducing something similar to—yet different from—a "Green Card" (i.e., a work permit): a "Love Card," allowing you to love. The idea was that if a Danish citizen were solemnly to declare that he or she loves a partner he or she has met abroad, then said partner should be awarded a "Love Card" allowing him or her temporary residence.[4] In the debate on Cities of Refuge, the DPP speaker—now in favor of a declaration on fundamental values—was reminded that he had dismissed the declaration of love with the words "people will sign anything to get into Denmark" (MP Henriksen, DPP, quoted by MP Ammitzbøll, soc.lib., 2008.05.23, 11:38).

Thus, rather than preventing parasitoids to abuse the host country, such a list of values represents an attempt to merge identity politics with security politics: It serves the construction of an existential threat—a radical Other—to legitimize extraordinary means to defend identity, an identity that paradoxically needs the Other to define itself (Wæver 1994). Even if the list of Danish values is carefully monitored by a respectable liberal intellectual—which the then Minister of Integration admittedly was—the very existence of the list, and the act of listing, are geared toward turning Muslims into Others. As Derrida, however, notes: "Ghosts haunt places that exist without them; they return to where they have been excluded from" (Derrida and Dufourmantelle 2000, 152).

The Difficulty of Making Muslims Other

The declarations and lists analyzed in this essay are but a couple of the results of a national obsession with the "fundamental values of Danish society" that Muslims are suspected to disregard and even undermine. The explication of such fundamental values as criteria for inclusion, however, implies a risk—the risk of excluding the wrong persons. During the debates on the Cities of Refuge, a recent parliamentary debate on the values of immigrants was brought to memory as a speaker for an opposition party exclaimed that "it would be a relief if the MPs from DPP would sign the [former] declaration in question" (MP Ammitzbøll, soc.lib., 2008.04.15, 15:05; cf. MP Clausen, red/green, 2008.05.23, 11:41).

In this earlier debate on April 26, 2007, special attention was awarded to one MP for the Danish People's Party, theologian Søren Krarup. During decades as a maverick right-wing intellectual, he had renounced or violated more than a couple of so-called fundamental Danish values. Among some of those that he had taken issue with in book-length showdowns were those of human rights and democracy; Krarup, however, concentrated his defense on newspaper reports accusing him (when asked questions carefully crafted to the purpose) of having failed to unambiguously accept homosexuality and to universally denounce the death penalty.

This problem is not new to Krarup; he has accustomed himself to explaining how his old, radical formulations are consistent with his present voting in parliament after he changed careers from self-styled intellectual outcast to de facto responsible for government policies. One of his argumentative strategies is a perfect illustration of the Lacanian concept of *jouissance* (reintroduced into English language political theory by Slavoj Žižek [1992] as "enjoyment"), defined as

> "pleasure in unpleasure"; . . . the paradoxical satisfaction procured by a painful encounter with a Thing that perturbs the equilibrium of the "pleasure principle". . . . The hatred of the Other is the hatred of our own excess of enjoyment. . . . [T]he fascinating image of the Other personifies . . . what . . . prevents us from achieving full identity with ourselves. (194–96)

A textbook example of *jouissance* is found in this quote by Krarup explaining his change in position on whether parents should be legally allowed to hit their children:

> What makes it so terribly difficult to talk about the right of chastisement today is that we have been swamped by a culture for which violence—the holy right of the man to beat his wife and children black and blue—is natural. This means that the Danish tradition for the right of chastisement has been more or less compromised by a Muslim tradition which is so different. (*Politiken* 2005.11.13)

In this case, protection of Danish identity requires us to painfully relinquish a piece of Danish culture. In most cases, however, Krarup would argue that the criticism of his digressions from political correctness amounted to hairsplitting—or that they refer only to highly hypothetical situations.

It seems, indeed, to be a difficult task to make the Muslim Other by listing values; the problem is, it still might work. Even if Søren Krarup's values may be characterized as un-Danish, nobody seriously wants to deport him or take away his citizenship. But when a young woman with brown skin, wearing a hijab or not, born and raised in Denmark, does not renounce the death penalty in the most hypothetical of all hypothetical societies (e.g., in an Islamic utopia, where everyone lives in perfect adherence to the will of Allah), then she is considered not Danish—she turns into the Other (Hervik 2002; Larsen 2007).

Hospitality as a Strategic Task

In *Of Hospitality*, Anne Dufourmantelle stresses the political role of philosophy in being granted the right to philosophize about absolute, utopian hospitality without a fixed purpose or a practical agenda (Derrida and Dufourmantelle 2000, 66). True: If we want to keep the political debate high-ceilinged, someone needs to keep the pillars supporting the ceiling erect and tall. So there is a role for speculative philosophy. We should, however, also heed Derrida's call for giving "place to a determined, limitable, and delimitable—in a word, to a calculable—right or law . . . to a concrete politics and ethics" of hospitality (147–48). In order to do so, we need to make ourselves familiar with the strategic terrain we intend to intervene. In the words of anthropologist Daniel Miller (2005, 15), though coined in a different context: "Having shown that we can be philosophers, we need the courage to refuse this ambition and return to ethnographic empathy and ordinary language."

Consequently, there is also an important role for what might be termed *strategic studies*, conceived of as identifying openings in the discourses of politics, of media, of everyday life—openings for articulating just a little more "real life" hospitality. We need to analyze the present processes of othering to identify opportunities for turning the Other into an other, a foreigner to whom conditional hospitality can—should—be offered.

This requires a turn away from essentializations, and toward hybridity: We need to insist that it is possible to be both Danish and Muslim, simultaneously a Democrat and a Muslim. But, as sociologist Birgitta Frello (2005, 101; my translation) warns: "If the concept of hybridity gives rise to an indifferent celebration of difference it creates blindness to the unequal power relations always involved." Thus, this turn also implies prioritizing some forms of hybridity over other forms: We need to include democratic Muslim Danes, and exclude non-democratic, non-Muslim Danes. Such a task needs to be based on analyses of the specific strategic terrain into which we choose to intervene; a terrain saturated with fears and strategies of defense. Utopian idea(l)s and moral principles alone will not do.

Appendix[5]

Declaration on Recognition of the Fundamental Values of the Danish Society

Name:

Foreign national's ID/Civil registry number:

I, the undersigned, hereby declare that I understand and accept the fundamental values of Danish society.

I thus declare as follows:

> I shall comply with Danish legislation and protect the Danish democratic principles in every respect.
>
> I respect the freedom and personal integrity of the individual, equal opportunities for men and women, and freedom of speech and religion, which are fundamental constitutional rights in Denmark.
>
> I understand and accept that discrimination on the grounds of race and skin color and threats and scorn against groups on the grounds of religion or sexual orientation is illegal in Denmark.
>
> I understand and accept that men and women have equal obligations and rights in Denmark and that both men and women shall contribute to society.
>
> I understand and accept that in Denmark all children shall be given equal respect and self-expression—be they boys or girls—in order for them to grow up and become active and responsible citizens who are capable of making their own decisions.
>
> I understand and accept that Danish society strongly condemns acts of terrorism and that any citizen has an obligation to fight terrorism amongst others by assisting the authorities through prevention and investigation.
>
> I understand and accept that active commitment to the Danish society is a precondition for democracy.

I also declare that I am aware that my stay in Denmark as part of the Cities of Refuge arrangement is temporary and that it is intended that I shall return to my homeland. The purpose of my stay is, hence, to allow me to practice my literary activities in Denmark for a period of time, while afterwards return to my homeland.

Date:

Signature:

The Aesthetics of Hospitality

Conviviality and Pilgrimage
Hospitality as Interruptive Practice

MIREILLE ROSELLO

Hospitality, Immigration, and Identity

When I first started thinking about hospitality almost ten years ago, I was wondering why it is even possible to discuss "immigration" as a facet of "hospitality." More specifically, I was looking for a productive way to critique the unformulated connection between immigration and hospitality. Like most people I know, I find it plausible to imagine the immigrant as a guest and the national as the host, and to posit that certain nations are "host countries." That certain lands, certain continents are seen as "hosts" and certain migrants as "guests" is such an obvious metaphorical move that I tend to forget that this type of thinking is a naturalized paradigm.[1] What greatly compounds the problem is the fact that the model of hospitality, which starts functioning when the guest is said to arrive, somehow persists long after the migrant has ceased to migrate. Sometimes, several generations after the original encounter between the host and the guest, those who can be traced back to a different past (i.e., ethnicity, religion, or culture) are treated as if they had inherited a sort of perpetual identity as guests.[2]

Politically, the grand narrative of the national as host who treats any other as an immigrant-guest is not intrinsically reactionary, but it certainly cuts both ways. Like any norm, such a narrative both constrains and enables multiple political positions within one system of legibility. The paradigm of hospitality can be usefully deployed whether one is arguing for pro- or anti-immigration policies. If I wish to argue against fortress Europe or against intra-European xenophobic policies, the discourses on hospitality that have circulated since the 1980s are very helpful: They are sophisticated and complex; they do not idealize hospitality as a principle without asking tough questions. When I use the word "hospitality" in this context, all the problematic issues that so many theorists of hospitality have brought to my attention get imported into my discussion.[3]

Such works teach us not to forget the constitutive violence that may be at work in the benevolent process of constructing the stranger as guest. As Jacques Derrida famously suggested, the issue of whether ownership or hospitality comes first is crucial: Is it because a territory is ours (say, by the contingency of having been born in a country that provides us with the rights attached to citizenship) that we have a right and a duty, to act as hosts? Or is it the other way around: Is it when I act as a host that I appropriate the here and now as my house, the place where I can welcome the other?

> To dare say welcome is perhaps to insinuate that one is at home here, that one knows what it means to be at home, and that at home one receives, invites, or offers hospitality, thus appropriating a space for oneself, a space to welcome [*accueillir*] the other, or, worse, welcoming the other in order to appropriate for oneself a place and then speak the language of hospitality. (Derrida 1999a, 15–16)

In other words, the paradigm of hospitality contains a critique of its own limits, which prevents me from idealizing it as the ideal instrument against anti-immigrant rhetoric. At the same time, I cannot dismiss the paradigm so easily. If I wish to point out that there is a certain performative arbitrariness in the way in which Europe and European citizens imagine themselves as hosts, as hospitable, and if I reject the metaphor, am I not simply denying that Europe has benefited from historical conditions, including different colonial pasts, which have given Europe and Europeans enough power to imagine themselves as hosts? And this power relation is still very much in place.

When hospitality becomes a grand narrative, it turns the paradigm into identity politics; some subjects are identified as hosts or guests, no matter what they do in a given context, on a microlevel. When we imagine that some agents are historically predisposed to be seen as guests and hosts, each position starts resembling an identity, and such identities tend to solidify. Yet, rather than bypassing the paradigm altogether, we may want to emphasize a different facet of hospitality. Would it not be more productive to look for what exactly, in our thinking about hospitality, emphasizes practices rather than identities? How can I talk about hospitality when I am interested not in who the guest and who the host is, but in how and when one acts as a guest or as a host? When I am interested in the dynamics of hosting rather than the identity of the host, in convivial practices that take the emphasis away from the host-guest dyad? If we shift our focus to practices, it is possible to emphasize different moments of hospitality during which the position of hosts and guests constantly fluctuate, as we theoretically know that they do. If our objects of analysis are moments when hospitality manifests itself instead of functioning as a generalizable paradigm, we will not be able to assume so easily that we know, ahead of time, who acts as the host in a particular context, and why or how he does.

In other words, I am not suggesting that we move to another grand narrative to critique what, in the hospitality model, may lead to self-defeating generalizations. I am not saying, for example, that we should talk about cosmopolitanism, multiculturalism, or globalization rather than about hospitality. If I look for models that enable me to think of cultures as always already hybridized so that I can concentrate on situations that completely bypass the host/guest paradigm, I may end up glossing over the specificities that continue to force certain agents into an imaginary scene where the roles of hosts and guests are predetermined.[4] How then can I talk about contemporary Europe as a historical moment where the constant interaction between subjects familiar with different cultures, religious practices, or ethnic models is haunted by the original encounter between a powerful, legitimate host and a minoritized, racialized, disempowered guest no matter what type of practices are observed in daily life?

I propose to address this question by going back and forth between what may appear as two disparate objects: a work of art on the one hand, a film directed in 2005 by French director Coline Serreau entitled *Saint-Jacques La Mecque (Santiago de Compostella-Mecca)*, and a theoretical model, the narrative of "conviviality" as proposed by Paul Gilroy in his 2004 *After Empire: Melancholia or Convivial Culture?* When those two objects are invited to cohabit and participate in the same conversation, they provide us with a vantage point that allows us to do two things. I first intend to identify what they have in common: To what extent does Gilroy's conviviality travel beyond his own object of study (i.e., beyond London, popular culture, and rap music)? Can we productively extrapolate and imagine a form of European conviviality as an alternative to European hospitality, something that Achille Mbembe (2008) has also recently called a "convivial nation"? In a second part, I will analyze the way in which these two narratives, when put next to each other, provide an interesting critique of each other's political value or conceptual limits.

Melancholia and Convivial Cultures

Gilroy (2004) offers a critique of multiculturalism and an antidote against what he calls "postcolonial melancholia." He suggests that the official discourse of multiculturalism, at least in an Anglo-Saxon context, has not kept its generous promises: The celebration of multicultural diversity is not hospitable because it is indistinguishable from a melancholic postcolonial syndrome that tends to reinscribe the ethnic other as a potentially dangerous subject (especially since September 2001). In other words, postcolonial melancholia constantly reiterates the construction of any ethnic other as guest who has just arrived and should be helped, educated, and civilized (as well as surveilled and contained). The State only pretends to welcome.

And yet, according to Gilroy, alternative configurations already exist: something that he calls practices of conviviality, and that he observes everywhere around him in London. They tend, however, to remain invisible and hard to read because "there is no governmental interest in the forms of conviviality and intermixture that appear to have evolved spontaneously and organically from the interventions of anti-racists and the ordinary multiculture of the postcolonial metropolis" (124). For Gilroy, this is the way out of what he calls the "machination of racial politics" (150). He asks us to notice and celebrate already-existing types of practices that have emerged in postcolonial urban centers where the principle of encounters replaces old formulations of cultural belonging and therefore dangerous forms of racialization. Comparing London to the Paris of Montesquieu's Persians, he studies artists who, like them, treat the city as a space that offers

> a fragmented and stratified location in which cultures, histories, and structures of feeling previously separated by enormous distances could be found in the same place, the same time: school, bus, café, cell, waiting room, or traffic jam. The results of this proximity are not always harmonious, but every notion of culture as property is broken and dispersed by the swirling, vertiginous motion of the postcolonial world . . . (70)

His book does not make any systematic attempt at defining "conviviality" and I suspect that this constitutes a deliberate avoidance of strong theory. He alludes to the "chaotic pleasures of the convivial postcolonial urban world" (151). His tactic is to analyze examples, that is, to provide us with stories that nurture his hope to hear

> other stories about "race" and racism to be told apart from the endless narrative of immigration as invasion and the melancholic blend

of guilt, denial, laughter, and homogenizing violence that it has precipitated. Those emancipatory interruptions can perhaps be defined by a liberating sense of the banality of intermixture and the subversive ordinariness of this country's convivial culture in which "race" is stripped of meaning and racism. (150)

When we choose to analyze the way in which groups and individuals already coexist and cohabit, the picture of the European welcoming the immigrant appears as an overgeneralization.

The paradigm of conviviality emphasizes encounters and practices rather than identity, which would enable us to get away from the stereotypical constructions of guest and host. On the other hand, conviviality is closely related to hospitality because it involves various forms of cohabitation, contact, and exchange between people who must articulate new definitions of their space, their territory, and their home. Gilroy focuses on the way in which positions of power and powerlessness can be deployed without completely depending on a given subject's cultural identity.

The examples that Gilroy selects belong to British popular culture. He watches television series such as *The Office*, reads the lyrics of Mike Skinner, a white rapper, and analyzes the satirical performances of Sacha Baron Cohen. Baron Cohen is particularly relevant here: he performs as "Ali G," a hilariously mad and maddening interviewer who practices and parodies two forms of hospitality. When he invites personalities, they are both included and implicitly treated as important guests due to the generic convention of the interview, but they are also radically excluded, relegated to some nonsensical noncommunity because of the general tone of the conversation and because of the way in which Ali G constructs his character. The questions that he asks are falsely naïve and calculated to ridicule both interviewer and interviewee, as well as the genre of the interview as such. When he talks to the head of homeland security, for example, he asks him if it would not be a good idea to reserve certain old buildings for terrorists so that they can have fun with them.[5] The ludicrous question, that the interviewer has no choice but to take seriously, mimics the fake multicultural dialogue in which the dominant seeks (in vain) to remain in control of what happens by assigning the other to a place that corresponds to one's own values and standards (old buildings can be destroyed for fun). The implication is that the West's gestures of hospitality are a form of polite acceptance of the other's imagined difference. Yet, that form of hospitality is unable to fathom that the other may not want to play the multicultural game according to these rules. The idea that the other would want and be able to resort to violence when integration is an alternative is ruled out. Ali

G's stupid questions make him sound stupid but also reveal the intrinsic limits of a kind of dialogue based on mutual bad faith and on the desire to preserve one's parameters.

The second type of hospitality that Ali G satirizes is a symbolic welcoming of a supposedly universal, or at least transnational, definition of ethnic identification markers. The interview with the head of homeland security starts with a short sequence during which Ali G appears naked, then is gradually dressed as a parody of a black ghetto kid, the stereotypical clothes and accessories being projected on his body as if to symbolize the violent process of human branding that such so-called choices imply. Ali G dresses, acts, and speaks as a globalized American thug, and Gilroy welcomes the outrageousness with which he makes the point that this sort of pseudo-hybridity is a self-destructive form of cultural hospitality. Ali G's identity, Gilroy explains, has become an obsession and

> the huge amounts of energy that were wasted worrying about whether Ali G is a white Jew pretending to be black, a white Jew pretending to be a white pretending to be black, a white Jew pretending to be an Asian pretending to be black and so on might have been better spent positioning his tactics in a proper historical and artistic sequence of strangers whose strangeness was functional and educative. (71)

Here, Ali G's fake hybridization is a critique of a form of togetherness and recognition based on superficial sameness (I dress and talk like you) rather than exchange (I talk to or with you). Ali G adopts a very specific form of race and class performance that, according to Gilroy, is "ridiculously inappropriate to the more innocent habits of marginal young Brits. [Ali G] makes the commitment to ghetto fabulous tastes and behaviors appear absurd. He is telling Britain that it had better find another way to go" (134). His satirical posturing responds to what Gilroy views as a reinscription of old ethnic, racial, or simply identitarian patterns that are much less important in a convivial culture. Ali G makes us imagine what a convivial culture would be where such markers would be mocked and parodied. The codes he pretends to adopt are, Gilroy writes, "stultifying U.S. styles and habits that have all but crushed local forms of the black vernacular and replaced them with the standardized and uniform global products for hip-hop consumer culture" (133).

What Gilroy calls conviviality is a hospitality based on togetherness rather than sameness or belonging; it is a different type, or perhaps a different moment of the hospitality paradigm. The scene of hospitality is multiplied and complexified: Instead of being a primary scene, it is played and replayed at many different levels, among a multitude of actors whose position of power and powerlessness is not only relative but also disconnected from their identity.[6] Gilroy's gesture is decidedly optimistic. He actively focuses on forms of transnational solidarities that refuse the paranoid reinscription of race and ethnicity without, however, celebrating the potentially homogenizing forces of globalization.

Coline Serreau's *Saint-Jacques La Mecque*

The audience who knows about Gilroy's examples may be unfamiliar with Serreau's works (except perhaps with the American remake of *Three Men and a Baby*). On the other hand, Serreau's fans have perhaps never heard of Ali G or Mike Skinner. Yet, I am suggesting that this film, which ignores Gilroy's book, and which Gilroy's book does not address, is worth looking at in this context because it deals with something that Gilroy does not actually interrogate.

Serreau's film does not celebrate already existing forms of conviviality that simply need to be found and observed in urban settings. Instead, the narrative suggests that in our melancholic postcolonial society, the routine of daily life must be interrupted for convivial practices to develop. Like most of Serreau's other films, *Saint-Jacques La Mecque* is a socially committed comedy. Lighthearted and optimistic,[7] it does not, however, present us with an idealized version of postcolonial France. Like Gilroy's London, it is populated by people from different ethnicities, different religions, and different social statuses, but in their daily interactions, these characters are posited as sources of difficulty and friction, at least at the beginning of the movie. The film introduces us to figures that could easily be allegorized or stereotyped (the capitalist upper-class white man, the secular feminist, the disenfranchised Muslim youth), characters who not only differ from each other, but also who find differences disturbing. Taken together, they exemplify what some French historians have called France's "colonial fracture" (Blanchard et al. 2005). Here, conviviality finally finds a way to develop; it is not only a promise or a horizon of hope, but also an interruption. Simply looking at a "school, bus, café, cell, waiting room, or traffic jam" (70) will not work because in Serreau's movie, conviviality is an exception that results from a long and difficult learning process. Convivial practices interrupt the norm. In *Saint-Jacques La Mecque*, conviviality will only become possible because something—a journey, a pilgrimage—will introduce a discontinuity. The practices that will develop can be described as chaotic or as "small triumphs" (150), but they are also returning us to the etymology of the word *conviviality*, which has to do with *convivium*, a feast, a banquet. A banquet is always an extraordinary moment, both part of your life and different from your daily life. It is about excess, not about work or hoarding, but at the same time it demands long preparations and a sort of potlatch mentality that requires expenditure and energy (Mauss [1925] 1990; Bataille [1946] 1991). But the etymological banquet also has a simple and down-to-earth side: *convivere* also means "to live with," except that the meaning of to live with is perhaps radically changed once we have understood that to cohabit, to share a house, demands more than the mere fact of physical proximity or promiscuity. Of course there are one or several hosts, but putting the emphasis on the banquet means focusing on how all the participants interact with each other.

Saint-Jacques La Mecque is an atypical road movie and more specifically a pilgrimage movie. The pilgrimage constitutes a radical moment of interruption in the characters' routines, but it is also a process that allows them to become aware of how their so-called normal lives and their subjectivity are constrained by forgotten rules and values. It is also a relatively atypical pilgrimage that troubles our assumption about what normally happens to pilgrims. This is not an intense religious experience thanks to which a national or transnational subgroup may express its common faith and assert the importance of this particular identification marker. In Ismaël Ferroukhi's *Le Grand Voyage*, for example, all the pilgrims who arrive at Mecca from so many different countries are bonded by their faith and their journey. In *Saint-Jacques La Mecque*, as the title lets us guess, Christianity and Islam are mutually creolized. Conviviality will not be the result of a preexisting link between strangers who already share the same religious beliefs; thus the pilgrimage does not create a smaller community whose members could, for once, forget that they are a minority. This film is not about celebrating minorities per se or about recognizing their rights to difference. Instead, it insists on the fact that the pilgrimage, which will be the occasion when new practices of conviviality develop, cannot be interpreted as a moment of authenticity. It is a chaotic endeavor, full of errors and farcical misunderstandings, but also of constraints and frictions.

We follow a group of pilgrims who walk together toward Santiago de Compostela and are forced to cohabit, exchange, share in a way that both resembles and differs from what happens in urban centers according to Gilroy. The conviviality they practice or refuse to practice is a mixture of what they had learned, prior to the journey, as individuals shaped by their own culture, politics, and socioeconomic backgrounds (including postcolonial melancholia), and of what they must invent when they find themselves cut off from their daily routines. The constant friction between the old rules and what they have to re-create as a new, temporary, and artificial community shows that both poles of Gilroy's construction (postcolonial melancholia and convivial culture) exist simultaneously, and are constantly superimposed upon each other rather than in mutual opposition.

All the characters going to Santiago together are a group of strangers who will have to cohabit for several months, although they are separated by every conceivable stereotypical sociological category. They are from radically different social classes (Pierre is a rich business man, his brother is chronically unemployed, permanently broke, and quasi-homeless). They belong to different age groups (four adolescents, several fifty-something adults, including three siblings, their guide, and a woman—and we cannot count on the young ones to provide us with obvious solutions). Ethnicity is fictionally marked (two of the adolescents are Arabs and the guide is black), religion is an issue (the two Arabs are Muslims, the others are culturally or religiously Christian), and they constantly bicker about politics. Clara, Pierre's sister, is an old-fashioned socialist who never misses an opportunity to accuse her rich brother of racism and paternalism, and she delivers feminist speeches that confuse radical secularism with individual freedom for women. They all speak French, but what is most obvious throughout the film is their inability to communicate: The three siblings are constantly yelling verbal abuses at each other, and it is significant that one of the young men is illiterate due to a bad case of dyslexia. His handicap ironically underlines the others' failure to understand each other or the other European pilgrims that they encounter on the way. Whatever conviviality this film fictionalizes is not a given.

The urban centers that Gilroy focuses upon are absent. Before the journey, these characters are part of a multicultural society that erects borders between them. They never shared the same house, they never invited each other, and they coexisted without interacting. If this community is representative of a certain multicultural France and Europe, then the lesson is that diversity is a mosaic of segregated differences. Conviviality malfunctions as long as it relies on preexisting codes of hospitality that force individuals to value sameness: the rich with the rich, the poor with the poor, since, as usual in Serreau's films, the implication is that global capitalism robs people of their ability to form other ties. What they will have to learn in order to be capable of welcoming each other, to "change while exchanging" (as Edouard Glissant [2006] famously puts it), is to unlearn what they knew.[8]

What is remarkable about the pilgrimage that Serreau stages is that it does not imply a moment of authenticity for a religious subgroup, a moment during which the pilgrims reassert their common faith.[9] In *Saint-Jacques La Mecque*, as the title indicates, there is something queer about the whole journey. Santiago de Compostela is not presented as the Christian equivalent to a trip to Mecca for Muslims. The way in which this particular trip is organized makes it impossible for the viewer to assume that this is simply a well-known ritual performed according to the rules. The *convivium* does not reinforce a bond between individuals who are already close to each other due to cultural and religious ties, and whose minority status isolates them within a larger group. Conviviality develops as the result of artificial and almost farcical circumstances.

The three siblings who participate in the journey are estranged. Their family is completely dysfunctional. They hate each other and have no contact prior to the pilgrimage that, moreover, they are embarking upon for completely a-religious reasons. They have reluctantly accepted to take part in it because their mother has recently died and left a will stating that she will leave all her money to charity unless the brothers and sisters agree to go to Santiago together. The desire to get her money, which is also, symbolically, the need to recover a lost heritage and filiation, is stronger than their hatred for each other. Conviviality is imposed and does not work miracles at first. From one perspective, they are not strangers to each other; they are biologically, racially, culturally as closely connected as anyone can be. And yet, the story presents them as inhospitable, and their inability to cohabit without yelling at each other or even beating each other up is one of the problems that the film stages and tries to find solutions to. Their constant fighting contaminates the group as a whole until the other members demand that they at least tolerate each other. Even postcolonial melancholia is schizophrenic: The strength of the biological bond between the white siblings, which could be interpreted as an allegory for the illusion of purity on the national level, can only be activated as a result of this long and painful experience of cohabitation.

Others are there by mistake. Ramzi, one of the Muslim youths, for example, thinks that he is going to Mecca. His friend Said, also a Muslim by culture but obviously not interested in the religious aspect of the pilgrimage, has tricked him. He has convinced him to borrow money from his poor mother to pay their way. Here, one young Muslim is taking advantage of his friend's almost incredible naïveté. He has managed to convince him that they are all going to La Mecque.

For Said, the pilgrimage is also a pretext, a format that exists and enables him to develop another narrative of encounter, something that we could call an interethnic and cross-economic love story. The reason why he absolutely wanted to join the group has nothing to do with religion: He has fallen in love with one of his classmates, a well-off bourgeois young woman, and upon overhearing that she was going to Saint-Jacques, he secretly booked the trip. His motivation could be analyzed as purely personal except that the film makes it clear that the distance they will walk together is what separates them both in terms of class (she is rich, he is poor) and of ethnicity (he is, as he thinks she has implied during a fight caused by a misunderstanding, a *frisé*, an Arab).

What kind of convivial practices does the film fictionalize as an answer to such problems? Serreau leads us in three counterintuitive directions. First, the film suggests that conviviality may well be the result of certain constraints: It does not privilege what occurs "spontaneously and organically" (Gilroy 2004, 124), but instead what forces people to be convivial. The characters must give each other time as well as space, and their patience involves enduring, being patient in the etymological sense of the term. Conviviality finally occurs because they have to tolerate something that they find painful and difficult. If the pilgrimage resembles, in any way, what Gilroy calls a "traffic jam" (70), it is because it interrupts the normal flow of life and thus constitutes a problematic but fruitful interruption of the norm. People meet but under circumstances that they deem undesirable. The urban centers that they left were not intrinsically convivial, but the artificial and nomadic space that they chart as they walk together contributes to the emergence of conviviality.

The pilgrimage takes the characters away from their usual residences, which means that the film could choose to erase forms of geographical segregation that other narratives must adopt as the horizon of verisimilitude. In films that represent disenfranchised French *banlieues*, for example, the bourgeois usually live in the city center while the periphery, where most of the housing projects were built in the 1950s and 1960s, is the territory of the ethnic other. In the case of *Saint-Jacques La Mecque*, the fact that the two Muslim youths do not come from a *banlieue*, that one of the brothers lives in a rich residential area, while the other is quasi-homeless, does not help them cope with the specific difficulties arising from the pilgrimage. But Serreau abstains from portraying the journey as a utopian space in which issues of promiscuity and space issues do not exist. Practically every night, the characters realize that they have to reinvent their territory because there is never enough room for all of them: either there are too few beds, the inn is booked, or they are forced to share rooms with other pilgrims. The norms of traditional distribution (e.g., separate male and female sleeping quarters or the principle of the individual room) collapse and no longer guarantee the borders that would provide a buffer between hostile individuals. Each night, the pilgrims must come up with a new solution, an imperfect and inadequate way of *convivere*. Lack of space is also a metaphor: The characters must learn how to share not only their sleeping quarters but also their values, their history; the ways in which their supposedly multicultural society inscribes each of them as a different type of subject depending on their ethnicity, gender, and class. The film shows that conviviality occurs simultaneously to the emergence of a rewriting of history that involves both an account of the colonial past and an integration of several strands of historical narrative.

In Serreau's film, the colonial past emerges as one of the hermeneutic grids that viewers can now apply to what first appeared as an exclusively Christian pilgrimage. Thanks to the collaboration between Clara, the school teacher, and Ramzi, who is eager to learn, their journey is rewritten as an encounter between Islam and Christianity. As the characters discover their own history, we learn to reinterpret Santiago not only as the Saint that Christians pay homage to, but also as the "matamoros"—the one who killed Moors, "des rebeus comme nous" [Arabs like us], as Ramzi explains, horrified. Still, Ramzi does not choose to discard him as a villain from the past. He does not suggest that the statue should be removed; he simply adds his own graffiti to the stereotype, greeting a Catholic priest with a heartfelt "Salaam Aleykum" or yelling "Allahu Akbar" from the top of another monument. He rewrites the pilgrimage as an opportunity to practice his own religion, in a *bricolée* and personal way.

Dramatically, however, the reason why it was so easy to deceive him plays an important role: If he is unbelievably dependent and powerless, it is because he has never learned how to read due to a bad case of dyslexia. In his case, as long as he is deceived, the pilgrimage can only be a cruel joke, but it is because Clara, the sister, teaches him how to read that his new knowledge of history will allow him (and us) to weave a tale in which contemporary Islam and contemporary Christianity cohabit in interesting ways.

Conviviality, however, is not always harmonious, and the film is perhaps less optimistic than Gilroy's book in that respect. *Saint-Jacques La Mecque* directly tests the potential but also the limits of conviviality as a way of resisting contemporary racism, a point worth exploring here since the issue of racialization and multiculturalism is crucial in *After Empire*. Serreau's pilgrimage is also a story about the (sometimes failed) interconnection between kinship and racism, foreignness and conviviality.

Racism and Inhospitality: Capitalism and Imperfect Hospitality

In a particularly violent scene, the reinscription of racial markers that Gilroy denounces is clearly articulated. Toward the end of the pilgrimage, they meet a Spanish priest who refuses to let the whole group stay for the night. He explains, in Spanish, that he does not have enough room to accommodate all the pilgrims. The guide, who is the only one who understands Spanish, translates, not so much the words, but the substance of the inhospitable statement for the group. He reveals the obviously racist subtext. This has happened before, he argues; the priest systematically excludes "bronzés" (brown men). Every year the same thing occurs: black and brown pilgrims are simply excluded from the list of guests.

Interestingly, the guide does not question the priest's obvious lie. He appears rather blasé and fatalistic about this blatantly racist attitude. But Pierre, uncharacteristically, confronts the priest in French. The elder brother—who has, until now, been suspected of harboring racist sentiments and been accused of treating the other members in a condescending and paternalistic way—is the only member of the group who refuses to put up with the priest's behavior. He attacks him as a Spaniard betraying both his history (the inhospitable host should have noticed that Franco died a long time ago, that fascism is no longer tolerated in Spain) and his religion ("We are sick," Pierre tells him, "of priests who give lessons and act like pigs").

Several elements are worth noting about the way in which the film frames this tirade. First of all, the system of address is radically flawed: The whole tirade misses the addressee because the priest either does not understand a word, or pretends not to. He repeats, "No hablo francés" or "¿Qué dices?" while Pierre asks, "What does he say?" The two characters are simply not communicating. On one level, nothing is happening (the priest will get away with his inhospitality and racism), on another one, the gist of the exchange is obvious. The priest is a racist, and when Pierre turns to his friends and asks "What does he say?" his brother replies: "Il se fout de ta gueule" [he is taking you for an idiot], which suggests that it is less important to understand the words than the racist subtext.

One of the most important aspects of this scene, however, is that it links the issue of racism to the narrative about broken "fraternité" that Pierre finds useful to invoke, much to the surprise of his siblings, who have never seen him act in any (traditional) brotherly way.[10] Clumsily, Pierre makes a connection between different types of estrangement that his intervention will somehow repair with a dose of hospitality. What he argues, vehemently, is that the group cannot be separated because they have become "brothers and sisters." According to him, this strong family bond has developed because "they have walked together." Given how the brothers and their sister have acted until now, his reference to some sort of natural solidarity among siblings is ironic to say the least. He does not seem to be aware that, according to his own behavior, brothers and sisters seem programmed to fight over everything and to despise each other. And yet, the contradiction or faulty reasoning is effective at least at one level. It provides him with the desire, strength, and means to refute the priest's lie. Of course, the latter has not explicitly stated that he does not want blacks and Beurs in his shelter. The reason he has invoked is reminiscent of all the political arguments about thresholds, about economic commonsense. According to the priest, there is simply not enough room to welcome all the pilgrims asking for hospitality. Pierre's reaction to this lie seems to miss both points: Race is blotted out from the picture altogether in his seemingly absurd argument about "family" ties, and the issue of whether or not there is enough room is not addressed at all. Pierre's response does not evoke race or of racism, either.

The third important element in this scene is the fact that the convivial solution offered in response to racism is far from ideal, considering the film's own professed mistrust for capitalist values and rules of conduct. When confronted with something identified as racist inhospitality, Pierre argues against the principle of exclusion, but both his discourse and his solution are tainted by ironic self-contradiction. The solution he proposes, once he realizes that he will not convince the priest, is to take the whole group to a hotel, for which he offers to foot the bill. In other words, one form of hospitality replaces one form of inhospitality. For the first time, the pilgrims will spend the night in an expensive hotel because the solution that the brother has found to their predicament is that he suddenly adopts the position of host. In other words, his solution reintroduces economic disparities, and we can either celebrate or deplore the fact that it is the white bourgeois who is entrusted with the responsibility of solving the problem of conviviality. His money compensates—perhaps overcompensates—for the priest's racism. The guardian of Christian values is exposed as a hypocrite, while the much-maligned capitalist logic that turns hospitality into commerce turns out to be the only way out. For the other members of the group, the nasty episode morphs into an evening of luxurious hot baths. The facilities they had become accustomed to and that they had to renounce to find their new selves, the loss they had accepted in order to gain this new sense of community, disappears, almost by magic. The night is, however, inscribed as a sort of exception to a new rule. It is of course problematic that the only solution that the film can offer to an obvious racial affront, which manifests itself as a hypocritical limit to hospitality, should be commercial. The film criticizes most forms of consumption even when they are not conspicuous, and the luxurious comfort provided by an expensive hotel seems to contradict the celebration of a simple and quasi-Spartan lifestyle. But even if this type of conviviality is tainted by a capitalist logic, the fact that the narrative compromises with its own ideals could been seen as another "small triumph" (Gilroy 2004, 150).

Interestingly, the film adds a postscriptum to Pierre's antiracist intervention, and in that scene, the viewer is warned against an overly optimistic interpretation of his already ambiguous gesture of conviviality. Maybe we should not believe in the neat distinction between the racist priest and the rich liberal. If, in the first scene, money is the answer to racism because one individual has decided to replace racism with conviviality, in the scene that I propose to read now, it is the other way around. This time, the broken, imperfect link between the siblings will be slightly repaired, but the convivial moment of "fraternity" is presented as a form of xenophobia. Brother and sister need each other when strangers disturb the group.

When the pilgrims finally reach Santiago, once again, and for the last time, they all stay in a hotel. And just as Clara and Pierre find their rooms, Pierre's hope to spend a quiet and peaceful night is shattered by the arrival of other Dutch pilgrims, characters that we have met before and that the film has constructed as those who will never become part of the community. Their form of conviviality consists of getting drunk and being rowdy. Like the main protagonists, they are Europeans; like them, they left their home to pilgrimage to Santiago, but they have not walked with the other protagonists. They are the others. They have been designated the "snoring Dutchmen," and they are very noisy indeed.

The spectator recognizes them: It is our second meaningful encounter with these undesirable others. When the group had to spend the night in an elementary school, these men had arrived late and kept everybody up with their loud snoring, forcing the group to give up on their night's rest and improvise a party. In the end, everybody was up, everybody was singing and dancing. In other words, during that first encounter, the strangers were troublemakers that someone else (the mayor of the village, the owner of a shared public space) had imposed upon our group. Having arrived first, they had to accept the presence of new guests but did not offer hospitality. On the contrary, the arrival of newcomers was interpreted as a serious disturbance.

Their difference was neutralized, however, thanks to another type of interruption, another type of *convivium*: They had not exactly eaten together but "danced together." A solution had been found, once more, to the fact that even hospitality means finding extra space, changing the function of rooms and buildings. Even after the school had been turned into a hotel room, it could not be completely appropriated. It is always possible that a new guest, a new immigrant will arrive and that this will require everyone to find yet other solutions, to continue to think creatively, and to accept several levels of interruption. In that first scene, the Dutchmen had inconvenienced the group as a whole, and it was as a group, and not as individuals, that the team had found a practice of conviviality.

In the last hotel scene, something different happens. The brother-and-sister narrative that Pierre opposed to the priest's inhospitable racism is put to the test. Although the relationship between the three siblings has definitely evolved since the beginning of the pilgrimage, they are still very far from the supposedly idyllic model that Pierre himself invoked to demand that they not be separated. Whereas all the other members of the group enjoy the comfort of their hotel room, Pierre, as luck or a carefully scripted scenario would have it, is facing the prospect of a sleepless night. The Dutchmen, he discovers, are going to occupy the room next to his.

The result is what we could call an example of reluctant hospitality. Anger and friction are still quasi-palpable between the brother and sister. Pierre stands in the corridor in front of his sister's room. Only the spectator gets to see that he is about to knock on the door, and then changes his mind. He obviously does not like to be put in the position of the guest. Just as he expresses his frustration by taking one step back, his sister opens the door and, without a word, invites him in with a sudden and authoritarian gesture. What they share, at this particular moment, is a narrative that constructs the other's other (the Dutchmen as the nonmembers of their community) as barely tolerable. She opens the door because she knows that her new brother (the one with whom she has walked, and whom she now feels responsible for) will have to put up with the intolerable presence of the snoring Dutchmen who are presented as incomprehensible barbarians whose language is not subtitled and whose caricatural portrayal does not even rise to the level of a national stereotype. They are just others, uncouth, annoying; they cannot be educated; they will just be a nuisance from which the sister decides to protect her brother. His room is next door to what will become theirs if he sleeps in her room, a no man's land will be created, a buffer that will absorb the others' noise, their undesirability. A border zone must be created, which is a no-contact zone. The sister's opening of the door before Pierre has made up his mind to knock again reveals that she subscribes to that narrative. Thus she agrees to be the ultimate host, to share the territory that he has originally helped provide even if, at this point, his prerogative obviously no longer gives him any special right. While Pierre loudly complained about having to share the women's dormitory in an earlier scene, he now acts as if he had forfeited any specific right. The relationship between the two siblings is still very tense, and the manifestation of hospitality is awkward, almost bordering on hostility. Both are silent; only the most rudimentary form of communication, a few gestures, replaces polite sentences. But they do kiss each other good night. What is important, however, is that the film forces us to read this good night kiss as the opposite of a traditional gesture. This is not hypocrisy (abiding by the appearance of rule and not by its spirit). As spectators having traveled with the two characters, and in the process having learned to decode their behavior, we now know that this moment can be read not as a poorly performed ritual of inhospitality but as a unique individual exchange of hospitable gestures (the host offers, the guest accepts, they both know why, they both know that they cannot expect much more from each other). Given their history, it is the best but also the only form of conviviality that can be constructed.

Conclusion

How, then, could we formulate what Gilroy's book and Serreau's film teach each other if they are invited to participate in the same conversation? Gilroy's intellectual move is a sort of sociological archaeology: He helps us identify already existing forms of conviviality, which, in our postcolonial societies, are not necessarily legible as such. In Serreau's film, conviviality is not a given. Her narrative focuses on the moment that precedes and prepares certain types of convivial practices rather than on the space in which they have supposedly already developed. The conviviality in question is imperfect and the characters must learn to endure and tolerate a significant level of discomfort before finding it. If they finally practice conviviality, it is because they have been forced to find a solution to a situation that made cohabitation painful, almost unbearable.

The fundamental difference between Gilroy's book and Serreau's film might then best be explained in terms of their respective forms of optimism. Gilroy splits his object of study (British postcolonial society) into two relatively compartmentalized realms. On the one hand, the official discourse on multiculturalism that remains haunted by postcolonial melancholia and, on the other hand, popular culture as a good example of convivial culture. He opposes the type of racialized discourse constantly reinscribed by the multicultural state's postcolonial melancholia, but also invites us to observe that forms of resistance to this reading of the world have already emerged in our urban centers. His optimism thus needs a quasi-disciplinary segregation between two types of discourses: the official and melancholic multiculturalism, and the convivial practices of popular culture. His paradigm does not need to articulate the difference between cultural politics and political culture. And we have seen that he does not try to elucidate the conditions of emergence of such convivial responses. His celebration of conviviality is thus rooted in a deeply pessimistic account: He posits that the state's failure must be redeemed by the discovery of micronarratives and microresistances that can only generate, in the reader, a prudent and limited form of optimism. We must accept the sociological fiction of an absolute difference between official multiculturalism and popular culture to be able to share Gilroy's enthusiasm for Ali G.

Serreau's film is a fictional account, which calls itself fiction, and which proposes a very different map of conviviality and postcolonial melancholia. Serreau's optimism results from her generic choice, and not from the topic she addresses. She has made a film on how the members of a European society might finally be able to *convivere* due to circumstances that interrupt the norm of separation between classes, genders, and ethnic communities. She suggests that melancholia and conviviality always coexist, and that they need not be assigned a given discourse or a given type of subject.

Comparing the book and the film thus allows us to read Gilroy's sociological narrative as a sort of fiction that can be adapted and modified, but also to interpret Serreau in terms of conviviality and multiculturalism. It also enables us to bring together sociology and film narratives, two realms that we tend to keep apart just as Gilroy distinguishes between popular culture and state discourse. The cautious optimism that Serreau's film may engender allows us to formulate two hypotheses. First of all, we need not search for conviviality beyond postcolonial melancholia and we need not assume that there exists a radical border between convivial urban centers on the one hand, and other ill-defined territories on the other, where we cannot (yet) find "school, bus, café, cell, waiting room, or traffic jams." Moreover, the imperfect and frictional practices of conviviality that Serreau stages do not emerge haphazardly or systematically. They are the effects of forms of constraint that might well be worth being theorized further.

Hospitality and the Zombification of the Other

NIKOS PAPASTERGIADIS

While hospitality was represented as a sacred duty in Homer's *Odyssey*, the status of the stranger was also framed by uncertainty. A Greek could never know in advance whether the stranger was an enemy or a god in disguise. The conventions of Greek hospitality were therefore laced with a mixture of self-interest and the desire to please the gods. To share food and offer gifts to a stranger was considered the highest form of civilization. By contrast, a monster like Cyclops preferred to devour his guests. Hospitality was a regulated mode of reception. The stranger was brought into the house according to various rules and customs that reflected the status of the stranger. The stranger's posture was critical: upright for the holy and prostrated for the poor. The determination over whether the stranger was a friend or enemy, and the willingness to reach out and touch the stranger, followed from the decision formed in the gaze of the host. The host looked and determined the status of the stranger in silence and then offered his hand. After the invitation to enter the house was made, the place of reception and seating arrangement again followed the protocols of status. It was only after food had been shared that speech commenced.

After 9/11, the cultural theorist Gayatri Spivak gazed at the images of the suicide bombers and observed that they "looked like ordinary graduate students."[1] For Spivak, these banal mug shots were not taken as the first sign of an unfathomable enigma, but as a prompt to ask the question: How can I imagine the suicide bomber as a person who shares the same human consciousness as me? Taking her cues from Kant's instruction that the aesthetic enables representation to proceed without objective concepts, she argues that the story of the suicide bomber can only enter the field of intelligibility after "the imagination is trained" to comprehend the other as an agent who is also a knowledge producer. The method for "accessing" such an understanding is not confined to contextualizing the agency of the suicide bomber within his or her sociopolitical history. Spivak stresses that figurative representations supplement the realm of reasoned debate and scholarly investigation. The most difficult part of this task is to surrender to the other as an equal, and from this imaginative outreach and assumed equality, or what she calls "the uncoercive rearrangement of desire," one can then learn about both a coercive belief system that already succeeded in persuading the young to want to die, and our own compulsion for "bestial" revenge. Through this method, Spivak (2002) proffers a warning that echoes Derrida's philosophy of hospitality: Suicidal bombing is a message inscribed in a body; "if we cannot hear the message, then we will not be able to alter the hospitality."

It is worth remembering that Derrida's conception of hospitality is not grounded in a strict code that can determine in advance who is worthy of sheltering and who is to be banished. The answer to the stranger's request for entry into the host's house is never determined in advance of the encounter. By keeping open the space of encounter, Derrida stresses that every culture has the capacity to be hospitable to the other (to receive them without question), and also to colonize the other by receiving them as a guest (to confine their admission through rules that confirm the authority of the host). This tension cannot be resolved in an absolute way, and Derrida recognizes that "unconditional hospitality" is impossible. However, he also insists that to lose sight of this principle of hospitality is to risk losing the marker of justice.[2] The gift of hospitality is held together with strings. An unconditional welcome, a concept that he concedes to be impracticable, is also posed against its opposite, the imperative of sovereignty. The right to mobility must be positioned alongside the hosts' right to authority over their own home. "No hospitality, in the classic sense, without sovereignty of oneself over one's home, but since there is also no hospitality without finitude, sovereignty can only be exercised by filtering, choosing, and thus by excluding and doing violence" (Derrida and Dufourmantelle 2000, 55).

In this essay I reflect on the tension between hospitality and sovereignty by examining the contemporary images of the stranger. I will argue that the names given to and taken by strangers, and in particular, the common appeal of the term *zombie*, is a reflection of the tendency to not only dehumanize the other but also of the withdrawal of the space of hospitality. Against this trend, I will also trace the efforts of migrants, activists, and artists to reclaim the dialogue between hospitality and human rights (Hlavajova and Mosquera 2004).

How Can There Be Hospitality for Zombies?

During the Fordist period of industrial expansion the dominant image of the stranger was expressed in terms of his or her function as a component in the machine. Images of strangers and even critics of exploitation drew on a common pool of metaphors of mechanical exploitation and alienation. In the 1970s migration was inextricably linked to the process of industrialization in the West. The identification of the migrant as a cog in the machine led many commentators to conclude that the alienation of migrants was also a metaphor for the general form of alienation under capitalism.[3] Theories of alienation referred to the reduction of humanity as it was objectified in the form of a mechanical part that generated profit for the master; hence, the alienation of the worker was always configured within the Marxist interpretation of the master/slave dialectic.

In the most recent statements by migrants and refugees the terms of self-identification have shifted decidedly toward the realm of the spectral. For instance, Arnold Zable's (2007) account of a hunger strike against the Australian government's policy of indefinite detention by Sri Lankan refugees on Nauru Island ends by drawing attention to the placards that the refugees composed, in which they describe themselves as "living corpses . . . walking zombies." Mohammed Sagar, an asylum seeker, who was held for seven years in an offshore camp, explained his predicament to a journalist in these terms: "I don't want to be happy, I just want my life back . . . whether it would be happy or sad doesn't matter. I just want it back. I want to be alive, that's all, because now I'm feeling like a dead living thing" (Gordon 2006). The fantasy of release from detention is therefore bound by the desire to return to the place of the "living." However, even this modest hope is presented as a chimera in refugee Richard Okao's (2006) account of living in Melbourne, "which is the city of the dead for me because it is the city where I realized that I was dead; that I wasn't living." Amal Masry was a survivor of the SIEV X—a people-smuggling boat that sank on its way to the Australian territory of Christmas Island. Three hundred and fifty-three people drowned in this disaster. Masry survived by clinging to a floating corpse. After being granted asylum in Australia Masry visited her son, who was exiled in Iran and recalled the horror of looking into the faces of the other refugees and thinking, "the color of their skin was bad, they were living but they were dead, like zombies."[4]

It is not just in the migrant's biographical accounts that we witness the use of the term *zombie*. Albert Memmi (2007, 74, 81), one of the pioneering theorists on the psychological dependencies that were forged under colonialism, has also searched for a new way of explaining the social effects of the "unstoppable human waves" of migration on the "besieged fortress of Europe. His scornful vision of the dislocative effect of migration gains focus as he zooms in on the identity of the immigrant's son:

> The son of the immigrant is a sort of zombie, lacking any profound attachment to the soil on which he was born. He is a French citizen, but he does not feel in the least bit French; he only partially shares the culture of the majority of his fellow citizens, and not at all the religion. For all that he is not completely Arab. . . . And in truth, he is from another planet: the ghetto. (119)

The rhetorical shift in the image of migrant subjectivity, from the wog/cog-mechanical to zombie-spectral metaphors provides a graphic register for seeing a contemporary form of dehumanization. The zombification of the other accentuates the extraction of the slave's functionality in the master/slave dialectic as it links the slave to a theory of the subject as a spectral entity. It no longer refers to the other as an object for use and exploitation, but as a redundant or purposeless thing. Given the recent transformations in both the structures of economic production and the mechanisms for disseminating cultural values, I contend that the stigmatic image of the migrant has been decoupled from the racial/mechanical image of being wogs/cogs in a vast industrial machine, and now draws upon a spectral symbolic economy.

The American anthropologists Jean and John Comaroff (2002) have also argued that the zombie tropes have been increasingly used as a way of making sense of the uncertainties associated with contemporary migration. They have argued that migrants have always been considered frightening because they usually look different; they sometimes make incomprehensible sounds, and since they are from elsewhere, there is a suspicion that they will not conform to the dominant moral categories. The dread evoked by the migrant is, according to the Comaroffs, akin to the experience of confronting a zombie because it is linked with the feeling of looking into the eyes of an alien being and not knowing whether your own image, thoughts, and hopes will be reflected back. The encounter with migrants is thus framed by the problems of sensorial appreciation and noncommunication. Taking as my starting point the argument offered by the Comaroffs, I will argue that the anxiety over the migrant's body, their silence, and their moral placelessness are linked to the broader transformations of postindustrial society and the global culture of ambient fear. The spectral logic that compares migrants and refugees to ghosts and zombies refers to a kind of abstracted identity that is stripped of national or ethnic markers, and a hijacking of agency by malicious and other-worldly powers.

Dogs in the Polis

During the 2005 French riots, a young unidentified boy from the housing estates in the northern suburbs of Paris was asked by an English journalist if he felt French. He replied: "We hate France and France hates us. I don't know what I am. Here's not home; my gran's in Algeria. But in any case France is just fucking with us. We're like mad dogs, you know? We bite everything we see" (Henley 2005, 17). The "mad dog" boy was part of a gang when he was interviewed. The "we" is this gang but also a more generic claim of defiance against the idea that the nation can create a "people." He despises that which despises him, but also recognizes that this hate leaves him without a place. He does not see himself as being at home in the same place as his parents. He knows that his gran's home is in Algeria, but where does this leave him? His fellow "gang" members reinforce this opposition against the French nation. It promises freedom, but all it offers is "*les keufs*, man, the cops." It declares that the republic is an open space, but leaves them stranded in what another gang member, Rachid, calls "shit dump." It presents equality as a right for all, but then his companion, Sylla, reminds the journalist that the former Minister of Interior and now French President Nicolas Sarkozy "calls us animals, he says he will clean the cities with a power hose. . . . Every car that goes up, that's one more message for him." The pyrrhic language is the marker of the deeper loss of faith in the neutrality and integrative power of the state. Republican ideals are seen as a façade that hides the entrenched values of the French. The gang suspects that they cannot enter the "open" space of the state as they are. The gang is not part of the "already French," and therefore would feel duped if they entered into such a social contract. Unlike their parents, who saw themselves as cogs in the state machine, these gangs find themselves without any function. They see no potential in a conciliatory dialogue with the state, and as other commentators have observed, the proposition that migrants must excise their identity in order to participate only inflames their sense of indignation, frustration, and anger.[5]

When the gang is left outside of the social contract, they are aware of being stranded in a no-man's land. They know that when the cops taunt and provoke them, their defiance is futile. "We're sinking in shit and France is standing on our heads. One way or another we are heading for prison. It might as well be for actually doing something." In their rage they can only become what the state tries to remove from humanity—animality. If France "hates" them, then the gang threatens to become what France fears most: an animal that is not bound by common ideals, values, and laws. By becoming animal, the "mad-dog boy" goes beyond comprehension of not only what he is, but where he is heading. Prison is not seen as the destiny for transgressors or as a space that provides deterrence, but as another marker of his own exclusion from social norms. It exists parallel—neither better, nor worse—to the world he already exists in.[6]

The violence of becoming an animal is not to be confused with juvenile rage. These bitter words were typical of the comments made by many of the rioting youths for whom police harassment was an everyday occurrence and who also expressed the sense that they had no place in the inner city (Schneider 2007, 530). In the public debates that followed the riots, most commentators concluded that the actions and statements of the youths were evidence of either the state's neglect, or the rioter's savage vandalism (Mishani and Smotricz 2005). However, this debate missed the most obvious question: How can the failure of the state, or the outburst of anger, strip people of their humanity to the extent that they either describe themselves as "mad dogs," or are perceived as "zombies"? The horror of a subject becoming animal can be traced throughout many philosophical attempts to distinguish between nature and culture, anarchy and civilization. Aristotle had no compunction in equating the natural slave with a domestic animal, while Giorgio Agamben (2000, 9) reminds us of Kojeve's lectures on the limits of civilization, in which he concluded that no animal can be a snob. Or put the other way around, the art of not "biting everything we see" is the achievement of the civilizing process.

Slavoj Žižek (2007a, 13) was among the few commentators who noted that the "mad-dog boy," while lacking a clear ideological agenda, was nevertheless articulating his fundamental human "insistence on *recognition*." This observation echoes precisely the claim made by the "mad-dog boy": "We burn because it's the only way to make ourselves heard. . . . Our parents should understand. They did nothing, they suffered in silence. We don't have a choice" (Henley 2005, 17). It is significant that the "mad-dog boy" feels both pity for the suffering and contempt for the silence of his own parents. He simultaneously elevates himself above, and also expels himself away, from his father's position. Detached, he is alone and confronted by the fear that he has no support. In his eyes the symbolic force of the father has been killed by the nation. He can neither identify with the symbolically dead father, nor with the deadly state. He knows that the return to "my gran's in Algeria" is pointless, just as becoming French is impossible. His own identity is thereby left without a place. It has nowhere to come from and nowhere to head toward. It withdraws into a position from which he can only recoil as an object: "I don't know what I am." Or again, as Žižek (2007a, 13) observed, the identity of the "mad-dog boy" is deadlocked because he is unable to locate the experience of his predicament into a meaningful Whole.

The experience of being entrapped in what the gang called a "shit dump" does not end with a rigid form of paralysis. On the contrary, the negative space is riven with a thrusting tension. While there is no grounding and binding for a social contract in which individual responsibility can take form, there is a paradoxical series of gestures through which the gang grinds out a defense of their hooded identity.[7] The spiraling flumes of the burning cars are evidence of both the "self-fulfilling sense of exclusion" (Schneider 2007, 529) and "the monstrous symptom of social and psychological devastation" that is hostile to society and yet expects "more subsidies" (Binswanger 2005). Yet, these retaliatory and self-destructive gestures are also expressive of the "worldless" vortex in which a boy becomes a mad dog. He does not seek to redeem himself by extracting some latent image in the national culture, or appeal to an image of a distant self that exists in a different place, but he does defend the (non)space in which his own self is embattled. It is a defensive-aggressive strategy that approximates that of a slave, as envisioned by Lu Hsun: "He rejects what he is, and at the same time he rejects any wish to be someone other than what he is" (Bharucha 2006, 65). The interview ends with the journalist, looking for a sign of hope, asking whether there is anyone the gang admires? The "mad-dog boy" points to Thierry Henry, a black French football star who was the greatest goal scorer for Arsenal, and then pours out this acid comment: "Henry never scores for France."

The haunting references to becoming an animal are also central to Agamben's influential essays on the human condition in modernity. Agamben begins his project by revisiting the classical philosophical claim that a human life is only worth living if it can transcend its original animal status. He draws out the Aristotelian categories that distinguish between a bare life, *zoe*, which is confined to the animal functions of nutrition and reproduction, and human life, *bios*, which proceeds with language and its capacity to develop aesthetic pleasure, moral principles, economic planning, and political order. Agamben observes that throughout the history of philosophy there is a consistent argument that humans realize their potential through the process of gaining representation within the law. In modern times, he argues, the sovereign—by extending the state of exception infinitely—has greater power to decide the conditions upon which the law can be suspended, and thereby to exclude people from the right of being a subject under law. As an outlaw, one's mode of being is reduced to that of bare life: He or she is excluded from the circuit of language and civilization.[8] The extreme example of this argument is the figure of the *homo sacer*—a subject under Roman law that could be killed with impunity, and whose existence can only be defined in biological terms. Their life, and more importantly the status of their life, is stripped of any cultural, moral, or political value. Agamben (1998, 185) provides numerous other examples of historical figures representing this animal state. Perhaps the most chilling one is his recall of Primo Levi's description of the camp inhabitant that was ironically called the "Muslim." This zombie-like figure "no longer belongs to the world of men in any way. . . . Mute and absolutely alone, he has passed into another world without memory and without grief." He is a being so stunted by fear that neither the threat of pain, nor the promise of pleasure, can register within him. Language no longer impacts upon consciousness. In this apathetic state the camp inhabitant is almost invisible; the guards cannot exert any more power over him, nor can the other inmates reach him. Agamben's evaluation of human life in the current political context is driven by a logic that identifies the negation of willpower, the collapse of a moral order, and the stripping away of all rituals that sustain cultural belonging with an inexorable state of bestialization. He argues that this slide into animality is accelerated and intensified by the sovereign's monopoly on power. This leaves the subject no space in which to forge any form of residual or resistant agency.

How far apart is the life of a camp inmate and that of the "mad-dog boy" in the *banlieues*? Agamben would claim that they are closer than one might imagine: They both inhabit the nonspace of bare life. From Agamben's perspective, it is not the "mad-dog boy's" transgressive acts of violence that have cast him beyond the law, but also the prior fact of being in a state of abandonment. He does not simply disagree with French values; he sees himself as being outside of the space of French culture. By being excluded from the functions that constitute human life, he has passed over to the indistinguishable zone of animality.[9] Similarly, Agamben (2000, 114–15) stresses that the *homo sacer* is not the extreme figure that only exists in the margins, but rather the exemplification of a generalized state of abandonment that everyone is subjected to in contemporary politics. Politics, he claims, begins with the threat of being held in this state of limbo, and he argues that, in "the most profane and banal ways," we are all virtually *homines sacri*. The spectacle of detention—which Agamben reminds us occurs not only in remote zones, but also in suburban sporting stadia and within the transit zones of metropolitan airports—is an expression of the power over the other that actually undermines the foundations of security and integration in society. The space in which the detainee is suspended is similar to the complex topology that the "mad-dog boy" claims for himself: It is both inside and outside society, the place where sovereign power is exerted to the maximum, but also one where the rule of law is reduced to a bare minimum. This double(d) location also exposes a threshold point from which, Agamben concludes, the citizen's worst fears emerge: The camp has subsumed the home and the city. The detainee is suspended in the camp not just to protect the citizen; he simultaneously manifests the fact that everyone can be abandoned. As the logic of the camp stretches over the whole of society, Agamben (2000, 188) concludes that the integrity of the boundary between human and animal is "taken away forever."

Is the "mad-dog boy" an example of Agamben's definition of the *homo sacer*? The one who is in limbo and will "bite at anything," and who for Agamben would serve as an example of lost humanity? The "mad-dog boy" declares himself to be in opposition to the dominant definition of humanity, but unlike Agamben, I do not see his words and gestures as markers of his expulsion. The position of the mad dog is more complex, as it both rejects the authority of the state, and also inverts the claim that his "savagery" renders him inhuman. To return him to the status of speaking subject is neither to redeem nor excuse his actions. My concern is not with justifications, but rather with an examination of the available categories for representing humanity. While the state now also revels in the use of spectral terms for representing refugees and terrorists, it is my aim to consider how this discourse also intimates more fundamental claims for identity amidst the loss in subjectivity.[10]

Spectral Others

Mad dogs, ghost prisoners, and zombie refugees—such stigmatic appellations have been ancient forms of addressing the enemy, foreigner, and even the deviant that lives within society.[11] However, it is now difficult to place the mad dogs, ghost prisoners, and zombies on the same continuum as the wogs that turned the cogs. These new names shift the position and the integrity of the boundary between humans and nonhumans. Even if the wog migrant was reduced to a cog, there still remained a begrudging admission of utility, and every migrant hung onto the hope that one day he would either return home to become a whole man again, or his own child's entry into society would redeem his sacrifice. At some point, the migrant wog imagined completeness. While the migrant-as-wog featured as a stigmatic figure in the nation-building narrative, the wog zombie languishes in, but then erupts as the ultimate threat to, the nation. In fact, the wog zombies are now being blamed for the destruction of the will to build a nation. This spectral image of the migrant as both a victim and the nation's victimizer is a popular literary trope and is used with great force, for instance in Christos Tsiolkas's recent novel *Dead Europe*.

It is worth recalling that the emergence of ghost stories in the modern era is linked to the Enlightenment and the French revolution. The Age of Reason sought to banish capricious myths, malevolent superstitions, and irrational belief systems. It sought to construct a transparent system of governance that was based on rational modes of explanation. It is now well accepted by cultural historians that the emergence of the ghost genre is a vehicle for expressing both the mysteries that exist at the edges of the illuminated spaces of reason, and the passions that elude the powers of rationality.[12] Malcolm Bull goes so far as to argue that the account of human consciousness in Hegel's master/slave dialectic ultimately relies on magnetic theory and the figure of the somnambulist. Hegel's account of the transition to full human consciousness begins with the slave's primal sense of deficiency, and despite his unequal struggle with the master, he gains a double recognition of himself and of his master's needs. It is through the act of labor that the slave produces both a sense of self and a sense of the self that exists in the other. In order to complete this theory of double consciousness, Hegel drew on popular scientific claims of the capacity of the magnetizer to influence a somnambulist to the extent that two separate individuals may come to function as one. Hegel also stressed that the flow of influence can be reversible, and it is by this process of open-ended mediation that the slave can rise to slay the master. Bull (1998, 240) further claims that W.E.B. Du Bois's rearticulation of Hegel's magnetic theory in his account of the African Americans' "veiled identity" and "gift of second sight," has also served as foundational point for subsequent generations of postcolonial and feminist perspectives on hybrid subjectivity. The spectral thus hovers throughout over theories of emancipation and revolution. Prior to 9/11, the rhetoric employed by the Bush administration was increasingly defined in terms of what his advisors framed as imperial realism. From this perspective, there was the firm belief that global reality could be shaped by American dreams.[13] However, when faced with the nightmarish image of Osama bin Laden, Bush's response was structured by a phantasmagoric "search for monsters and ghosts" (Devetak 2005, 622).[14]

In the literary and horror film genre, the status of zombies is not confined to aliens that haunt the borderlands, but also encompasses figures that embody the suppression of the other under capitalism (Wood 1986, 213). In anthropological accounts, there is the similar observation that the depiction of migrants as zombies not only provides convenient scapegoats, but also heightens the vulnerability of social laws, norms, and values (Comaroff and Comaroff 2002, 796). Their mobility is presented as if it were a liberation from the rules that bind people to the laws of a place; hence, the anxiety over the migrant's arrival is not confined to the initial transgression at the border, but extends to an unbounded fear that migrants, like zombies, possess an insatiable appetite and predatory behavior that will destroy all forms of social control. It is therefore worth pausing to consider the link between the dehumanizing image of wog zombies and what the American anthropologists Jean and John Comaroff (ibid.) call the "experiential anomalies and aporias" in the dominant sources of power.

The zombie is a figure that appears to be alive but is also dead. In folkloric and anthropological literature it has been noted that the figure of the dead coming back to seek revenge against the living has recurred in almost all cultures. Archetypically, the zombie can move but has neither memory nor will. Their primary senses have been either mutilated—the tongue is cut and the voice seems to come from the nose—or stunned: The eyes are open but the stare is remote. Deprived of these senses, they lack the means for communication. The image of the zombie often oscillates between that of a dead person returned to life, and a body whose soul has been stolen and forced to work for an evil master. Even the meaning of the word is uncertain. It is akin to the Kongo word *nzambi*, meaning "god." However, it could be derived from either the French word for shadows, *les ombres*, or traced back to the West Indian term for ghost, *jumbie* (Ackerman and Gauthier 1999, 466–94).

In postcolonial literature, the appearance of zombies has been linked to the sudden upheaval of social structures, collapse of traditional forms of moral authority, and the rapid collisions between different worldviews such as colonialism, industrialization, and the Great Wars. Most recently, Jean and John Comaroff have noted an unprecedented increase in the reports on the existence of zombies in the turbulent post-Apartheid period in South Africa. The reports ranged from tales and rumors that circulated in small communities, to journalistic investigations and state commissions that investigated the motivations for the outburst of violence against migrant laborers. In line with earlier associations between zombies and violent social rupture, the Comaroffs posited a link between the proliferation of these reports and the social and moral implosion caused by neoliberal capitalism. They argue that both the imagery of zombies and the flows of capitalism are governed by a spectral logic. The increasingly "opaque, even occult" conditions for the production of wealth in contemporary society have, according to the Comaroffs (1999, 279–301), left people unable to find a rational understanding of the social change and led them to resort to supernatural imagery as a form of social explanation.

The Comaroffs argue that the experiential conditions of neoliberal capitalism are framed by a spectral logic because the "hand" of capital is not only invisible, it is also the omnipotent force for social change—no one can point to "it," but "it" is the only thing that makes things happen. The mysterious presence and force of this "it" has defied any model of explanation that relies on a direct connection between cause and effect. The Comaroffs (2002, 782) claim that radical shifts in the process of economic production, and the new forms of conspicuous wealth, have disrupted traditional modes for explaining the exchange value between human labor and human life; hence, the proliferation of "the disquieting figure of the zombie" is an attempt to explain the otherwise inexplicable contradictions in social value. In short, when the traditional and rational systems for defining exchange value have been rendered defunct, the allure of zombie narratives gains greater currency. These writers also make the more general claim: that the zombie is not just an instance of eccentric and local fears, but also an index of a broader cultural anxiety. In each instance, the Comaroffs (2002) argue:

> The living dead comment on the disruption of an economy in which the productive energies were once visibly invested in the reproduction of a situated order of domestic and communal relations; an order through which the present was literally kept in place. And the future was secured. (795)

By focusing on the reportage of zombies, the Comaroffs are seeking to address the broader cultural upheavals that arise from the transition of an industrial to a postindustrial society. During the period of heavy industrialization, the place and function of the workplace was, in large measures, defined by reference to the heavy tools and solid structures of the machine age. It was no coincidence that the graffito "wogs turn cogs" also protested against the alienation of the migrant in the language of the machine. In the postindustrial phase, the imagery of the workplace has switched toward light practices, or what Bauman (2000) calls the "liquid" flows of capital. The goals of capital have thereby shifted from the concentration of energy into a unified system, to the generation of multiple platforms for the dissemination of energy flows. The place of production and the determination of a company culture are no longer fixed to the territory or norms of a specific place, but unleashed into a global field of perpetual reinvention. In this field no one has the promise of being a lifelong cog in the machine. For when global capital pursues its objective of maximizing surplus and minimizing cost, it should come as no surprise that it is also responsible for provoking a violent competition between the mobile and immobile agents.

The process of zombification that the Comaroffs observed in Post-Apartheid South Africa is used as a metaphor for the pattern of dehumanization that characterizes the neoliberal world order. As mobility and uncertainty become the dominant features of everyday life, the Comaroffs argue that society tends toward apocalyptic scenery in which there is a total rupture of the symbolic bonds and the reduction of humans to senseless zombies. This process of dislocation is represented as being of a different order than a migrant's experience of alienation in the era of preindustrial labor. As a consequence, the counterreactions are represented as more radical. Unlike the wogs that turned cogs—who, as "mad-dog boy" pointed out, "suffered in silence"—the zombie has the potential for demonic and unpredictable reaction against the machine. The fear of the zombie lies in the fact that it is perceived to be beyond animal, for it not only "bites," but also needs to "eat human flesh." Zombification becomes a metaphor for the neoliberal order because in this era the migrant has no hope of being permanently resettled, and the global economic forces have severed any link between productive energy and cultural meaning. In this context, the Comaroffs offer the melancholic conclusion that migrants are irreversibly dehumanized and also imply that, by "becoming" zombie, the migrant may wreck neoliberal capitalism and thereby rescue everyone from its nightmare.

While Agamben defines the essence of humanity in relation to the articulation of will, the Comaroffs stress that human value is forged in the integration of productive energy within an embedded cultural context. Both perspectives assume a territorialized vision of human life and thereby identify the value of a migrant life in a negative binary. From this perspective, there is not only a dehumanizing logic but also a fatalistic account of the consequences of mobility. All the examples of wogs as cogs or zombies have a negative presumption against the forces that have catapulted people out of their previous states of security and certainty. For while each of these images captures the extent to which the migrant sees his or her body as an entity whose motion is controlled by an external force, they simultaneously conceal the possibility that energy is also emitted from the "bodies" of the automaton, beast and living dead. Central to the argument posed by Agamben and the Comaroffs is the claim that neoliberal capitalism is an incomprehensible process of change because its operating forces are remote, obscure, and volatile, and as a result, no form of coherent agency can survive in its wake. The spectral figure of the monstrous enters when rational principles and civilizational institutions everywhere are in ruins. Against this plaintive conclusion, I want to turn to a different view on the relation between mobility and identity, and then suggest an alternative reading of the metaphor that couples migrants and zombies.

Cyborg Wog

After the 2005 riots in Paris, immigrant activist Nico Squiglia (2005) declared: "I am a migrant. I do not want to integrate. I want to be who I am."[15] This is precisely the kind of comment that makes cultural conservatives and progressive multiculturalists panic.[16] The rejection of integration is immediately seen as either a failure of the state to offer a stronger basis for national affiliation, or the inability of multiculturalism to generate more inclusive modes of cultural belonging. When Nico Squiglia declares "I want to be who I am," he could be considered a threat to the national demand for solidarity and for dismissing the civic promise of equality.[17] Squiglia's comment at first glance seems to justify the fear that there is now a generation of youth out there that has turned its back on the state. They neither seek to gain access to more of its resources, nor try to reform its operational logic. On the contrary, they are creating new imagined communities that have no relation to the territorial and bounded form of a national society. Squiglia's declaration is both a rejection of the state and a proclamation that there is an alternative space for the realization of the self. He already claims possession of the fullness of the "who I am," while also protesting against the forces that block his wish to become who he wants to be. His identity proceeds by rejecting the city and nation as places that would allow identities to be formed by coming together—"I do not want to integrate"—and proclaims an identity that is perpetually in motion: "I am a migrant." These paradoxical declarations also occur in the context of both a fight against the populist backlash that minorities now experience, and an assertion of their awareness of the state's dependency on foreign labor and investment.[18] However, this claim of rejecting integration and demanding the autonomy of identity is also expressive of an agency that occupies a complex topology.

Nico Squiglia was born in Argentina and now lives in Spain. He is a member of the project Indymedia Straits of Gibraltar, a group composed of activists, artists, and cross-disciplinary thinkers.[19] The codename for the project is Fadaiat, which means in Arabic "through space," "satellite dish," and "space ship." Located in a medieval castle on the edge of the militarized southeastern border of the European Union, this project considers itself as a mirror-territory of the transformations taking place in the world.

The idea of the project is both utopian and instrumental: Through its coalition of artists and activists it has created a No-Border media laboratory that is engaged in mapping border flows, critiquing the new militarized border economies, and developing links with both local protests on migration issues and international human rights organizations.

Throughout the diverse actions of Fadaiat, the free flow of information is seen as the "connector" between people from different places, and for people on the move. Given linguistic differences between the various members, the project has also embarked on an ambitious effort to devise a communication system based on universal spatial-visual symbols. This project has set out to learn from and hijack the symbolic codes that have been developed to promote global capital, and to redirect them toward the interests of migrants. While this collective is opposed to the existing modes of regulating migration, its method of opposition is not an outright confrontation with global capitalism, but a form of resistance that reassigns value back to the activities that migrants execute in their everyday lives. This method of resistance draws from a system that is generated by diasporic networks, and in this new social space the collective claims to forge a "new territory for global democracy." Such rejection of the state thus creates a space very different from the void in which zombies roam. The ambivalence of place that Squiglia articulates as his identity is in fact a consequence of what Ulrich Beck (2002, 24) calls the zombification of the state. As Squiglia claims to be in, but not of, the place, he simultaneously affirms the identity that comes in the context of mobility and asserts a right to define his human value in terms that exceed state-centric parameters. Squiglia decrees his right to preserve identity as a universal one. This proclamation takes a double twist: He claims to have access to rights that are defined by the state, but also insists that his identity rests on rights that are above and beyond those of the state. By rejecting integration into the mechanisms of the state, he does not disavow the hope of realizing his identity in the context of others; he simply rejects the claim that the context of his community is confined to the coordinates of the nation-state.

Squiglia's affirmation of his identity as a migrant, and his desire to define his being in the ongoing process of becoming mobile, is not just an expression of narcissistic individualism but corresponds to a new discourse of migrant subjectivity.[20] The homepage of Indymedia describes migration as a result of a complex interplay of forces, rather than the product of linear or mechanistic structures. The group argues that migrants are not simply pushed or pulled by one command, or driven out of their homes by the structural imbalances in the world system. On the contrary, they perceive migrants as autonomous political agents who are also self-organizing in relation to specific pressures. There is no singular or overdetermined force that regulates—"decides for"—the direction or destiny of the migrants. They are all engaged in complex decision-making processes. Rather than being "cogs" in the machine, they move in order to "dignify their life conditions." This experience of mobility, informality, and volatility, accentuated by the migrant condition is, they argue, also a feature becoming characteristic of working life in general. It is from this vantage that they claim that everyone is "becoming migrant," and conclude that the paranoid metaphors of "Fortress, USA, Europe, Australia" are misleading because they are built upon the illusions of a splendid isolationism.

Squiglia's depiction of his identity, and this new discourse on migration, are examples of what Harald Kleinschmidt calls a shift from the "residentialist" sources to the regional relations that define the self.[21] Identity is no longer connected to an exclusive territory, or the product of a unified community; it rather arises from a process of interaction with diverse influences and exists within an elastic border. The Fadaiat collective rejects the conventional definition of the border as simply a demarcation point that separates different entities. It is not just an imaginary line that becomes a geopolitical division, but rather a "crossed-place" where mixtures intensify and new "social practices put pressure on established limits"; hence, the border is not a fixed location where one form ends and another begins, but a threshold in which transformation occurs in multiple and unpredictable ways. This vision of a border identity is linked to the ambition of hijacking the info-capital networks in order to create a new ecology between bodies and communication systems. In this utopian model, the Fadaiat collective claims that agency is shaped by the freedom of the cyborg: "Our modernity has its own mobile borders, which, as always, are in search of the other: the external other that we call nature, and the internal other—subjectivity, ourselves in plural."

Much of the discussion on the cyborgian transformation of subjectivity has revolved around the unhelpful category of the "post-human." The incorporation of technology to extend communication is often interpreted through a sci-fi vision of the machine becoming one with the flesh. It resurrects the fantasy that Elizabeth Wilson (1988, 38) explored so exquisitely in relation to the childish wish that dolls can become alive, and the fear that humans can slip into mechanical states. I would argue that the use of new communicative technologies does not announce a break, but extends the struggle for the realization of humanity. If the central feature of humanity is the capacity for language, then the search for a common language and the means to communicate with everyone marks the most profound humanist ambition. A universal language and the free flow of information is the necessary but unrealizable dream of humanism. It is a dream that is forever born in multiple and incommensurable translations. Barbara Creed (2003) has also argued that the banal reality of globalization has presented a new ground for thinking about the political and ethical relations in global communication networks. The perception of the world as an interconnected place and the use of new media have, she claims, not only proliferated the flow of information and heightened the awareness of global forces; they have also transformed the individual's perception of the self. In Creed's view, this transformation has led to a politicization of the self. Individuals are more likely to search for an understanding of the causes and consequences of social problems, and they are seeking explanations that can relate local conditions to global forces. She argues that by tracing the complex contours of social issues, and comparing them to distant situations, individuals now see themselves as being at the crossroads of multiple sources of information. This has led to new categories, perspectives, and standards for the understanding of specific events. Creed (2003, 193) concludes that this engagement with information that connects people in the virtual world, but also requires direct intervention within local contexts, has produced a new "global self." She sees this transformation in subjectivity as a positive force that will overcome the cultural chauvinism and petty territoriality of the nationalist self, as well as offering an alternative to the imperialistic view that globalization will only strengthen tribalism.

Creed's claim that the Internet and the new "global self" will lead to a genuine cosmopolitanism is one of the most optimistic voices in the new discourse on identity and belonging. This reclamation of cosmopolitan values and humanist desires is also central to Paul Gilroy's (2004, 28) argument that a new "planetary humanism" is evident in the contingent and multicultural interactions that have transformed both the conditions of everyday urban conviviality and the rise of translocal human rights movements. The Fadaiat project is one of many collective art projects that have emerged in the context of neoliberal society. A common characteristic in many collectives from this period has been the identification of the transversal relationship between subjectivity and location. The fullness of subjectivity is no longer presented as an achievement to be gained only after the overcoming of alienation, or even in the process of being connected between different places, but rather it is conceived as occurring in the midst of the subject's movement across and through space; hence, the forms of solidarity that emerge from these encounters follow from a prior commitment that cross-cultural communication can produce a recognition of mutual human worth, rather than proceeding from the quasi-mystical assumption that being born in a specific place and having acquired specific cultural traits constitutes the basis of one's exclusive identification with "a people." It is no longer where you are from, or even where you are at, that matters; it is about how and with whom we communicate.

The Diaspora: At Home Outside Its Home

Speaking at the opening of Refugee Week in Melbourne, John Pandazopoulos, a former state minister responsible for multiculturalism, connected the plight of the refugees held in detention with the experiences of earlier migrants who had arrived in Australia.[22] He spoke with moral indignation against the then-federal policies on border protection, and with genuine empathy for the plight of people who, like his own parents, were forced to leave their homes. He observed a deeper moral connection with refugees and expressed his belief that this would lead to more than a plea for tolerance toward outsiders. He claimed that "the wheel has turned on these issues," and concluded that as a consequence most people now consider the refugee's story a part of the nation's historical narrative.

Pandazopoulos was able to acknowledge the refugee story by first establishing a commonality with the founding myths of the nation. This connection both allays the guilt over the harm done to the refugee and reinstates hospitality as a central feature of the national narrative. By contrast, John Howard, the former prime minister of Australia, consistently denied that guilt was a necessary emotion for either reviewing the legacies of the past or establishing a connection with refugees. His stance on immigration focused on defending the absolute priority of national security over humanitarian concerns. He also pushed an agenda that reduced social services and dismantled cultural policies previously directed toward promoting a multicultural society. In general, he insisted that migrants should integrate into mainstream society and rejected multiculturalism as a dangerous and divisive experiment. This position encouraged his ministers to make pejorative remarks about the so-called "mushy" principles of multiculturalism (Garnaut 2006),[23] as well as singling out for ridicule the grandmothers that dressed in black and refused to learn English (Robb 2006).

The response to these remarks on the ethnic community radio programs was described by one of the hosts as a form of "wailing" anger.[24] One respondent, an old and frail woman who had emigrated from Mexico said: "We came here with nothing. My English is still bad. However, I did what I could, and with my now dead husband worked very hard to bring up a good family." Even at the age of seventy-five, she also expressed great pride in her children, both of whom are doctors: "They cure people now," she said. In response to the suggestion that her failure to learn English is a sign of her unwillingness to join mainstream society, and an expression of disdain of common values, she turns the challenge back to the prime minister: "Just ask him to come to my place to teach me about values. I'll teach him where he should go."[25]

Even with her "bad" English, whence is she offering to teach the prime minister a lesson on values? It is not from outside or elsewhere, but from within "my place." This place is her home. By placing the values lesson in her home, this woman claims both her equal place inside the nation and her equal right as a person who can speak the language of human values. The language and place from which she enters this debate may seem uncanny to the sovereign who assumes a monopoly over defining national values, and yet, it is this assertion of relative autonomy that is the seat of its anxiety, and a glimpse of a value system that privileges the human above any other category. The government's complaint over the failure of immigrants to integrate is contradicted by the response from this old woman, who believes she has succeeded in retaining her human dignity. In her opposition there is both a rejection of sovereign authority and an assertion of her own cultural value as an absolute human right. She reinstates that she is the master of her own house. The Prime Minister is warned that she remains unmoved by his authority. "Now Australia is my country, I can't go back where I came from. I don't like this but I am not going anywhere." For this "poor Mexican migrant" who admits that she "speaks with an awful accent," there is the realization that there is no home to return to, and that life is to be drawn from the very landscape that is foreign to her, even if in this landscape there are voices that condemn her as being among the dead ones. In a letter to photographer Frédéric Brenner (2003, 21), Jacques Derrida noted that "the diaspora is at home outside its home, it remains outside its home at home, at home at the other's." The "mad-dog boy" in Paris, the artists in the new collectives, and the old woman from Mexico may respond to the challenge in different ways, but they all proceed from the same insistence: I am who I am, and the national values are not the absolute containers of my humanity. Let me repeat the warning issued by the old woman to the Prime Minister: "Just ask him to come to my place to teach me about values. I'll teach him where to go." Like the "mad-dog boy," she is angry at the lack of respect. She also proclaims that she has the moral authority to "teach him where to go."

Translation and Universality

In the modern period, the power of sovereigns has increasingly been defined by their ability to encroach into the private lifeworld of their subjects. Hidden inside the government's complaint about the old migrant stuck in his or her ghetto is another fear—that it is failing to gain influence over these communities as they are gaining new connections with other worlds. With satellite dishes pointing elsewhere, there is a new fear of the death of national culture as it is bypassed and even vilified in the pursuit of an imaginary life in diasporic cultures. This fear that the nation will fragment into antagonistic ghettoes, combined with the supposed intergenerational gulf that is evident in the nihilistic rage of the "mad-dog boy," is indicative of what Albert Memmi (2007, 111) calls a new social divide. Sociologists have always recognized that the corollary of modernization is detraditionalization.[26] However, as James Rosenau (2003) argues, the fragmentation of traditional forms of authority is also a stimulus for the reintegration into new social collectives and a redistribution of individual rights.

Rosenau's "optimistic" approach toward the crisis in authority is consistent with the new paradigm of migration that adopts a transnational and complex feedback perspective. This perspective is not a utopian promise to overcome alienation, but it does offer an alternative to the melancholic disposition toward the decline of the nation-state and it avoids the denigration of migrant subjects as figures of death and destruction. Butler, Laclau, and Žižek also argue that there is a need for an alternative approach toward the understanding of the universal rights of the human subject in the context of cross-cultural communication and global mobilities. Butler contends that, if translation can now be thought of as an unending exercise unleashed from the binary of original and copy, then this also provides a new framework for grasping the dynamic interplay between particularity and universality that would accompany the move from spectral humanity into the political. This implies that within each invocation of becoming animal, or turning into a zombie, there must be also be a rearticulation of what it means to be human. However, as Butler (2000) states, this movement also requires a new kind of language:

> Another universality emerges from the trace that only borders on political legibility: the subject who has not been given the prerogative to be a subject, whose modus vivendi is an imposed catachresis. If the spectrally human is to enter into the hegemonic reformulation of universality, a language between languages will have to be found. This will be no metalanguage, nor will it be the condition from

which all languages hail. It will be the labour of transaction and translation which belongs to no single site, but it is the movement between languages, and has its final destination in this movement itself. Indeed, the task will not be to assimilate the unspeakable into the domain of speakability in order to house it there, within the existing norms of dominance, but to shatter the confidence of dominance, to show how equivocal its claims to universality are, and, from that equivocation, track the break-up of its regime, an opening toward alternative visions of universality that are wrought from the work of translation itself. (178–79)

Rethinking universality through the prism of cultural translation opens up the vexed relationship between human rights and cultural difference. Hospitality is now poised in a more complex terrain. What are the visual signs that represent the status of the stranger? When do we touch each other? What is the point at which dialogue commences? It is obvious that declaring multiculturalism a failure provides no answers to these questions. In Australia this dead-end is predicated on constructing the "wog-grandmother" as the image of death. The "wog- grandmother" is singled out as this deathly force that must be eliminated in order to preserve the integrity of the nation. And yet, she turns the images of death and life into and around each other. It may have been a translation error, when she boasted that alongside "my now dead husband I worked very hard to bring up a good family," but it is this linguistic error that reveals the interplay between death and life in the diasporic imaginary.

Herein lies the paradox that was first touched upon in Marx's understanding of alienation, and also suggested by Derrida in his revision of the border between human and animals: It is those who were regarded as mad dogs, mutes, and zombies that now make a stand for all humanity. They are not asking for their dignity to be returned, or for greater access into the national imaginary; they recognize the futility of both requests, and are making a more perplexing summons for the recognition of a humanity that is already embodied in their presence but not yet represented. They are not justifying their equal right because they believe that they are already like, or want to become like, those who possess national citizenship—rather, they issue this plea from a bodily claim of equal human existence. Their body is already here. He or she has a singular existence that needs to be acknowledged as being part of a whole. If the body is the only possession, the only means by which the excluded can make themselves visible and audible in public space, then it is also the body that must become the site in which the protest occurs. By being in a place, he or she exists in relation to others. As bodies, with inherent biological functions and human values, the real and fictional figures that I have explored in this essay do not simply represent the depths of dehumanization but also express a process of rehumanization. In the struggle to make themselves heard, they are articulating a form of political resistance that Žižek (2007b, 70) calls the "embodiment of society as Such, as the stand-in for the Whole of Society in its universality, against the particular power interests."

Even in this far-reaching phrase by Žižek we can see the struggle that theorists encounter when they seek to give form to the complex interplay between dehumanization and rehumanization. The effort to dehumanize the other always reveals much about the fears that lurk in the self. From the examples I have surveyed in this essay, we can witness the way migrants are perceived as automata, animals, and zombies. As Hayden White (1978, 152) has argued, this "ostensive self-definition by negation" is an ancient strategy. It is a paltry attempt to achieve superior dignity by impugning the identity of the other. However, it is also worth recalling that this strategy is pushed to its most extreme limits during times of heightened vulnerability. The suspicion, contempt, and hostility now projected toward migrants testify to a deeper ambivalence toward mobility. The fear of the migrant is always expressed through the suspicion that he or she causes harm and then moves on. However, underlying this fear is a presumption that the migrant has rejected a settled life, and the citizen then is forced to consider: What sort of a human wants to be on the move, and to what extent is society dependent on mobility? The challenge of living together is averted by answering that only cogs, animals, and zombies live on the move. A human on the move is a perceived threat to the citizen not only because of the initial transgression at the border, but because the possibility of ongoing mobility renders the totality of the experience and every future encounter uncertain. This uncertainty cannot be resolved by pinning his or her identity back on the place of origin. The dread caused by migrants is not confined to the fact that they are from somewhere else, but is increasingly linked to the anxiety that they and everyone else must exist in an unbounded state of global roaming. So who are they, and what will happen to us if they enter? What would it mean to accept that they too are humans with bodies and dreams?

These questions haunt the national imaginary because they reveal a subject that claims to possess an identity that is both fully formed and unsettled. This cosmopolitan subject appears both full in its proclamation of humanity and spectral because it does not seek to be regrounded in the form of the national citizen. I began this essay with the graffito of "wogs run cogs." Under the conditions of national capitalism the migrants' alienation was expressed, as their labor was appropriated from their body and rendered as a cog in the machine. Marx argued that the alienated man is torn from his own body, nature, productive capacities, and human essence. The emancipation of man is also a successive "return" to a state of "species being" where the individual man has absorbed in himself a state of being in a politically equal society and possessing an equal humanity. According to Marx, it was this negation of identity that also created the proletarian class that he saw as the agent of change. Under global capitalism, the migrant's alienation appears like a ghost in search of the machine. Hardt and Negri have extrapolated the Marxian axiom to argue that the new deterritorialized proletariat will become the agent of freedom in the name of a global humanity. This is a big call and I do not reject it as mere idealism, because at the center of the stories on automata, animals, and zombies that I have surveyed in this essay is the dialectic between alienation and freedom. In these narratives, there are traces of the cosmopolitan yearning and the demand for the migrant's right to be here that relies on nothing more or less than his or her humanity.

The Art and Poetics of Translation as Hospitality

PAOLA ZACCARIA

> ... the value of tolerance is no longer sufficient to the task. And we appeal to another concept of hospitality.
> —Jacques Derrida, "Displaced Literatures"

I

I come from Bari, a city located on Italy's southeastern shores, and, in 1991, the site of one of the most dramatic events to prove our unpreparedness to deal with mass exoduses. The event was called "the Albanian emergency," in which the word "emergency" was already used as a synonym for danger of invasion, flooding, or border crisis. I am evoking and invoking one of the most outrageous and shocking sights resulting from the breakdown of a totalitarian hegemony inside the last post–Cold War European communist state, Albania. I am evoking the exodus of a large portion of people—until then confined—toward the borders of the country they, thanks to media lies, dreamt of as the land of freedom and bounty. I will recall here the images forever imprinted in my memory: the arrival.

As soon as the overcrowded ship shaped by human bodies had landed in Bari harbor, all compassion, embodied in so many narratives of exodus that this sight evoked (Noah's ark, our Saint Nicholas, and various Madonnas arriving from Eastern or African lands on boats) notwithstanding, the landing was suddenly and dramatically transformed into a deportation to, and the detention in, the city's stadium, which, at this time of the year, resembled a roasting desert.[1]

That sight, that blistering wound inflicted upon hospitality—a practice ingrained in Southern Italian culture—blew to pieces the optimistic vision of my region as a welcoming, sheltering harbor for refugees, displaced populations, and migrants. It disgraced the institutions and struck an everlasting blow to many people's trust in governmental policies. It undermined the belief in the Italian Foreign Office and Ministry of Social Security, which relegated the Southern Mediterranean areas such as North Africa and Albania—but also the area in which I live, Apulia, as well as the Sicilian island of Lampedusa—to "loopholes" in the South through which faceless and nameless "masses" tried to gain access to the land of hope. On the other hand, however, this event appealed in a certain way to civil consciousness and required a new social and cultural thinking; it called for new practices capable of transforming cultural perceptions and social values (i.e., the ability to perceive and address the changing architecture of international relations initiated by the fall of the Berlin Wall and the shift toward globalization and change).

This preamble is designed to offer a first orientation into the epistemological frame required to analyze a "fortress mentality" and the burgeoning of apartheid practices in Italy (one of the European nation-states confronted with mass immigration). It is also intended to clarify that the subtext or background of my considerations are the geography and politics of migration in the South of Italy, with its landing shores on the coasts of my home region, and in Lampedusa, Italy's southernmost island, which Rutvica Andrijasevic (2006, 32) has described as "the Southern Gate to Fortress Europe." This area, which is actually a Southern border designed to protect Western Europe—just as the Spanish coast, facing Morocco, triangulates with the Maghreb coast and with Libya. This Southern gate is the point of entrance for migrants whose primary regions of origin have been identified by nongovernmental organizations (ARCI and *Médecins Sans Frontières*) as the Middle East (Iraq and Palestine), the Maghreb (Morocco, Tunisia, and Algeria), the Horn of Africa, and Sub-Saharan Africa.

When Italian media and politicians speak of migration, they spread and perpetuate the myth of "invasion." In my country—or should I say the place that I happen to live in, since I am very critical of the term "nation-state," and hence of the word "country"—the system of law and order justifies the segregation of "irregular" migrants. It constitutes a type of apartheid that follows a policy of "preemptive" seclusion-exclusion in so-called temporary holding centers (in Italian: *Centri di Permanenza Temporanea*, which I will hereafter refer to as CPT), out of considerations labeled "crime prevention." The semantics of lawfulness and punishment in the name of resident citizens' security is instrumental in cashing in on the consensus of conservative, racist tempers, and to keep the more vulnerable portions of the population quiet.

On the shores of Southern Italy, where I live—or, to echo Derrida, in *la demeure je demeure*—our contemporary wretched of the earth land on boats without even a steersman, or die in the deep sea in sunken, twentieth-century slave ships. Actually, in the age of slavery, ships were better equipped than these boats of despair, because slaves at least had some monetary value, whereas the migrant desperately trying to reach Southern Europe's shores has, in the eyes of many politicians, no value: he or she is "refuse" (in the double sense of the word), a nonrecyclable shell to be disposed of, a life that can disappear together with the worn-out vessel he or she embarked on without anybody claiming it. And in our contemporary, unethical age, even "it" might be too much to say, as even a thing can claim a price, can be an exchange commodity, whereas the immigrant trying to enter the South of Europe is bodiless, voiceless, faceless, valueless, and, as such—waste.

II

With these unbearable images in my mind, and the subsequent bad conscience they aroused, words such as escape, exile, (e)migration, expatriation, dislocation, exodus, diaspora, and asylum entered my vocabulary and started resounding inside and around me—words which evoke images of individuals and multitudes on the move, on the road, on the run.

At the beginning of this process I told myself: I have to try to discern the differences, try to systematize these words and conditions, try to accord them their place. After so many years of incessant questioning, I have learned that it is impossible to trace or place, in a clear-cut, finite manner, the terminological and material boundaries around these words and conditions, which exude rupture and agency, which evoke mourning and resurrection, and which indicate farewells that already yearn for and invoke welcomes.

I felt that what the semantics of forced expulsion required me to do was at least some kind of border crossing—border demolition being illegal; that is, to resort to a deconstructive inventiveness, which, as Derrida (1989, 60) wrote in *Reading de Man Reading*, "can consist only in opening, in unclosetting, in destabilizing foreclusionary structures, so as to allow the passage towards the other." On the other hand, both literally and theoretically, I wondered whether, after all, the very drive which keeps the migrants and the stateless in any time and culture moving is not the drive to trespass borders. This first question by necessity leads to a second one: is not the drive to cross, to cut across, to pass through, to intersect (fields, disciplines, and discourses) an experience that *fronterizos*, dislocated people, experience physically, and contemporary migration analyses set at the core of their investigations?

What I call migration theories and analyses are surveys that focus upon the linguistic, spatial, cultural, disciplinary, and philosophical points of juncture and disjuncture, which are located at the threshold and, with subtle distinctions, have been termed "third space," "interstitial" (Bhabha 1990a), *nepantla*[2] or border crossing (Anzaldúa 1993, 2002), contact zone (Pratt 1991), etc. At their core, the analyses and semantic fields I am speaking of address the topic and condition of hospitality, the question of how the host can and should accept the *arrivant*. Unconditionally? Without questioning him or her? Without setting boundaries, as Derrida postulates?

When Derrida (2005a, 67) writes that hospitality is "an art and a poetics," does he mean that it pertains first of all to the domain of the aesthetic, or should we say that for Derrida the aesthetic stance should precede the ethical and political stance, or that aesthetic constructions are forbearers of, and give shape to, ethical and political stances?

In my book *La lingua che ospita* (*The Hospitable Tongue*, 2004), I claimed that very often poetry and art envision courageous political perspectives much earlier than political thought and politics itself, although politics, and sometimes also philosophy and ethics, do not usually take into account the subtle new views and ideas expressed by art. Moreover, if art is a gift that, according to Derrida's (1992b, 30) commentaries on the aporia of the genuine gift, implies that it escapes the economy of giving and receiving, offering and acknowledging; if art, consequently, does not (or should not) ask for reward, not even for a "thank you," then hospitality, as an art and a poetics, should first of all make room for welcomes, without asking for returns, raising borders, or establishing limits, rules, requests for assimilation, or norms.[3]

Hospitality as art, as poetics; hospitality as poetry: I want to dwell on this, notwithstanding the implicit Derridean assumption that genuine hospitality—which, together with genuine gift and genuine forgiving, constitutes the triad of possible-impossible aporias—is impossible.

Several years ago I envisioned literature, poetics, and that peculiar linguistic and cultural practice called translation as a hosting gesture, and the translator as the one who dwells on the borders.[4] I theoretically approached the question whether a translation without assimilation, without cannibalism, is possible, a translation that receives the other at its best when it has the humility of acknowledging that not everything can be translated (i.e., when it accepts that cultural differences entail, at a linguistic level, untranslatability: when it accepts disorientation).

Although the title of my study, *The Hospitable Tongue*, has a Derridean theoretical and linguistic flavor to it, in that book my analyses mainly resorted to Derrida's idea of the trace—at least that was what I thought until a few months ago. But while I started rereading Derrida on cosmopolitanism and hospitality, I realized that, thanks to his reflections, it is possible to represent the translator as he or she who oscillates between unconditionally surrendering himself or herself to the (hospitality of the) other's language, and complying to the conditions posed by his or her own native language and culture. In my book, I ventured the hypothesis that translation forms the basis of hospitality (i.e., the groundwork for new, uncovered paths). It can take the translator—who is constantly tracking the source text and moving between borders—into an intercultural transnational/transitional/relational space that is not exactly identifiable with his or her own native parameters: the process and practice of translation teaches the hospitable translator not to rely completely on his original language, culture, and norms, not to rely on nation(ality) as such.

As unconditional hospitality allows any guest in, because he or she carries a promise, the elation of "what is yet-to-come", *à venir*, so translation, in the hands of a hospitable translator, allows new imaginary and material wor(l)ds to enter the hosting wor(l)d, because there is promise and exhilaration in letting oneself be touched by these brave new wor(l)ds. With hospitality, as with the translation of foreign works, new forms of communities, new relations, new architectures enter the host's—that is, the translator's—world. Thanks to translation, the borders of the host's world, the borders of the translator-acting-as-a host, will be deconstructed and forever changed. He or she who undertakes the task of crossing into another tongue, another text, another culture, will be crossed by that journey in turn. Thanks to translation, aesthetic, ethical, and cultural transformations enter the world.

And yet, if this were just so, if we thought about translation as (always) an opportunity for opening up, this would imply that the possible-impossible aporia—unconditional hospitality—was fulfilled. It would mean that one of the first requirements of the notion of conditional hospitality—that there is a master of the house (of language), someone who maintains the power to host in his home/city/country/national language—has been canceled. But then, if there were no masters, no borders, no controls, no checkpoints, we would not speak of hospitality, because the earth without the scars of wires, walls, and wars would accept anyone regardless of race, gender, social status, or religion. Thus, just as Derrida envisions unconditional hospitality within what Darko Suvin (2004, 106) would define as a "utopianistic horizon,"[5] translation as hospitality, as transformation, is the horizon foreseen by the traveler-translator who, in his or her journey, drawn by the desire for understanding, undertakes the process of untying himself or herself from the fetters of "mastering" the language/the text/the other in order to achieve "radically better forms of relationship between people." Translation as hospitality tends toward unconditional hospitality; it is a task that can never be fulfilled. It is a promise, to use Derrida's (1996) vocabulary in *Le Monolinguisme de l'autre*, a call for what is still *à venir*, to come.

While reading Mireille Rosello's (2001) *Postcolonial Hospitality: The Immigrant as Guest*, I came across a passage in which she remarks that for Derrida the issue of language cannot be dissociated from the most basic level of hospitality. The stranger's discomfort with the new language is emphasized in the following passage from Derrida's dialogue with Anne Dufourmantelle in *Of Hospitality* that Rosello also refers to:

> the foreigner who, inept at speaking the language, always risks being without defense before the law of the country that welcomes or expels him; the foreigner . . . has to ask for hospitality in a language which is by definition not his own, the one imposed on him by the master of the house, the host, the king, the lord, the authorities, the nation, the State, the father, etc. This personage imposes on him translation into their own language, and that's the first act of violence. That is where the question of hospitality begins: must we ask the foreigner to understand, to speak our language, in all the senses of this term, in all its possible extensions, before being able and so as to be able to welcome him into our country? (Derrida and Dufourmantelle 2000, 15)

The foreigner's condition as described by Derrida—the discomfort with the "national" language of the guest country, the disempowering condition the newcomer finds himself thrown into as soon as he arrives, the impossibility of articulating his name, his needs, etc.—turns the arrivant into a stranger, a dispossessed, rootless and violated being caught in a "tongueless" discomfort zone: exiled, emigrated beings experience the painful and excruciating condition of having their tongues cut. Contemporary citizenship and residency laws that establish who is welcomed and who is not are evidence of the fact that decolonization is far from being accomplished: in Western "democracies" the rules of inclusion/exclusion, denegation/acceptance are tainted by traces of colonialism—discrimination, violence, and coercive conformity.

In my view, this excision of the tongue (i.e., the violence of a welcome that requires from the newcomer the immediate acquisition of the new language)—the penalty for noncompliance being the impossibility to represent oneself symbolically, resulting in powerlessness, lack of agency, and control—this, and all the economic, social, racist, and gender inequalities that add to the migrant's devastating experience form "the materiality" that any hospitable translator should always have in mind, as they constitute the threshold, the frame, from where he or she enters the process of translation. In order to unconditionally host the other's tongue, the translator, who knows how it feels to live in the discomfort zone where you cannot find the words to express name and needs, should practice a constant journey between his or her own familiar native language and the guest's dislocated and nameless one. In so doing, he or she is able to offer a pattern for new and diverse laws of hospitality, thus saving hospitality from being reduced to one unique form and venturing beyond any "faithfulness" to one's own national-hosting language, culture, and law. Thus translation provides the opportunity to circumvent the state's restrictions to unconditional hospitality and to invent new forms of hospitality that arise from cross-cultural and transcultural contacts—or, to put it in the words of a Palestinian-Italian song, to conceive of hospitable translation as a practice of "enamorment," of "*lingua contro lingua*"[6]: tongue interlaced with tongue, as in a kiss, the gesture that expresses mutual trust, mutual attraction—the gesture performing an unconditional, mutual hospitality.

Translation as hospitality requires the translator to establish more than a dialogue, a conversation with the text as guest. As Luz Garcia Gomez (2009) affirms in her essay "The Arab Other: Gender, Interculturality and Languaged Language," dialogue is a specific form of conversation, an exchange of ideas and opinions, whereas conversation is "narration, recuperation and communication of knowledges within an open process," which turns conversation into a language imbued with sensibilities, affections, empathy, and understanding.[7]

Finally, I would like to add one more consideration on the differences in the prefixes of the words dia-logue and con-versation: the first, dia-(logue), implies the separation of I/other, whereas the prefix *cum-* of conversation not only introduces the idea of togetherness, but also broadens it through the meanings of *vertere*: to address, to go toward the other, in cum-versation. The entwinement between *cum* and *vertere* can serve as a signpost to remind those thinking about the subject of translation as hospitality that translation as conversation has a chance of opening up toward and hosting the other's tongue, as it requires understanding, affection, and sensibility. If we take translation to be a practice of conversation, we will also realize that translation is "gendered": a hospitable translation testifies that the subject doing the translating—be it man or woman—has experienced, traversed the discomfort zone, has crossed the boundaries of nationality. He or she is thus able to genuinely address, to go toward the other offering him or her his or her own address, which, in being not a national(istic), "owned" home, but a place of refuge—the uncertain terrain of the in-between, the elastic line between host and guest—is not suffered by the newcomer as a type of hospitality that requires belonging and integration. In that elastic position between hosting and guesthood, nobody should have to undergo the (linguistic) experience of ex(ap)propriation—another word-concept coined by Derrida.

Derrida's statement about the condition of the dispossessed—"the first and last condition of belonging, language is also the experience of expropriation, of an irreducible exappropriation. What is called the 'mother' tongue is already 'the other's language'" (Derrida and Dufourmantelle 2000, 89)—entails that, exiled from his own land and language, the migrant (the exiled) and the translator alike learn that ex-appropriation was with them since the beginning. They received their own language, their linguistic matrix, from somebody who, although usually coinciding with the mother, is nonetheless an other. When leaving their own place, the multitudes on the move leave behind the (other's) matrix and are left without properties, without names. The translator, living in the discomfort and yet composite zone of global political, cultural, economic, and linguistic intertwinements knows that in the very act of entering the threshold of the other's textuality, he or she has to learn to speak without the assurances of the mother tongue, has to make space for polylogical, plurilingual, composite languages and yet lend an ear in order to give voice to specific singular accents against the hegemonic drive to homologation and (linguistic, gendered, cultural) normativity.

As the exiled realizes that it is impossible to shelter forever the mother tongue in order to own a "unique" cultural identity at least through language, so the translator learns that, in being simultaneously the host and the guest of the other's language, he or she undergoes the disquieting experience of being expropriated of his or her own language and cultural identity: he or she makes the experience of ex-appropriation.

The translator's unstable condition offers a good opportunity to experience the irreducible interrelation between host and guest necessary to enacting hospitality. He or she experiences the ambiguously dual and contradictory impulses Derrida defines on the one hand as the Law of unconditional, absolute hospitality toward the foreigner and to any "other," and on the other, the laws of hospitality of one's own culture that, in being codified rights, are conditional and open to the foreigner only as the invited, expected guest. The translator is a host in that he or she receives the other('s) text but, at the same time, is the guest in that he or she finds refuge in the other's text. Moreover, the translator oscillates between unconditional acceptance of the other's word and world and the laws of his or her own language, which, in being codified, condition his or her openness to fully welcome the other's voice. This makes it possible to think of translation as gauging the resonances of another language in the mother tongue; as the mother tongue is both one's own language and the echo of the mother's tongue, so the translated text is at the same time written in one's own tongue and yet bears echoes of the other's (the matrix's) tongue.

The translator's peculiar experience of hospitality, of being the locus where the dual impulses converge, make of him or her one of the figures who can enhance Derrida's (2001a, 8) utopianist dream "of another concept, of another set of rights for the city, of another politics of the city"; it opens up "new horizons of possibility previously undreamt of by international state law."

All of this reinforces my view of the centrality of translation in today's not-yet-decolonized world, because in order to make the world more hospitable, in order to help widen the gates of state law and of national languages, in order to help promote interculturality, the translation of the "texture" of the other must be acted out with the awareness, on the part of the one who translates, that he or she is in conversation with him or her who is being translated: "conversational" translation—although in this case it is apparently a one-way performance (since only one of the idioms spoken in the conversation is translated)—should be an experimentation in transcribing the other's word in one's own language, which, nonetheless, makes room for the guest's voice. Translation as hospitality transforms one's own "natural" tongue in "illegitimate" ways in order to overcome the silence that is usually the lot accorded to the guest, to the newcomer. Translation as hospitality is a process reminiscent of what Elias Canetti (1990), in the first volume of his autobiography, *The Tongue Set Free*, has called the "salvaged tongue." Canetti, a writer born in a multicultural town in Bulgaria, chose to be an exile and not to write in his "national" language but in German—the foreign language his parents used as their private, love tongue in order to retain some intimacy in a home, which, although very large, did not allow for intimacy because it was usually overcrowded.

The rules of the game, however, can also be turned around; simultaneous to conceiving of the translator's function as a pattern to mold hospitality, I can also try to assess whether and how it could be fruitful for the host to encourage the newcomer to conceive of himself or herself as a translator.

However, if the host assumes the position of a translator, he or she has to experience the in-betweenness of linguistic, social, psychological, and cultural positionalities; he or she has to engage in a conversation in the other's language, and not in his or her own; he or she has to experience the partiality of translation-hospitality, how it feels to not be able to entirely translate oneself to the other and the other to oneself, to be compelled to adopt the other's language, to realize that any translation is always partial, provisional, unaccomplished, and fractured.

Thus translation should serve as a passageway, a connector, a conduit that, in opening languages and cultures to each other, builds bridges, helps undermine protective nationalistic perspectives, heals wounds, and aids in uncovering and appeasing dualisms and mistrust because, as Chicana thinker and poet Gloria Anzaldúa (2002) wrote in the preface to *This Bridge We Call Home*:

> To bridge means loosening our borders, not closing off to others. Bridging is the work of opening the gate to the stranger, within and without. To step across the threshold is to be stripped of the illusion of safety because it moves us into unfamiliar territory and does not grant safe passage. To bridge is to attempt community, and for that we must risk being open to personal, political and spiritual intimacy, risk being wounded. (3)

With the perspective available to a border crosser, we enter another semantic and philosophical area that Derrida himself connects to hospitality: forgiveness, reconciliation as a precondition for encouraging acts of hospitality. Besides, in reading Anzaldúa on *mestizaje*, interculturality and translation, the sentence "Bridging is the work of opening the gate to the stranger, within and without" reminds me of Derrida's semantics in *On Cosmopolitanism*, *Of Hospitality*, and *Le monolinguisme de l'autre*: If the analysis and semantic field offered by Anzaldúa and the interculturality and translation issues I am speaking of address, at their core, the topic and condition of hospitality, Derrida's reflections on translation, from his early work to the later, more explicitly political studies, point to an understanding of language as dialogue, hospitality, and a means for reconciliation.

If borders are erected and conditions posed when hospitality is offered, separation, discrimination, and exclusion inevitably sneak in. A borderless hospitality, just like the border(less) transitional and transnational positionality Anzaldúa speaks of, is openness and opening; it carries with it the breathing of things to come: new poetic, ethical, and political relationships. It offers the possibility to reinvent one's own political identity and categories (the host's and the guest's alike); it requires trespassing preexisting models. Every one of us can easily see how all of this applies to translation as well.

III

> Is not hospitality an interruption of the self?
> **Derrida,** *Adieu to Emanuel Levinas*

In what follows, I would like to address the enormous question Derrida posed about how to translate the ethical demand for a borderless, unconditional hospitality into specific political or juridical practices:

> The law of hospitality, the express law that governs the general concept of hospitality, appears as a paradoxical law, pervertible or perverting. It seems to dictate that absolute hospitality should break with the law of hospitality as right or duty, with the "pact" of hospitality. To put it in different terms, absolute hospitality requires that I open up my home and that I give not only to the foreigner . . . but to the absolute, unknown, anonymous other, and that I *give place* to them, that I let them come, that I let them arrive, and take place in the place I offer them, without asking of them either reciprocity (entering into a pact) or even their names. *The law of absolute hospitality commands a break with hospitality by right, with law or justice as rights*. Just as hospitality breaks with hospitality by right; not that it condemns or is opposed to it, and it can on the contrary set and maintain it in a perpetual progressive movement; but it is as strangely heterogeneous to it as justice is heterogeneous to the law to which it is yet so close, from which in truth it is indissociable. (Derrida and Dufourmantelle 2000, 26, 28; second emphasis mine)

I would like to intersect Derrida's views with Wendy Brown's (1997, 87) observation about gender studies, the latter of which I would like to extend to emigration studies and hence to translation and transcultural studies. It is not enough to use multicultural and postcolonial analysis and its tropes such as contamination, plurality, contradiction, and fracture in order to counter subjection and disparity (Brown), xenophobia, or, at its best, tolerance (Derrida). We can no longer presume a "coherence" and "equivalence" in the formations of different subjects, even when they belong to the same community. As Brown points out, it is necessary to take into account the different stories, "the genealogies of particular modalities of subjection." Both for Derrida and for Brown, the focus of their analyses is on a double knot, an "undecidable crossing of the ways" (Derrida and Dufourmantelle 2000, 26). On the one hand, there is the relational-political issue of the other and of justice; on the other, there is the juridical-political issue of norms, rules, laws, or "pacts" (Benveniste's [1969] expression, which presupposes reciprocity): Should the host-guest relation become unbalanced, the host has the right to maintain discretionary ownership of everything. Basically, the paradox at the heart of the issue of hosting the foreigner, the anonymous other, stems from this double bind, from this schizoid play between justice and rights—two paradigms often in conflict with each other: the irreconcilability between unconditional and conditional hospitality determines the status of the arrivant as either legitimate guest or as illegitimate-parasite-clandestine-alien. This undecidable double bind and the consequences of the controversial opposition justice/laws we are presently witnessing in Italy and elsewhere, makes us fear that even when and if Europe acknowledges the present phenomena of mass displacement as the backlash of coloniality, the aporia will lead to the closure of the gates of hospitality.

Since we are living in times of new imperialisms and economic oppression, in the last years many of us have been stressing the necessity for linguistic practices to host the foreign voice, the other's word. The centrality I have been according to translation as the locus and the tool of encounter and understanding, at first born out of my need to use semiotic and literary theories as means of mediations, has been confirmed and nourished by my recent rereading of Derrida's thoughts on cosmopolitanism, polylinguism, hospitality, and translation. The conjugation of his thinking with Mesoamerican decolonizing theories has supported my view of translation as a crucial tool for enhancing a transnational cultural project aiming at mutual discovery, understanding, trust, and intercultural encounters between cultures, subjects, and communities. To risk translatability, even at the cost of writing on the borders, of verging on untranslatability, is the first step toward the enactment of interculturality: it is an act of hospitality.

If the "text in the process of being translated" forces the translator to incessantly be aware of the other on the other side of the "text as looking glass," if the translation process makes the translator move back and forth between his or her and the other's side, and if it makes him or her oscillate between two planes, two languages, this allows us to draw comparisons to the host's oscillations between his or her plane-language culture and those of the guest, and to consider both conditions—the host's as well as the translator's—as states of in-betweenness. But is being in-between enough? Can it offer and ensure the discovery and understanding of the other('s tongue)?

Host and guest, if they want to dwell in hospitality, should perhaps try an alternative space, which might be less intimate than the one in-between, but one that certainly leaves room—or should we say ensures the proper distance?—between the "I" and the other. Only from a nonfusional relation the "third" (cf. Bhabha 1990a; 1990b; 1994, especially 36–39), that which escapes duality, can see the light. As the translator's journey toward the other's voice-world-work-world is a crossing of cultural, gender, and geographic distances, hospitality requires the host to similarly engage in the guest's voice experience, all the more so when the guest's voice might be silenced by devastating experiences, or when he or she arrives speaking no "national language" for which the host can find a translator. The guest only commands the "mother tongue," which can be, for example, a dialect for which there is no translation because in a global world that does not want to acknowledge the impossibility to save the borders of the nation-state, dialects are being delegitimated, destabilized, and erased precisely because they attest to a disquieting ("pervertible or perverting") statelessness; that is, they embody a realm that escapes the laws of belonging (to the norm, the state, the law, or to a "national" language, although they attest to other forms of belonging). And what if the arrivant does not tell his or her name because the horror he or she has experienced prior to the departure and during the passage has robbed him or her of his or her identity, or altered it considerably? Or when he or she is the "absolute arrivant," without any ID or visa?

IV

At this point, as the witness of history and of his/story and her/story, I feel the need to pose a few questions, not to the guest, the refugee, or the exiled, but to those who try to use Derrida's provocative thought to cope with the age of new slaveries and oppressions: how can we move from a model of relations imbued with violence and oppression born out of colonialism—a model that racially marked the relationship between colonizers and colonized along classifications organized in terms of race, class, and gender—to a different model of relations between (ex-/im)migrants and residents?

To tell the truth, although the terms are reversed (it is the ex-colonized who makes a move from his or her own land to Europe and not the ex-settler who goes to take possession of the other's land), we do witness that the so-called postcolonial, not yet entirely de-colonized subjects are still oppressed: those who in the past took possession of their lands and bodies now refuse to offer hospitality to the children of the formerly colonized, which are called clandestines, illegals, aliens, or *sans papiers*, because they arrive at our doors without the permits of the masters of the world—and, above all, without visa and MasterCard.

Were there any visas or permits required when Europe colonized the Americas, Africa, parts of Asia, Australia, New Zealand, and so forth? Where was the visa when Russia took control of Eastern Europe and the United States started its expansion beyond its borders, to neighboring South America and the Far East?

In times of closure and vulnerability, even when postcolonial subjects who have reached the borders of Europe do get a visa, they are seen as constituting a threat to resident citizens imprisoned by paranoid fears and ideologies spread by "democratic" governments that have a vested interest in maintaining the dichotomies of self and other, host and guest, mine and yours, citizenship and temporary residency. Hospitality is offered provided that "the other follow our rules, our way of life, even our language, our culture, our political system, and so on" (Derrida 2003, 128). In the best of cases, the guest is offered conditional hospitality that expects, if not requires, his or her gratefulness and conformity to the local values. This is "hostpitality" (Derrida and Dufourmantelle 2000, 45), a neologism derived from Latin *hostis* and *potis* (to have power). Any relation created between host and guest is imbued by gestures of attack or defense, is inflected with relations of power and ownership, and is paralyzed by fear of hostility.

In such a "hostipitable" encounter, the opposition between self and other, resident and arrivant cannot be abolished. The declaration of the impossibility of an absolute hospitality that gives shape to the aporia of conditional/unconditional hospitality excludes any possibility to devise new models of living together through hospitality, because the assumption of ownership of and belonging to a house/space/land/country—however tolerant or "hos(ti)pitable" it might be—will forever maintain the newcomer in a position of distance.

The notion of ownership of the homeland, strictly linked to notions of nation and nationality, will forever entangle the concept-practice of hospitality in the nets of an imbalance of power and rights. When the host welcomes the guest, when a nation welcomes the exiles and emigrants, the host and nation "insinuate that one is at home here, that one knows what it means to be at home, and that at home one receives, or offers hospitality, thus appropriating for oneself a place to welcome the other" (Derrida 1999a, 15–16). It is a way of showing that I am in control of the place/home/nation: this is my place and I am generous enough to welcome you in (or as inhospitable as to refuse asylum).

However, when dealing with hospitality and translation, the matter is even more complicated: both translation and hospitality deal with the issue of the other. Moreover, both can involve the fear of being held hostage by the other's language or culture, in one's own language, in one's own home. Derrida (1998, 14) himself, arguing about identity, ipseity and hospitality, highlights the danger when he speaks of "the semantic chain that works on the body of hospitality as well as hostility—hostis, hospes, hosti-pet, posis, despotes, potere, potis sum, possum, pote est, potest, pot sedere, possidere, compos, etc." In a footnote to this semantic survey, Derrida (77) suggests to deepen the semantic resonances by reading Benveniste's chapter on "Hospitality." In fact, his account of hospitality starts from Benveniste, who, in *Le Vocabulaire des institutions indo-européennes*, discussed the contradictory nature of a cluster of concepts: host, guest, and stranger. In Latin, the guest, being a stranger, was called both *hospes* (whence the etymological root of hospitality) and *hostis*, which means "enemy." Benveniste (1969, 87–89) argued that the notion of favorable stranger evolved into guest, while a hostile stranger was considered an enemy. It is more than obvious that nowadays in the countries faced with large numbers of immigrants, governments are passing laws that define a priori (i.e., based not upon a case-by-case inquiry, but upon discriminatory, very often racial[ized] parameters)—those cultures/conditions/bodies to be denied or expelled; define, that is, who is to be considered hostile or hospitable. Practiced in this manner, hospitality can result in repression, hostility, even the erasure of identities and bodies.

If both hospitality and hostility have their roots in host—the one who can shelter and can attack—the roots of the undecidability between unlimited hospitality and the laws of hospitality are most probably due to the antinomy created by what Derrida calls hospitality of invitation and not visitation (in this case the guest is seen as *hospes*) and unwilling hospitality (*hostis*), although in Roman times *hostis* did not just refer to the stranger as enemy, but also to foreigners who brought to the city gifts, thus creating mutual obligation, but also asking for laws to regulate this status.[8]

Thus the welcome of the arrivant is limited by jurisdiction and reasserts the mastery of the host over his space, his home, his nation. The laws of hospitality, or conditional hospitality, being the result of the chain family-nation-state-law, are antinomic to the practice of unconditional hospitality as the precondition for genuine interculturality and transculturality, transformation and translation—translationscapes.

Michael Cronin (2006, 37), in his *Translation and Identity*, which comments on Benveniste and Derrida retracing the etymology of hospitality, that is, the semantic chain linking *hospes* to *hostis*—what he calls "the uneasy proximity that sees open welcome give way to nervous xenophobia"—assumes that translation "can be the ultimate expression of linguistic hospitality welcoming new languages, cultures and ideas into the mother tongue, or it can be a fortress of hegemonic difference translating people into the language of dominant cultures and annihilating difference."

The aporia governing the notion of hospitality can be found at the heart of translation practices as well: hospitality and translation can try to overcome ownership, mastery, discrimination, and erasure of difference only if practiced with an interrelational, supra- or transnational and intercultural horizon in mind, one aware of the new conditions of hospitality: cohabitation without closure, fear, or requirements for uniformity and assimilation. Fissures, chinks, cracks effected by the hands (acts) and minds (political creativity) of border people—dissidents, dislocated wanderers, exiles and emigrants, translators and refugees—in the divide between the law of unlimited hospitality (and of open, noncannibalistic translation) and the rules imposed by the state to govern inbound arrivals (and languages), grow larger and more powerful every day, thus offering a decolonized, transnational, and hospitable landscape called earth to a new kind of multilingual people, who willingly pass from one language to another, with none of them being the "national," the "source" tongue, with some of them moving straight toward the "target" tongue. Not citizens, but peregrini, path-crossers, streetwalkers; not authors, but translators; not masters, but equals; not natives with rights over other people, but wanderers or apatrides with duties toward the (unconditionally) hospitable earth.

Undoubtedly, the main points expressed by Derrida in *On Cosmopolitanism*, *Of Hospitality*, and *Le monolinguisme de l'autre* can be adopted as guidelines to discuss, in all its complexity, contemporary migration, the migrant/national relationship—which in Derridean thinking is the host/guest relationship—and the as-yet-not-sufficiently addressed return of hierarchization and reproletarization to the Western metropolises. Nonetheless, I venture to express a doubt, or, rather, make a critical comment on Derrida's (2001a, 5–6) analysis of hospitality. The figure in the background of his analysis, the refugee he has in mind, is the public intellectual, as he states in *On Cosmopolitanism*: "the victims [of terrorism, persecution, and enslavement] . . . are . . . what one refers to as intellectuals, scholars, journalists and writers—men and women capable of speaking out (*porter une parole*)—in a public domain." And here is where my reservation comes in: are the cities of refuge conceived only for exiled intellectuals? Can we really equate the conditions of the intellectual persecuted by censorship to the conditions of the emigrants persecuted by hunger, poverty, civil wars, and economic and class exploitation?

In order to understand the implications of this question, it might also be important to raise the question whether Derrida's views—based as they are on concepts derived from a Western system of knowledge, or as he says, from our heritage (Hannah Arendt and Kant) and their deconstruction—can help to reconfigure the relationship between host and guest, reconfigure it in the light of what we are experiencing at present, the dichotomy between the rich, Western, liberal ex-colonizer who is still the hegemonic resident, and the often poor, Southern, ex-colonized immigrant and asylum-seeker, dispossessed by liberalism and stripped of democratic opportunities. The question and the challenge that Derrida confronts us with is the demanding task of negotiating between the imperative for an unconditional hospitality and the one for a conditional hospitality, and of transforming their aporias into specific political or juridical practices.

In my view, this aporetic and contradictory relation between the order of the unconditional and the order of the conditional, their irreducibility to each other, which sounds ethically crucial, is at the heart of all human relationships, comprising gender, sex, class, race, or culture. Negotiating what seems irreconcilable is, perhaps, the way out of dichotomic, oppositional, contrastive views of knowledge and community; it is one of the political and ethical forms of resistance we are left with on this planet, one we can offer our coinhabitants of the earth coming from afar by opening up the gates and sharing with them the exercise of agency and the right to keep moving on.

Notes

Introduction: "Taking Place"—Conditional/Unconditional Hospitality
Thomas Claviez

1. For a very informed critical analysis of the mutual influence of Levinas and Derrida, especially as regards the concept of hospitality, cf., among others, Still, *Derrida and Hospitality*.

2. For a closer analysis of the connection between the polis and Aristotle's ethics, cf. Claviez, *Aesthetics & Ethics*, 53–111.

3. That Irigaray's notion of reciprocity is based upon not only a gendered, but also a biological distinction between the sexes, is also a point made by Still, *Derrida and Hospitality*, 133–35.

4. For further discussion of the French emigration laws, cf. Derrida, *On Cosmopolitanism*, 16–17.

5. On this, cf. Claviez, "Democracy: À Dieu, à Venir, or au Revoir?" 108–11.

6. On the history of this projection, cf. Claviez, "What Is a European?"

7. If anything, conviviality as "practice interrupting the norm" should alert us to the fact that, contrary to Levinas's and Derrida's radical hospitality, the "hospitality industry" that has developed around what Craig Calhoun (2002) has so aptly termed "frequent-flyer cosmopolitanism," characterized by its increasing homogeneity, is designed to protect us from any otherness/Otherness we might encounter, giving us the illusion of "being at home" wherever we are. Which begs the question why we leave home in the first place . . .

8. There is a fine irony in the fact that, if Hobbes's metaphor holds, we are all wolves to each other—which implies that we are basically the same; wolves usually do not attack each other. Moreover, the treaty that he presumes would help

185

overcome this "state of nature" is highly unstable: Who would trust a wolf signing such a treaty? And what is worse: With such a treaty, the contingency of wolf-like human nature is not only locked out, it is encapsulated inside society as well. One could, however, argue that Hobbes's formulation "homo homini lupus" indicates a difference between wolves and man. That, however, then begs the question what "man" in a Hobbesian context can still mean.

Hospitality—Under Compassion and Violence
Anne Dufourmantelle
1. "Autrui qui se révèle précisément—et de par son altérité—non point dans un choc négateur du moi mais comme le phénomène originel de la douceur." Levinas, *Totalité et Infini*, 161.

Transcending Transcendence, or: Transcend*ifferances*: Limping Toward a Radical Concept of Hospitality
Thomas Claviez
1. For a compact assessment of this debate, cf. Mouffe, *Deconstruction and Pragmatism*.
2. Cf. Rorty, "Objectivity, Relativism, and Truth," 13.
3. Cf. Claviez, *Aesthetics & Ethics*, 31–35.
4. Cf. Llewelyn, "Am I Obsessed by Bobby?" 236.
5. And it is in this instance, when Irigaray (2008a 2, 15) reconnects the two transcendences with an "is," that she comes dangerously close to essentialize "man" and "woman" into the one "universal dialectics that supersedes all others," as when she claims that "one difference at once appears as universal: sexual, or better, sexuate, difference," or urges us to "take charge of what woman really is and what is proper to her." Such an approach reduces the potentially infinite number of transcendences to two that structure all the others.
6. Cf. Derrida, *Writing and Difference*, 129–31.
7. Cf. Žižek, "Neighbors and Other Monsters," 134–89. What defines monsters, if anything, is that they are "improper" and thus "incalculable" in the many senses of the term.
8. This is Cheah's rather Machiavellian conclusion, as I read it; cf. Cheah, *Inhuman Conditions*, 178.
9. Cf. Kant, *Grounding for the Metaphysics of Morals*, 29.
10. Cf. Kant, *Critique of Judgment*, 68.
11. It seems, at least, to enrich our *Bildung* to read Kafka.
12. Cf. Žižek, "Neighbors and Other Monsters," 137–39; Butler, *Kritik der ethischen Gewalt*, 58–61. This concept of exposure, however, forms, if slightly modified, the basis for Jean-Luc Nancy's concept of an alternative community based not on the sameness ensured by the nation or culture, but by the shared exposure to otherness. Cf. Nancy, *Inoperative Community*, 25–29.
13. Cf. Claviez, *Aesthetics & Ethics*, 31–35 and 202–18.

14. I assume that, from a Lacanian perspective à la Žižek, the "Parliament of Things" that Latour outlines and opts for at the end of *We Have Never Been Modern* cannot but constitute a mixture between a monsters' ball and a freak show.

15. Cf. Agamben, *State of Exception*.

Toward a Mutual Hospitality
Luce Irigaray

1. Contrary to my custom, I use "gender" and not "sex" in this text. I want to suggest that "gender" and "genealogy" share the same etymology, and also that I am talking about a sexuate identity and not only about a sexual belonging. The context of this paper clearly indicates that I am not referring to an already gendered construction but to a natural identity that still needs an appropriate culture.

2. Cf. Irigaray, *Sharing the World*, 15; *Way of Love*, 52.

3. Cf. Irigaray, *Sharing the World*, 43.

4. Cf. Irigaray, *I Love to You*, 138–39.

5. Cf. Irigaray, *Luce Irigaray: Teaching* and *Sharing the World* (especially the chapter "Distance in Nearness").

6. I heartily thank Stephen Pluháček for his accurate and respectful rereading of my own English translation of this text.

To Open: Hospitality and Alienation
Pheng Cheah

1. "Host" and its Latin etymology are immensely rich in meaning and always imply relations of force and power. Depending on the context, *hospes* can mean "host," "guest," "stranger," or "foreigner." *Hospes* is also related to *hostis*, which also means "enemy." In Medieval Latin, it referred to an army or warlike expedition; hence, *host* can mean "an armed company or multitude of men." However, it can also mean a victim for sacrifice, from the Latin *hostia*, a term often used to refer to Christ. This is its religious meaning, where it refers to "the bread consecrated in the Eucharist, regarded as the body of Christ sacrificially offered."

2. Here, as in all other following quotations, the first reference is to the German edition, while the second is to the English translation.

3. This theme is found throughout Marx's corpus and as early as the *Economic and Philosophical Manuscripts* of 1844.

4. Here, as in all other following quotations, the first reference is to the German edition, while the second is to the English translation.

5. On the total and therefore universal and borderless character of appropriation, cf. Marx, *Deutsche Ideologie*, 57–59; *German Ideology*, 92–94.

6. Arendt's (1968, 297–98) grounding of human rights in the right to hospitality means that her account of human rights is neither republican nor liberal. The plural field of human existence in which words and actions take place precedes rational-critical political participation and is in fact its precondition. But it is also

not merely a natural condition of human individuals who possess prepolitical rights by virtue of natural law. In her view, the eighteenth century theory of natural rights cannot adequately explain the predicament of stateless peoples in the twentieth century because it considers human dignity as independent of human community and plurality.

7. In Arendt's view, the Marxist materialist characterization of this intersubjective world as a superstructure overlooks the real effects of the disclosure of subjects. Cf. Arendt, *Human Condition*, 183.

8. Cf. ibid., 257; Arendt, *Origins of Totalitarianism*, 298.

9. For Arendt, this utilitarian logic is a consequence of the loss of an absolute standard supplied by religion and natural law as a result of modern secularization. In *The Human Condition*, she makes the slightly different argument that a more general loss of faith in modernity throws men upon themselves instead of upon the world.

10. See Derrida's (1992b, 162) discussion of how the true gift must break with generosity: "If it is not to follow a program, even a program inscribed in the *phusis*, a gift must not be generous. Generosity must not be its motive or its essential character."

11. See, for instance, Giorgio Agamben's (1998) ubiquitous account of the exclusion of bare life and Judith Butler's (1990) account of heteronormative subjection. The various intellectual sources for this schema include Julia Kristeva's idea of abjection, psychoanalytical accounts of repression, and the prohibition of the law, Schmitt's account of the sovereign exception, and a misreading of Foucault's account of biopower that focuses solely on its disciplinary aspects and ignores Foucault's critique of the juridico-discursive model of power and the repressive hypothesis.

12. This paragraph is slightly revised from Cheah (2008, 203).

13. For a discussion of the transnational traffic of migrant sex-workers from and to Thailand, see Phongpaichit et al., *Guns, Girls, Gambling, Ganja*, chaps. 8–9.

Proximity and Paradox: Law and Politics in the New Europe
Bonnie Honig

1. This is a revised and expanded version of chapters that have previously been published in Honig, *Emergency Politics*, and Benhabib, *Another Cosmopolitanism*.

2. CNN. "1988 Presidential Debates." August 25, 2008. http://www.cnn.com/ELECTION/2000/debates/history.story/1988.html.

3. I have in mind here Kant's famous discussion of the absolutism of the prohibition against lying, even to save the life of someone who has sought sanctuary with you, a topic attended to in some detail by Derrida, who casts it as a violation of hospitality. *Cosmopolitics* is the term under which Cheah and Robbins (1998) gather a collection of essays exploring themes of hospitality, transnational debt, and international engagement. Derrida identifies Kant with a mere cosmopolitics and notes that Levinas never used that term, or the more usual *cosmopolitanism*,

preferring instead: *universalism*. Derrida (1999a, 88) suggests that Levinas abjured the term *cosmopolitanism* or *cosmopolitics* (Derrida does not here distinguish the two) for two reasons: "first, because this sort of political thought refers pure hospitality and this peace to an indefinite progress [which also always "retains the trace of a natural hostility," which is its point of departure in Kant]; second, because of the well-known ideological connotations with which modern anti-Semitism saddled the great tradition of a cosmopolitanism passed down from Stoicism or Pauline Christianity to the Enlightenment and to Kant."

4. Derrida 2005, 173n12, citing *Of Hospitality, On Cosmopolitanism*, and *Adieu*.

5. In a way, this is analogous to or even a version of the domain problem explored in David Miller, "Democracy's Domain."

6. Elsewhere, he also notes that the French term for hosts [*hôtes*] is the same as the term for guests, denoting another register of undecidability (Derrida 2002a).

7. This is reminiscent of Rogers Smith's (1993) effort to identify ascriptive moments in U.S. history, not with the liberal tradition but with alternative ascriptive rivals to that tradition. On Smith, see Stevens, "Beyond Tocqueville," and Honig, *Democracy and the Foreigner* (chaps. 1 and 5).

8. As Derrida (2001b, 253) puts the point in "Force of Law": "The undecidable remains caught, lodged, as a ghost at least, but an essential ghost, in every decision, in every event of decision. Its ghostliness deconstructs from within all assurance of presence, all certainty or all alleged criteriology assuring us of the justice of a decision."

9. A similar point is made by Balibar (2003, 120), who says that Arendt's "'right to have rights' does not feature a minimal remainder of the political, made of juridical and moral claims to be protected by a constitution; it is much more the idea of a maximum. Or, better said, it refers to the continuous process in which a minimal recognition of the belonging of human beings to the 'common' sphere of existence (and therefore also work, culture, public and private speech) already involves—and makes possible—a totality of rights. I call this the 'insurrectional' element of democracy, which plays a determinant role in every constitution of a democratic or republican state." (Note that democracy is here, quite properly, not cast as insurrectional, but as having an "insurrectional element.")

10. For another take on the paradox of rights, see Brown, "Suffering the Paradoxes of Rights."

11. Indeed, Benhabib (2006, 75n8) herself confesses in the final version of the lectures that she may have been, with regard to the French headscarf case, overly optimistic, given events in the year since. Balibar (2003, 122), by contrast, is not less optimistic. He is cutting: The Maastricht definition of European citizenship that awards EU citizenship to nationals of any constituent national state, he says, "immediately transforms a project of inclusion into a program of exclusion," given the size of the resident alien population in Europe at the time and given the dependence of Europe on that population's labor.

12. See Balibar, *We, the People of Europe?*, 122, 162, and passim. For example, "European citizenship, within the limits of the currently existing union, is not

conceived of as a recognition of the rights and contributions of all the communities present upon European soil, but as a postcolonial isolation of 'native' and 'nonnative' populations" (ibid., 170).

13. I am thinking here of Arendt's (1985; pt. I, chap. 4; pt. II, chap. 9) discussion of the Dreyfus case as well as her argument that police powers developed to deal with the stateless after World War II would, if left unchecked, soon be used against the general population.

14. In her discussion of the French Marianne, Benhabib (2006, 59–61) leaves the terrain of law altogether to mark out the importance of cultural politics, with which I agree. In only one instance does Benhabib leave the terrain staked out by the binary of formal law versus democratic contestation to acknowledge the abundant powers of administrative discretion. The example she mentions is a positive one of discretionary power used to the good: "Although officially the wearing of the 'turban' (a form of headscarf worn by observant Muslim women) is banned [in Turkey], many faculty members as well as administrators tolerate it when they can" (79). On discretion and the rule of law, see Honig, *Emergency Politics*, chap. 3.

15. Here, Benhabib seems almost to echo Julia Kristeva, whose (more) French universalism is criticized in detail in Honig, *Democracy and the Foreigner*, chap. 3.

16. On the paradox of politics, see Honig, *Emergency Politics*.

17. This claim is one I defend at length *vis-à-vis* Rawls and Sandel in *Political Theory and the Displacement of Politics*, chap. 5. In this context, it makes sense to note as well that such political claim-making would be undercut and not just aided by the successes of universalism since such successes may attenuate lines of accountability and participation, privileging courts as venues of adjudication over popular participation.

18. On the paradox of democratic legitimation, see Honig, *Emergency Politics*, chap. 1, and Benhabib, "Deliberative Rationality."

19. Compare with her earlier casting of the paradox: "Rousseau's distinction between the 'will of all' and 'the general will,' between what specific individuals under concrete circumstances believe to be in their best interest and what they would believe to be in their collective interest if they were properly enlightened, expresses the paradox of democratic legitimacy. Democratic rule, which views the will of the people as sovereign, is based upon the regulative fiction that the exercise of such sovereignty is legitimate, i.e., can be normatively justified, only insofar as such exercise of power also expresses a 'general will,' that is, a collective good that is said to be equally in the interests of all" (Benhabib 1994, 28–29).

20. For a powerful critique of this claim, from Dahl to the present, see David Miller, "Democracy's Domain."

21. Another response might stress the importance of diminishing international inequalities such that it would matter less from a moral and material point of view where one was born. Such a response would highlight the power relations and inequalities that govern the international sphere and subject some nations and nationals to the will of others.

22. See Honig, "Between Decision and Deliberation" (revised as chapter 1 in *Emergency Politics*).

23. On this point, see also Critchley, *Infinitely Demanding*, 144. He says: "[I]t sometimes seems to me that the only thing in which American leftists believe . . . is law, particularly international law. International law is a very nice thing, but if it fails to have an anchor in everyday social practices then it leads to a politics of abstraction."

24. Benhabib finds it likely that the experience of standing up to the state will provide the girls with the resources to "engage and contest the very meaning of the Islamic traditions that they are now fighting to uphold."

25. On the chrono-logic of rights, see Honig, *Emergency Politics*, chap. 2.

26. In Canada, alien suffrage was ended at the same time, as some women (military wives) were first given the vote (1917–18). Until then coresidents were assumed to share a fate, a shared future, if not a past. This is different from the German court's invocation of "fate" in its decision on alien suffrage, in which, it seems, the fact that people moved once (in a cross-border migration; presumably other residents had moved too but not across national borders), was taken as license to script those people as always about to leave. (This, it seems to me, is the real offense, insofar as it bespeaks the unimaginability of real immigration. They may have come here but they are never really here because, having come from elsewhere, they will certainly leave; will they be called home? or expelled, deported?) In other words, the fact of proximity, so important in this chapter, is radically undone by a symbolic politics that scripts the immigrant not as one who is here but rather as one who is always on his way out (evidence for which, as it were, is that he came here in the first place).

27. At the lectures, Benhabib responded, as Habermas also has to objections like this one, by acknowledging the fact of the regress, saying, "Okay, one step forward, two steps back." This response is different from the double gesture called for here insofar as it rescues progress from any evidence against it, and preserves the linearity of its timeline: progress and regress are two sides of the same coin and regress is suffered here due to the promise of progress. Thus, the alternative to progressive time is not regress but rather plural temporalities, an idea developed by Connolly (2005) (along with some useful thoughts on cosmopolitanism) in his recent work, *Pluralism*, and commented upon in Honig, *Emergency Politics*, chap. 2.

28. On the productive and symbolic politics of foreignness in social welfare politics, see Honig, *Democracy and the Foreigner*, chap. 4.

29. I take Brown (2002) to have something like this approach in mind when she talks about "suffering the paradoxes of rights" in *Left Legalism, Left Critique*.

30. The same might be said as well for the new human rights regime itself, which, as Derrida points out, is a new site of sovereignty and counters sovereignty with sovereignty, not with nonsovereignty.

31. On the camps, see Balibar, "Europe as Borderland."

32. On the politics of (non)seriousness, see Honig, *Emergency Politics*, chaps. 1 and 2, with regard to Holmes and Slow Food. See also Critchley, *Infinitely*

Demanding, 124, who knows that "comical tactics can hide a serious political intent" (though, I would add, sometimes the tactic *is* the intent).

33. For a brief in favor of irrelevance, see Honig, "Against Relevance."

34. One example may suffice: I write that we should "approve of movements like Free Ibrahim, and of those that demand alien suffrage for co-residents—'because they are here.' But advocates of an agonistic cosmopolitics would work at the same time to prevent the energies of those movements from being lost once their state-centered and state-affirming goals are won" (Honig 2008, 119).

35. I discuss this is more detail in *Emergency Politics*, chap. 1.

Conditions for Hospitality or Defence of Identity?
Writers in Need of Refuge—A Case of Denmark's "Muslim Relations"
Ulrik Pram Gad

1. To facilitate the participation in the International Cities of Refuge Network, two bills were needed: One, presented by the Minister for Culture, amended the Literature Act to allow municipalities to spend money on hosting the writers; another, presented by the Minister of Refugee, Immigration, and Integration Affairs, amended the Aliens Act to allow the writers in question into the country in the first place. This analysis is based on the government presentations of these bills, the parliamentary debates, and the reports of the parliamentary committees scrutinizing them, as well as the consultative statements by NGOs, etc., and the ministers' answers to the committee's questions made public in the reports.

2. Less polite characteristics by international organizations and media reports are summarized by political scientist Hans-Jørgen Nielsen (2004, 15–17, 63–81, 152–177), who finds the picture painted by these foreign observers too grim.

3. Two notes on the translation of this excerpt: First, the passive Danish form of "it is intended" is kept in the English version, since it is a way of camouflaging agency and responsibility typical of Danish bureaucracy. Second, the extension of the sentence "while afterwards return to my homeland" does not grammatically make sense in Danish, but serves the purpose of including the return in the purpose of the stay.

4. Currently, this is not always possible even if you marry your beloved, since for family reunification to be granted, the provisions of the Alien Act require that the joint affiliation of the couple to Denmark be greater than to any other country—which, by simple math, it is not if you have met your partner in his or her home country and he or she has never been to Denmark.

5. The translation from Danish is partly copy-pasted from the "Declaration on Integration and Active Citizenship in Danish Society" on the official home page of the Ministry of Refugee, Immigration, and Integration Affairs. Where the "Declaration on Recognition of the Fundamental Values of the Danish Society" differs from this original declaration, the author has done the translation. The "understand and accept" of the official English version presented to writers to sign is more specific and binding than the Danish *anerkende*, which covers both the English "recognize" and "acknowledge."

Conviviality and Pilgrimage: Hospitality as Interruptive Practice
Mireille Rosello

1. When I assume that Europe plays the role of a host while countries such as Morocco or Algeria send guests, I forget that hospitality functions as a naturalized grand narrative. Cf. Rosello, *Postcolonial Hospitality*.

2. The minority ethnic stranger, the racialized subject, the exotic other, even if he or she has always been your neighbor, is internally colonized as the imaginary second- or third-generation immigrant-guest.

3. I am especially thinking of Jacques Derrida and Anne Dufourmantelle (Derrida 1997a & b; 1998, 1999a, b & c; Derrida and Dufourmantelle 2000); Emmanuel Levinas (1961), Seyla Benhabib (2006), Bonnie Honig (2006), and all the rereadings of Imanuel Kant's (1991, 93–130) promise of "perpetual peace" and "universal hospitality."

4. See the debate between scholars who address the issue of cosmopolitanism from different perspectives, a conversation that sometimes resembles the tensions within hospitality discourses. The issues of idealization and generalization run through the work of Appiah, Beck, Cheah, and Robbins.

5. See the video at: http://www.youtube.com/watch?v=fNfSQA6ZRsc&feature=related.

6. Not only is it impossible to reduce multiculturalism to the encounter between the national and the immigrant but it also becomes clear that such a paradigm imposes a simplified reading of the stranger as immigrant. This type of conviviality resists the vision of the melancholic.

7. The film is different, for example, from Stephen Frears's *Dirty Pretty Thing*, where only minority and disenfranchised agents can be counted on to act hospitably.

8. "Je peux changer en échangeant avec l'autre, sans me perdre pourtant ni me dénaturer. C'est pourquoi nous avons besoin des frontières, non plus pour nous arrêter, mais pour exercer ce libre passage du même à l'autre, pour souligner la merveille de l'ici-là" [I can change while exchanging with the other without losing myself or my nature. Which is why we need borders, not to stop us but to let us exercise this passage from the same to the other, to underscore the marvel of here-to-there] (Glissant 2006, 25). "Changing while exchanging" is one of Edouard Glissant's favorite formulas. It reappears in countless texts and interviews. For recent quotations, see Glissant, "Il n'est frontière qu'on outrepasse" and "Les revues culturelles et l'Europe."

9. In Ferroukhi's *Le Grand Voyage*, for example, the film builds up toward the arrival at Mecca, where people from all over the world congregate and are united by their belief in the meaningfulness of the trip that they have just taken.

10. Sisterhood is just as important as brotherhood in the story, but it is also significant to remember that "fraternité" is aligned with "liberté" and "égalité" in the mantra of the French Republic.

Hospitality and the Zombification of the Other
Nikos Papastergiadis

1. These observations and comments were formed in a number of essays by Gayatri Spivak (2004a; 2004b).

2. Cf. Derrida and Dufourmantelle, *Of Hospitality*.

3. The most influential account was by Castles and Kosack (1973).

4. This quote is taken from a documentary film entitled *Hope: A Documentary Film about Amal Basry and the SIEV X Disaster*, Dir. Steve Thomas (Flying Carpet Films, 2007).

5. See also Bowen, *Why the French Don't Like Headscarves*. In "Comment on Paris Riots," Alain Tourraine supports the view that French republicanism was "riddled with prejudices" and is therefore not surprised that the gangs are forming identities "based on aggression." However, he also notes, "we can no longer pretend that France is the protector of universal value, and that in this mission it has the right to make second-class citizens of anyone who doesn't fit the bill of this ideal 'national ego'" (*Berliner Zeitung,* November 9, 2005).

6. In his novel *Landscapes After the Battle* (Trans. by H. Lane, London: Serpent's Tail, 1987), Juan Goytisolo offers a prescient scenario that is closer to the worldview expressed by this gang. Goytisolo represents the city of Paris as being in a state of turmoil. Overnight an insurgent gang of immigrants had switched all the street signs from French into Arabic. Goytisolo suggests that republican chauvinism, combined with denialism over postcolonial humiliations, produces both indifference toward the foreigners that live in, but are excluded from, French culture, and a vacuum that attracts its own violent counterforce.

7. As noted by Jacques Rancière (2007, 266): "During the riots in the Parisian *banlieue* in the fall of 2005, these hoods covering the heads of Arab and black youth, became stigma: they were compared to both terrorists' masks and to Muslim girls' veils. The hoods became the symbol of a population locked up inside its own idiocy. Now in Chris Marker's film *Revenge of the Eye* (2006) they transform the young people into medieval monks."

8. Agamben proposes three chilling theses that haunt the norms of liberty, governance, and belonging: First, the constitutive force in politics is expressed in relation to the ban; second, the fundamental activity of sovereign power is the production of bare life; third, the camp has subsumed both the polis and the home as the paradigmatic space of biopolitics. Cf. Agamben, *Homo Sacer*, 181.

9. Malcolm Bull provides a useful analysis of this alienating passage between human and animal in "Vectors of the Biopolitical," 10.

10. See for instance Stephen Grey's (2006) account of the history of rendition, in particular his critique of the dissembling vocabulary that was invented to portray these prisoners as ghosts, and the airflights known as "ghost places." He noted that the apprehension of the suspects is referred to as "snatching"; their transfer, usually by means of an outsourced network of private Gulfstream jets, and piloted by people who refer to themselves as "taxi drivers." These "ghost

prisoners" have been sent to such destinations as the infamous prison in Syria known as the "Grave" because its cells are little larger than coffins. See also Xan Rice, "Africa's secret trail of 'ghosts,'" *Guardian Weekly* April 27–May 3, 2007, 3; and Rachel Meeropool (ed.), *America's Disappeared: Secret Imprisonment, Detainees and the "War on Terror."* (New York: Seven Stories Press, 2005).

11. Hayden White (1978, 150–82) argues that this practice "arises out of the need for men to dignify their specific mode of existence by contrasting it with those of other men, real or imagined, who merely differ from themselves." In his brief history of the figure of the wild man, he notes that while this figure recurs in history its meaning shifts.

12. Cf. Timothy Roberts, "Dead Ends: The Spectre of Elitism in the Zombie Film," *Philament: Liminal* 9 (December 2006): 75. For a more general discussion of the appeal of natural authority and supernatural forces as a negation of humanist perspectives, see Kenan Malik, *Man, Beast and Zombie: What Science Can and Cannot Tell Us About Human Nature* (Rutgers: Rutgers University Press, 2002).

13. Cf. Burbach and Tarbell, *Imperial Overstretch*.

14. See also Cynthia Weber, "Flying Planes Can Be Dangerous," *Millenium: Journal of International Studies* 31.1 (2002): 129–47. This shift in vocabulary and its relation to social transformation is also evident in Frankel's concluding volume of his trilogy on Australian politics. See Boris Frankel, *Zombies, Lilliputians and Sadists: The Power of the Living Dead and the Future of Australia.* (Freemantle: Curtin University Books, 2004).

15. All further references to the Fadaiat project are drawn from: http://observartorio.fadaiat.net/tiki and http://www.aminima.net/fadaiateng.htm.

16. Cf. Phillips, *Londonistan*.

17. Olivier Roy argues that "rootless Muslim youth" see themselves as excluded from the mainstream, but he also suggests that they take an active role in importing a "psychological frontier" into their own location in the cities. It is this oscillation between the perception of discrimination and resentment that fuels neofundamentalism. According to Roy, this ideology is a product of the digital diaspora. He argues that it adopts a polemical interpretation of multicultural rhetoric as a means to reject integration, and through the circuits of the new communicative technologies it is able to invent a new transnational worldview. Roy concludes that neofundamentalism pretends to offer a new identity, but effectively resurrects old adversarial binarisms that seek to "represent tradition, when in fact they express a negative form of westernisation." From Roy's perspective the trajectories of Muslim youth are on a collision course with Western society. See Roy, *Globalised Islam: The Search for a New Ummah.* (London: Hurst, 2004).

18. Cf. Phoenix, "Remembered Racialization."

19. For new critical accounts of similar collectives, see Gerald Raunig, *Art and Revolution: Transversal Activism in the Long Twentieth Century* (Los Angeles: Semiotexte, 2007); Blake Stimson and Gregory Sholette (eds.); *Collectivism after Modernism: The Art of Social Imagination after 1945* (Minneapolis: University of

Minnesota Press, 2007); and Grant H. Kester, *Conversation Pieces* (Berkley: University of California Press, 2004).

20. For examples of this new discourse, see Linda Basch, Nina Glick Schiller, and Cristina Szanton Blanc, *Nations Unbound*, New York: Gordon and Breach, 1994; and Iain Chambers, *Migrancy, Culture, Identity* (London: Routledge, London, 1994).

21. For a critique of the residentialist theories of identity and culture, see Harald Kleinschmidt, "Introduction" in Harald.Kleinschmidt (ed.), *Migration, Regional Integration and Human Security*, (Aldershot: Ashgate, 2006), 2–8.

22. Refugee Week was launched at Carillo Gantner Theatre, University of Melbourne, October 19, 2006.

23. Asked to explain his new term, Costello replied: "Well, mushy multiculturalism is the kind of multiculturalism that says it is important for migrants coming to Australia to retain the love of the country of their origin and their culture and their language, but it makes no demand on such people to show a similar loyalty or a higher loyalty I would argue to Australia and its people. . . . I am emphasising Australian values . . . We don't just expect lip service, we expect people to mean it." Paul Murray, *Radio Interview with Peter Costello*. 6PR, Australia, February 24, 2006.

24. Similar responses could be found on these blogs: in September 2006, the Federal Government released Ethnic Communities' Council of Victoria, ECCV Submission to the Discussion Paper, *Australian Citizenship: Much More than a Ceremony* November 15, 2006, http://eccv.org.au/doc/ECCVCITSUB.pdf; Graham Matthews, "Testing times for 'Australian values,'" in *Green Left Online, Issues,* November 17, 1993, http://www.greenleft.org.au/2006/685/8111; Syed Atiq Ul Hassan, "Blaming Muslims Equals More Votes," *The Forum, Online Opinion's Article Discussion Area*, September 19, 2006, http://www.forum.onlineopinion.com.au/thread.asp?article=4912; Ruy Diaz, "Australia: John Howard Stands by his 'Muslims Must Integrate' Comment," *Western Resistance*, September 1, 2006, http://www.westernresistance.com/blog/archives/002861.html; Andrew Norton, "The Citizenship Test for Hyperbolia," *Andrew Norton Blog Archive*, December 12, 2006 http://www.andrewnorton.info/blog/2006/ 12/12/the-citizenship-test-for-hyperbolia/; Socialist Equality Party, "Militarism and Howard's 'Australian values' Campaign," *World Socialist Website,* September 29, 2006, http://www.wsws.org/articles/2006/sep2006/aust-s29.shtml; "Italian Migrants Disprove Need for Language Tests," *The Australian, Letters Blog,* September 18, 2006, http://blogs.theaustralian.news.com.au/letters/index.php/theaustralian/comments/italian_migrants_disprove_need_for_language_tests/.

25. See Trumper, "The Australian Values: The View from Howard World" on Radio Austral, Wednesday 20 September 2006. All further quotes in this text refer to this program.

26. Cf. Paul Helas, Scott Lash, and Paul Morris. (eds.), *Detraditionalization: Critical Reflections on Authority and Identity* (Oxford: Blackwell, 1996).

The Art and Poetics of Translation as Hospitality
Paola Zaccaria

1. There exist two video clips that forever captured the shame: the shocking images of the ship entering Bari harbor, where the exodus had the astounding shape of a beehive, with the asylum seekers clinging even to the top of the ship funnel, and the images of the refugees locked in the city stadium in hot, sunny weather, who, as if they were war refugees or lepers, received food and drink from helicopters.

2. In her essay "Chicana Artists: Exploring Nepantla, el Lugar de la Frontera," Anzaldua (1993, 163) defined "Nepantla" as a "Nahuatl word for an in-between state, the uncertain terrain one crosses when moving from one place to another, when changing from one class, race, or gender position to another, when traveling from the present identity into a new identity."

3. Seyla Benhabib (2004) distinguishes four different phases in the migratory process: emigration, that is, the first entrance in a foreign country; civil, economic, and cultural absorption; incorporation, that is, residency in the same place for quite a long time; and naturalization, that is, acquiring political citizenship. Of course this step-by-step process has as its ideological background a type of emigration aiming at integration and belonging.

4. The reference here is to my book *La lingua che ospita. Poetica Politica Traduzioni* (Roma: Meltemi, 2004), but the seeds of this study have been sown in my previous essays; cf. Zaccaria, "Narrare dalla soglia" and "Vivir en la Frontera."

5. In his essay "Sul concetto di utopia in epoca moderna," Darko Suvin introduces some important distinctions between utopia, utopianism, utopian, and utopianist.

6. *Lingua Contro Lingua* is the title of a CD published by Radiodervish, an Italian-Palestinian band, in 1998.

7. I am quoting here from Luz Gomez Garcia's manuscript "The Arab Other: Gender, Interculturality and Languaged Language," later published in G. Covi, J. Anim-Addo, and A. Karavanta (eds.), *Interculturality and Gender* (London: Mango Publishers, 2009). Cf. also Giovanna Covi et al. (eds.), *ReSisters in Conversation: Representation Responsibility Complexity Pedagogy* (York: Raw Nerve Books, 2006).

8. ". . . it is as though the laws (plural) of hospitality, in marking limits, power, rights, and duties, consisted in challenging and transgressing the law of hospitality, the one that would command that the 'new arrival' be offered an unconditional welcome" (Derrida 2000, 77).

Works Cited

Ackermann, Hans-W., and Jeanine Gauthier. "The Ways and Nature of the Zombi." *The Journal of American Folklore* 104.414 (Autumn 1991): 466–94.
Agamben, Giorgio. *Homo Sacer: Sovereign Power and Bare Life*. Translated by Daniel Heller-Roazen. Stanford: Stanford University Press, 1998.
———. *The Open: Man and Animal*. Translated by Kevin Attell. Stanford: Stanford University Press, 2000.
———. *State of Exception*. Translated by Kevin Attell. Chicago: University of Chicago Press, 2005.
———. "We Refugees." http://www.egs.edu/faculty/agamben/agamben-werefugees.html.
Anderson, Benedict. *Imagined Communities*. London: Verso, 1991.
Andrijasevic, Rutvica. "The Southern Gate to Fortress Europe." *Policy Perspectives: Islam and Tolerance in Wider Europe*. Edited by Pamela Kilpadi. Budapest and New York: Open Society Institute, 2006. 30–50. http://www.policy.hu/ipf/policypersp/.
Annan, Kofi. "Powerful Message Needed to Counter Extremism, Overcome Misperceptions between Islam, West, Says Secretary-General in Doha Remarks." Press Release No: L/04/2006 [SG/SM/10359], February 27, 2006. Accessed December 18, 2006. http://www.unescap.org/unis/press/2006/feb/l04.asp.
Anzaldúa, Gloria. "Chicana Artists: Exploring Nepantla, el Lugar de la Frontera. " *NACLA Report on the Americas* 27.1 (1993): 37–43.
Anzaldúa, Gloria, and Analouise Keating, eds. *This Bridge We Call Home: Radical Visions for Transformation*. New York: Routledge, 2002.
Appiah, Kwame Anthony. *Cosmopolitanism: Ethics in a World of Strangers*. New York: Norton, 2006.

Arendt, Hannah. *The Human Condition*. Chicago: University of Chicago Press, 1958.

———. *On Revolution*. New York: Penguin Books, 1963.

———. *The Origins of Totalitarianism*. Second edition. New York: Harcourt, 1968.

———. *The Human Condition*. New York and London: HBJ, 1973.

Badiou, Alain. "The Scene of Two." *Lacanian Ink* 21 (2003): 42–55.

Balibar, Etienne. *We, the People of Europe?* Translated by James Swenson. Princeton: Princeton University Press, 2003.

———. "Europe as Borderland." Paper presented as the Alexander von Humboldt Lecture in Human Geography, University of Nijmegen, November 10, 2004. http://socgeo.ruhosting.nl/colloquium/Europe%20as%20Borderland.pdf.

Bataille, George. *Accursed Share, Vol. 1: Consumption*. [1946]. Translated by Robert Hurley. London: Zone Books, 1991.

Bateson, Gregory. *Steps to an Ecology of Mind*. New York: Bantam, 1972.

Bauman, Zigmunt. *Liquid Modernity*. Cambridge: Polity Press, 2000.

Beck, Ulrich. "The Cosmopolitan Society and Its Enemies." *Theory, Culture & Society* 19.1–2 (2002): 17–44.

———. *Cosmopolitan Vision*. London: Polity Press, 2006.

Benhabib, Seyla. "Deliberative Rationality and Models of Democratic Legitimacy." *Constellations* 1.1 (December 1994): 26–52.

———. *The Rights of Others. Aliens, Residents, and Citizens*. Cambridge: Press Syndicate of the University of Cambridge, 2004.

———. *Another Cosmopolitanism. The Tanner Lectures*. Edited by Robert Post. New York: Oxford University Press, 2006.

Benveniste, Émile. *Le Vocabulaire des institutions indo-européennes*. Paris: Minuit, 1969.

Bhabha, Homi. "The Third Space: Interview with Homi Bhabha." *Identity, Community, Culture, Difference*. Edited by Jonathan Rutherford. London: Lawrence & Wishart, 1990a. 207–21.

———. "DissemiNation: Time, Narrative, and the Margins of the Modern Nation." *Nation and Narration*. Edited by Homi K. Bhabha. London: Routledge, 1990b. 291–322.

———. *The Location of Culture*. London: Routledge, 1994.

Bharucha, Rustom. *Another Asia*. New Delhi: Oxford University Press, 2006.

Binswanger, Daniel. *Die Weltwoche*, November 10, 2005.

Blanchard, Pascal, Nicolas Bancel, and Sandrine Lemaire. *La Fracture coloniale. La société française au prisme de l'héritage colonial*. Paris: La Découverte, 2005.

Bowen, John R. *Why the French Don't Like Headscarves: Islam, the State, and Public Space*. Princeton: Princeton University Press, 2006.

Brenner, Frédéric. *Diaspora: Homelands in Exile*. New York: HarperCollins, 2003.

Brown, Wendy. "The Impossibility of Women's Studies." *Differences* 9 (1997): 79–102.

———. "Suffering the Paradoxes of Rights." *Left Legalism/Left Critique*. Edited by Wendy Brown and Janet Halley. Durham: Duke University Press, 2002. 420–34.

Bull, Malcolm. "Slavery and the Multiple Self." *New Left Review* 231 (Sept/Oct 1998): 225–45.

———. "Vectors of the Biopolitical." *New Left Review* 45 (May/June, 2007): 7–25.

Burbach, Roger, and Jim Tarbell. *Imperial Overstretch: George Bush and the Hubris of Empire*. London: Zed Books, 2004.

Butler, Judith. *Kritik der ethischen Gewalt*. Frankfurt: Suhrkamp, 2007.

———. *Gender Trouble*. New York: Routledge, 1990.

———. "Competing Universalities." *Contingency, Hegemony, Universality. Contemporary Dialogues on the Left*. Judith Butler, Ernesto Laclau, and Slavoj Žižek. London: Verso, 2000. 136–81.

Calhoun, Craig. "The Class Consciousness of Frequent Travelers: Toward a Critique of Actually Existing Cosmopolitanism." *The South Atlantic Quarterly* 101.4 (Fall 2002). 869–97.

Canetti, Elias. *The Tongue Set Free*, New York: Farrar, Straus, and Giroux, 1990.

Castles, Stephen, and Godula Kosack. *Immigrant Workers and Class Structure in Western Europe*. London: Oxford University Press, 1973.

Cheah, Pheng. *Spectral Nationality*. New York: Columbia University Press, 2003.

———. *Inhuman Conditions: On Cosmopolitanism and Human Rights*. Cambridge: Harvard University Press, 2006.

———. "Crises of Money." *Positions: East Asia Cultures Critique* 16.1 (Spring 2008): 189–219.

Cheah, Pheng, and Bruce Robbins, eds. *Cosmopolitics: Thinking and Feeling Beyond the Nation*. Minneapolis: University of Minnesota Press, 1998.

Claviez, Thomas. *Aesthetics & Ethics: Moral Imagination from Aristotle to Levinas and from Uncle Tom's Cabin to House Made of Dawn*. Heidelberg: Winter, 2008.

———. "What Is a European? Letters from a European Americanist." *Literature for Europe?* Edited by Theo D'haen and Iannis Goerlandt. Amsterdam: Rodopi, 2009. 79–100.

———. "Democracy: À Dieu, à Venir, or au Revoir?" *Annals of Scholarship* 19.3 (2010): 107–25.

Comaroff, Jean, and John Comaroff. "Occult Economies and the Violence of Abstraction: Notes from the South African Postcolony." *American Ethnologist* 26.2 (May 1999): 279–301.

———. "Alien-Nation: Zombies, Immigrants, and Millennial Capitalism." *The South Atlantic Quarterly* 101.4 (Fall 2002): 779–805.

Connolly, William E. *Pluralism*. Durham: Duke University Press, 2005.

Creed, Barbara. *Media Matrix: Sexing the New Reality*. Crows Nest: Allen & Unwin, 2003.

Critchley, Simon. *Infinitely Demanding: Ethics of Commitment, Politics of Resistance.* London: Verso, 2007.
Cronin, Michael. *Translation and Identity.* New York and London: Routledge, 2006.
de Ville, Jacques. *Jacques Derrida: Law as Absolute Hospitality.* New York: Routledge, 2011.
Derrida, Jacques. *Writing and Difference.* Translated by A. Bass. London: Routledge, 1978.
———. "Des Tours de Babel." *Difference in Translation.* Edited by Joseph F. Graham. Ithaca: Cornell University Press, 1985. 165–207.
———. "Psyche: Inventions of the Other." *Reading De Man Reading.* Edited by Lindsay Waters and Wlad Godzich. Minneapolis: University of Minnesota Press, 1989. 25–65.
———. *The Other Heading: Reflections on Today's Europe.* Translated by Pascale-Anne Brault and Michael B. Naas. Bloomington: Indiana University Press, 1992a.
———. *Given Time: I. Counterfeit Money.* Translated by Peggy Kamuf. Chicago: University of Chicago Press, 1992b.
———. *Aporias: Dying-Awaiting (One Another at) "the Limits of Truth."* Translated by Thomas Dutoit. Palo Alto: Stanford University Press, 1993.
———. *Le monolinguisme de l'autre.* Paris: Galilée, 1996.
———. *Cosmopolites de tous les pays, encore un effort!* Paris: Galilée, 1997a.
———. "Quand j'ai entendu l'expression 'délit d'hospitalité.'" *Plein droit* 34 (April 1997b): 3–8.
———. *Monolingualism of the Other or The Prosthesis of Origin.* Translated by Patrick Mensah. Stanford: Stanford University Press, 1998.
———. *Adieu to Emmanuel Levinas.* Translated by Pascale-Anne Brault and Michael Naas. Stanford: Stanford University Press, 1999a.
———. "Une hospitalité à l'infini." *Autour de Jacques Derrida: Manifeste pour l'hospitalité.* With the participation of Michel Wieviorka. Edited by Mohammed Seffahi. Paris: Paroles daube, 1999b. 97–106.
———. "Débat: Une hospitalité sans condition." *Autour de Jacques Derrida: Manifeste pour l'hospitalité.* With the participation of Michel Wieviorka. Edited by Mohammed Seffahi. Paris: Paroles daube, 1999c. 133–42.
———. *On Cosmopolitanism and Forgiveness.* Translated by Mark Dooley and Michael Hughes. New York: Routledge, 2001a.
———. "Force of Law: The Mystical Foundation of Authority." *Acts of Religion.* Edited by Gil Anidjar. New York: Routledge, 2001b. 228–98.
———. "Hostipitality." *Acts of Religion.* Edited by Gil Anidjar. New York: Routledge, 2002a. 356–420.
———. "Politics and Friendship." *Negotiations: Interventions and Interviews 1971–2001.* Translated and edited by Elizabeth Rottenberg. Palo Alto: Stanford University Press, 2002b. 147–98.
———. "Autoimmunity: Real and Symbolic Suicides: A Dialogue with Jacques Derrida." *Philosophy in a Time of Terror: Dialogues with Jürgen Habermas and*

Jacques Derrida. Edited by Giovanna Borradori. Chicago: University of Chicago Press, 2003. 85–136.

———. *Rogues: Two Essays on Reason*. Translated by Pascale-Anne Brault and Michael B. Naas. Stanford: Stanford University Press, 2005a.

———. *Paper Machine*. Translated by Rachel Bowlby. Stanford: Stanford University Press, 2005b.

———. *The Politics of Friendship*. London: Verso, 2006.

Derrida, Jacques, and Anne Dufourmantelle. *Of Hospitality: Anne Dufourmantelle Invites Jacques Derrida to Respond*. Translated by Rachel Bowlby. Stanford: Stanford University Press, 2000.

Devetak, Richard. "The Gothic Scene of International Relations: Ghosts, Monsters, Terror and the Sublime after September 11." *Review of International Studies* 31 (2005): 621–43.

Døving, Runar. "Vaffelhjertets makt - en analyse av norske kvinners hushold." *Varene tar makten*. Edited by Siri Meyer and Erling Dokk Holm. Oslo: Ad Notam Gyldendal, 2001.

———. *Rype med lettøl. En etnografi fra Norge*. Oslo: Pax, 2003.

Emerson, Ralph Waldo. *Selected Essays, Lectures, and Poems*. New York: Bantam, 2007.

Eriksen, Thomas Hylland. *Bak fiendebildet: Politisk islam og verden etter 11. september (Behind the Enemy Image: Political Islam and the World after 9-11)*. Oslo: Cappelen, 2001.

"Folketingets forhandlinger." Parliamentary negotiations of April 26, 2007, April 15, 2008, May 23, 2008, June 12, 2008. Reports from parliament Committee on Integration of May 13, 2008 concerning bill L131 and from parliament Committee on Culture of May 14 and 28, 2008 concerning bill L137. Accessed August 4, 2008. http://www.ft.dk.

Foucault, Michel. "Different Spaces." *Aesthetics, Method, and Epistemology*. Edited by James D. Faubion. New York: The New Press, 1998. 174–85.

Fox, Jonathan. "Clash of Civilizations or Clash of Religions: Which Is a More Important Determinant of Ethnic Conflict?" *Ethnicities* 1.3 (2000): 295–366.

Frello, Birgitta. "Hybriditet: Truende forurening eller kreativ overskridelse." *Kultur på kryds og tværs*. Edited by Henning Bech and Anne Scott Sørensen. Århus: Klim, 2005.

Fukuyama, Francis. *The End of History and the Last Man*. New York: Avon, 1992.

Garnaut, John. "Costello to Violent Muslims: Get Out." *Sydney Morning Herald* (February 24, 2006): 1.

Gilroy, Paul. *After Empire: Melancholia or Convivial Culture?* London and New York: Routledge, 2004.

Glissant, Edouard. "Il n'est frontière qu'on outrepasse." *Le Monde diplomatique*, October 2006. Accessed December 2008. http://www.monde-diplomatique.fr/2006/10/GLISSANT/13999.

———. "Les revues culturelles et l'Europe: Quelques considérations sur les périodiques culturels." (November 26, 2008). Accessed December 2008. http://www.eurozine.com/articles/article_2008-11-26-glissant-fr.html.

Goethe, Johann Wolfgang von. *On Art and Antiquity*. Vol. 3, Issue 1 (1821).

Gómez-García, Luz. "L'Altro Arabo: genere, interculturalità e una lingua che si fa lingua." *Interculturality and Gender*. Edited by Giovanna Covi, Joan Anim-Addo, and Mina Karavanta. London: Mango Publishers, 2009. 161–81.

Gordon, Michael. "Living in Limbo." *The Age* (September 30, 2006): Insight Section, 1.

Gray, John. "Easier Said Than done." *The Nation* (January 30, 2006).

Grey, Stephen. *Ghost Plane: The True Story of the CIA Torture Program*. St. Martin's Press: New York, 2006.

Gullestad, Marianne. "Invisible Fences: Egalitarianism, Nationalism and Racism." *Journal of the Royal Anthropological Institute* 8 (2002a): 45–62.

———. *Det Norske sett med nye øyne*. Oslo: Universitetsforlaget, 2002b.

Haahr, Jens Henrik. "'Our Danish Democracy': Community, People and Democracy in the Danish Debate on the Common Currency." *Cooperation and Conflict* 38.1 (2003): 27–45.

Habermas, Jürgen. "Constitutional Democracy: A Paradoxical Union of Contradictory Principles?" Translated by William. Rehg. *Political Theory* 29.6 (December 2001): 766–81.

Hardt, Michael, and Antonio Negri. *Empire*. Cambridge: Harvard University Press, 2000.

Hegel, Georg Wilhelm Friedrich. *Enzyklopädie der philosophischen Wissenschaften. Zweiter Teil: Die Naturphilosophie*. Werke in zwanzig Bänden, Vol. 9. Frankfurt am Main: Suhrkamp, 1970a.

———. *Enzyklopädie der philosophischen Wissenschaften. Dritter Teil: Die Philosophie des Geistes*. Werke in zwanzig Bänden, Vol. 10. Frankfurt am Main: Suhrkamp, 1970b.

———. *Philosophy of Nature. Part Two of the Encyclopaedia of the Philosophical Sciences* (1830). Translated by A. V. Miller. London: Clarendon Press, 1970c.

———. *Philosophy of Mind. Part Three of the Encyclopaedia of the Philosophical Sciences* (1830). Translated by William Wallace. Oxford: Clarendon Press, 1971.

Henley, Jon. "We Hate France and France Hates Us." *Guardian International* (November 9, 2005): 17.

Hervik, Peter. *Mediernes Muslimer. En antropologisk undersøgelse af mediernes dækning af religioner i Danmark*. København: Nævnet for Etnisk Ligestilling, 2002.

Hlavajova, Maria, and Gerardo Mosquera, curators. *Cordially Invited*. Utrecht: BAK, 2004.

Honig, Bonnie. *Political Theory and the Displacement of Politics*. Ithaca: Cornell University Press, 1993.

———. *Democracy and the Foreigner*. Princeton: Princeton University Press, 2001.

———. "Against Relevance." Paper presented at the Perestroika Reception during the annual meeting of the American Political Science Association, Boston, Mass., September 2002.

———. "Another Cosmopolitanism: Law and Politics in the New Europe." *Another Cosmopolitanism*. Edited by Robert Post. With Jeremy Waldron, Bonnie Honig and Will Kymlicka. Oxford: Oxford University Press, 2006. 102–27.

———. "Between Decision and Deliberation: Political Paradox in Democratic Theory." *American Political Science Review* 101.1 (March 2007): 1–17.

———. *Emergency Politics: Paradox, Law, Democracy*. Princeton: Princeton University Press, 2009.

Huntington, Samuel. *The Clash of Civilizations and the Remaking of a World Order*. New York: Simon and Schuster, 1996.

Irigaray, Luce. "Questions to Emmanuel Levinas: On the Divinity of Love." *Re-Reading Levinas*. Edited by Robert Bernasconi and Simon Critchley. Bloomington: Indiana University Press, 1991. 109–18.

———. *I Love to You*. London and New York: Routledge, 1996.

———. *The Way of Love*. London: Continuum, 2004.

———. *Sharing the World*. London: Continuum, 2008a.

Irigaray, Luce, and Mary Green, eds. *Luce Irigaray: Teaching*. London: Continuum, 2008b.

Kant, Immanuel. "On a Supposed Right to Lie Because of Philanthropic Concerns." *Grounding for the Metaphysics of Morals*. Translated by J. W. Ellington. Indianapolis & Cambridge: Hackett Publishing Company, 1981.

———. "Perpetual Peace: A Philosophical Sketch." *Political Writings*. Edited by H. S. Reiss. Translated by H. B. Nisbet. New York: Cambridge University Press, [1795] 1991. 93–130.

———. *Critique of Judgment*. New York: Cosmo, 2007.

Kepel, Gilles. *Chronique d'une guerre d'orient*. Paris: Gallimard, 2002.

Lacan, Jacques. *The Seminar of Jacques Lacan, Book VII. The Ethics of Psychoanalysis, 1959–1960*. Translated by Dennis Porter. New York: Norton, 1992.

———. *The Seminar of Jacques Lacan, Book XX. Encore*. Translated by Bruce Fink. New York: Norton, 1999.

Larsen, Rasmus Skov. "Asmaa Abdol Hamid - en ufattelig indre fjende?" *Faklen* (2007).

Latour, Bruno. *We Have Never Been Modern*. Translated by C. Porter. Cambridge: Harvard University Press, 1993.

Levinas, Emmanuel. *Totalité et Infini: Essai sur l'extériorité*. La Haye: Nijhoff, 1961.

———. *Totality and Infinity*. Pittsburgh: Duquesne University Press, 1969.

———. *Ethics and Infinity*. Pittsburgh: Duquesne University Press, 1985.

———. "The Trace of the Other." *Deconstruction in Context*. Edited by Mark Taylor. Chicago: University of Chicago Press, 1986. 345–59.

———. *Beyond the Verse*. Bloomington: Indiana University Press, 1994.

———. *Difficult Freedom: Essays on Judaism*. Baltimore: The Johns Hopkins University Press, 1997.

Llewelyn, John. "Am I Obsessed by Bobby? (Humanism of the Other Animal)." *Re-Reading Levinas*. Edited by Robert Bernasconi and Simon Critchley. Bloomington: Indiana University Press, 1991. 234–45.

Maalouf, Amin. *Les identités meurtrières*. Paris: Livres de poche, 2001.

Malka, Salomon. *Lire Levinas*. Paris: Cerf, 1984.

Marx, Karl. *Deutsche Ideologie. Marx/Engels Gesamtausgabe*, Vol. 1.5. Edited by Vladimir Adoratskij. Berlin: Marx-Engels Verlag, 1932b.

———. *The German Ideology*. Edited by C. J. Arthur. New York: International Publishers, 1970.

———. *Das Kapital, Kritik der politischen Ökonomie. Erster Band* (Hamburg 1890). In *Karl Marx Friedrich Engels Gesamtausgabe (MEGA)*, Vol. 2, 10. Edited by Institut für Marxismus-Leninismus. Berlin: Dietz, 1973a.

———. *Ökonomisch-philosophische Manuskripte. Zweite Wiedergabe*. In *Karl Marx Friedrich Engels Gesamtausgabe (MEGA)* Vol. 1, 2. Edited by Institut für Marxismus-Leninismus. Berlin: Dietz, 1973b.

———. *Economic and Philosophical Manuscripts. Early Writings*. Translated by Rodney Livingstone and Gregor Benton. Harmondsworth: Penguin, 1975.

———. *Capital: A Critique of Political Economy*. Vol. 1. Translated by Ben Fowkes. Harmondsworth: Penguin, 1976b.

Marx, Karl, and Friedrich Engels. "Manifest der Kommunistischen Partei" (February 1848). *Marx/Engels Gesamtausgabe*, Vol. 1.6. Edited by Vladimir Adoratskij. Berlin: Marx-Engels Verlag, 1932a.

———. "Manifesto of the Communist Party." *The Revolutions of 1848. Political Writings, Vol. 1*. Edited by David Fernbach. Harmondsworth: Penguin, 1976a.

Mauss, Marcel. *The Gift: The Form and Reason for Exchange in Archaic Societies*. Translated by W. D. Hall. London: Norton, [1925] 1990.

Mbembe, Achille. "La France peut-elle réinventer son identité?" *Histoire et colonies* (August 25, 2007). Accessed July 2008. http://www.ldh-toulon.net/spip.php?article2221.

Memmi, Albert. *Decolonization and the Decolonized*. University of Minnesota Press: Minneapolis, 2007.

Miller, Daniel. "Materiality: An Introduction." *Materiality*. Edited by Daniel Miller. Durham: Duke University Press, 2005. 1–50.

Miller, David. "Democracy's Domain." *Philosophy and Public Affairs* 37.3 (2009): 201–28.

Mimouni, Rachid. *De la barbarie en général et de l'intégrisme en particulier*. Paris: Le pré aux clercs, 1992.

Ministry of Refugee, Immigration, and Integration Affairs. http://www.nyidanmark.dk and http://newtodenmark.dk, official homepages of Ministry of Refugee, Immigration, and Integration Affairs. Accessed August 4, 2008.

Mishani, Dror, and Aurelia Smotricz. "What Sort of Frenchmen Are They? Interview with Alain Finkielkraut." *Ha'aretz*, (November 15, 2005).

Mouffe, Chantal, ed. *Deconstruction and Pragmatism*. London: Routledge, 1996.

Nancy, Jean-Luc. *The Inoperative Community*. Minneapolis: University of Minnesota Press, 1991.

Ngugi wa Thiong'o. *Decolonizing the Mind: The Politics of Language in African Literature*. London: Heinemann, 1986.

Nielsen, Hans Jørgen. *Er danskerne fremmedfjendske? Udlandets syn på debatten om indvandrere 2000–2002*. Århus: Aarhus UF/Rockwool Fondens Forskningsenhed, 2004.

Okao, Richard. "Black Heart." *The Big Issue* 256, (June 19–July 4, 2006): 16.

Patočka, Jan. *Platon et l'Europe*. Translated by E. Abrams. Paris: Lagrasse Verdier, 1983.

———. *Liberté et sacrifice*. Grenoble: Jérôme Millon, coll. Krisis, 1990.

———. *Heretical Essays in the Philosophy of History*. Translated by E. Kohák. Edited by James Dodd. Chicago: Open Court, 1996.

Phillips, Melanie. *Londonistan: How Britain Is Creating a Terror State Within*. London: Gibson Square, 2005.

Phoenix, Anne. "Remembered Racialization: Young People and Positioning in Differential Understandings." *Studies in Theory and Practice*. Edited by Karim Murji and John Solomos. Oxford: Oxford University Press, 2005.

Phongpaichit Pasuk, et al. *Guns, Girls, Gambling, Ganja: Thailand's Illegal Economy and Public Policy*. Chiang Mai: Silkworm Books, 1998.

Pratt, Mary Louise. "Arts of the Contact Zone." *Profession* (1991): 33–40

Rancière, Jacques. "Art of the Possible." *Artforum* XLV.7 (March 2007): 256–69.

Reinhard, Kenneth. "Toward a Political Theology of the Neighbor." Žižek, Slavoj, Eric L. Santner, and Kenneth Reinhard. *The Neighbor: Three Inquiries in Political Theology*. Chicago: University of Chicago Press, 2005. 11–75.

Ricoeur, Paul. *Oneself as Another*. Chicago: University of Chicago Press, 1992.

Robb, Andrew. "In Support of a Formal Citizenship Test." Address to the Jewish National Fund Gold Patron's Lunch, Mercantile Rowing Club (October 25, 2006).

Rogin, Michael. *Ronald Reagan, the Movie*. Berkeley: University of California Press, 1987.

Ronell, Avital. *The Test Drive*. Urbana: University of Illinois Press, 2005.

Rorty, Richard. "Objectivity, Relativism, and Truth." *Philosophical Papers,* Vol. 1. Cambridge: Cambridge University Press, 1991.

Rosello, Mireille. *Postcolonial Hospitality: The Immigrant as Guest*. Stanford: Stanford University Press, 2001.

Rosenau, James. *Distant Proximities: Dynamics Beyond Globalization*. Princeton: Princeton University Press, 2003.

Rosenzweig, Franz. *The Star of Redemption*, Translated by Barbara E. Galli. Madison: University of Wisconsin Press, 2005.

Santner, Eric. *On Creaturely Life: Rilke, Benjamin, Sebald*. Chicago: University of Chicago Press, 2006.

Sassen, Saskia. *Globalization and Its Discontents*. New York: New Press, 1998.

Schneider, Cathy Lisa. "Police Power and Race Riots in Paris." *Politics and Society* 35.4 (December 2007): 523–49.

Sjørslev, Inger. "Integrationens paradoks og den kulturelle træghed." *Integration: Antropologiske Perspektiver*. Edited by Karen Fog Olwig and Karsten Pærregaard. København: Museum Tusculanum, 2007. Chapter 5.

Smith, Adam. *An Inquiry into the Nature and Causes of the Wealth of Nations*. Chicago: University of Chicago Press, 1976.

Smith, Rogers M. "Beyond Tocqueville, Myrdal, and Hartz: The Multiple Traditions in America." *American Political Science Review* 87.3 (September 1993): 549–66.

Soguk, Nevzat. *States and Strangers: Refugees and Displacements of Statecraft*. Minneapolis: University of Minnesota Press, 1990.

Spivak, Gayatri Chakravorty. "Can the Subaltern Speak?" *Marxism and the Interpretation of Culture*. Edited by Cary Nelson and Lawrence Grossberg. Urbana: University of Illinois Press, 1988. 271–313.

———. "Keynote Lecture." Congress CATH on "Translating Class, Altering Hospitality." Leeds, June 23, 2002.

———. "Terror: A Speech After 9-11." *Boundary* 2 31.2 (2004a): 81–111.

———. "Globalicities: Terror and Its Consequences." *The New Centennial Review* 4.1 (2004b): 73–94.

Squiglia, Nico. "Transit Migration." International Symposium, Kölnischer Kunstverein, Cologne, November 10–13, 2005.

Stevens, Jacqueline. "Beyond Tocqueville, Please!" *American Political Science Review* 89.4 (December 1995): 987–95.

Still, Judith. *Derrida and Hospitality*. Edinburgh: Edinburgh University Press, 2010.

Suvin, Darko. "Sul concetto di utopia in epoca moderna." *Nuova secondaria* 5 (gennaio 2004): 105–11.

Todorov, Tzvetan. *Mémoire du mal, tentation du bien*. Paris: Robert Laffont, 2000.

Trumper, Ezequiel. "The Australian Values: The View from Howard World." Radio Austral, Wednesday, September 20, 2006.

Tsiolkas, Christos. *Dead Europe*. Sydney: Vintage, 2005.

Wæver, Ole. "Insecurity and Identity Unlimited." *Working Papers* 14, Copenhagen: COPRI, 1994. Also accessible as Wæver, Ole. "Insécurité, Identité: Une Dialectique sans Fin." *Entre Union et Nations: L'État en Europe*. Edited by Anne-Marie Le Gloannec. Presses de Sciences Po, 2008. 91–138.

White, Hayden. "The Forms of Wilderness: Archeology of an Idea." *Tropics of Discourse*. Baltimore: Johns Hopkins University Press, 1978. 150–82.

Wilson, Elizabeth. *Hallucinations: Life in the Post-Modern City*. London: Radius, 1988.

Wood, Robin. *Hollywood: From Vietnam to Reagan*. New York: Columbia University Press, 1986.

Zable, Arnold. "Australia's Very Own Devil's Island." *The Age*, 7 (September 2007): 13.

Zaccaria, Paola. "Narrare dalla soglia." *Incontri di culture: la semiotica tra frontiere e traduzioni*. Edited by Patrizia Calefato, Gian Paolo Caprettini, and Giulia Colaizzi. Torino: Utet, 2001a. 134–43.

———. "Vivir en la frontera". *Representar-representarse. Firmado: mujer*. Edited by Ramirez and Mercedes Arriaga. Huelva: Artes Graficas Giron, 2001b. 643–53.

———. *La lingua che ospita. Poetica Politica Traduzioni*. Roma: Meltemi, 2004.

Žižek. Slavoj. "Eastern Republics of Gilead." *Dimensions of Radical Democracy*. Edited by Chantal Mouffe. London: Verso, 1992.

———. "Neighbors and Other Monsters: A Plea for Ethical Violence." *The Neighbor: Three Inquiries in Political Theology*. Žižek, Slajov, Eric L.Santner, and Kenneth Reinhard. Chicago: University of Chicago Press, 2005. 134–90.

———. "Some Politically Incorrect Reflections on Urban Violence in Paris and New Orleans and Related Matters." *Urban Politics Now*. Edited by BAVO. Rotterdam: NAi Publishers, 2007a. 12–29.

———. "The Lesson of Rancière." *Jacques Rancière. The Politics of Aesthetics*. Translated by G. Rockhill. London: Continuum, 2007b. 69–79.

Contributors

Pheng Cheah is Professor of Rhetoric at the University of California, Berkeley. He has published extensively on the theory and practice of cosmopolitanism. He is the author of *Inhuman Conditions: On Cosmopolitanism and Human Rights* (2006) and *Spectral Nationality: Passages of Freedom from Kant to Postcolonial Literatures of Liberation* (2003) and the coeditor of several books, including *Cosmopolitics: Thinking and Feeling Beyond the Nation* (1998), *Grounds of Comparison: Around the Work of Benedict Anderson* (2003), and *Derrida and the Time of the Political* (2009). He is completing a book on theories of the world and world literature from the postcolonial peripheries in an age of financial globalization and a related book on globalization and the three Chinas as seen from the perspectives of the independent cinema of Jia Zhangke, Tsai Ming-Liang, and Fruit Chan.

Thomas Claviez is currently Professor for Literary Theory and Director of the Center for Cultural Studies (CCS) at the University of Berne. He is the author of *Grenzfälle: Mythos—Ideologiee—American Studies* (1998) and *Aesthetics & Ethics: Moral Imagination from Aristotle to Levinas and from Uncle Tom's Cabin to House Made of Dawn* (2008). He is the coeditor of *"Mirror Writing": (Re-)Constructions of Native American Identity* (2000), *Theories of American Studies/Theories of American Culture* (2003), *Neo-Realism: Between Innovation and Continuation* (2004), and *Aesthetic Transgressions: Modernity, Liberalism, and the Function of Literature* (2006). He is currently working on a monograph with the title *A Metonymic Society? Towards a New Poetics of Community*.

Anne Dufourmantelle is a philosopher and psychoanalyst and teaches at the European Graduate School in Saas-Fé. She is a member of Le Cercle Freudien

211

(Paris) and the association Apres-Coup (New York). Her most recent publications include *Intelligence du Rêve* (2012), *Fighting Theory: Interviews with Avital Ronnel* (2011), *Blind Date: Sex and Philosophy* (2009), *Negri on Negri: Antonio Negri in Conversation with Anne Dufourmantelle* (2007), and, with Jacques Derrida, *Of Hospitality: Anne Dufourmantelle Invites Jacques Derrida to Respond* (2000).

Thomas Hylland Eriksen is Professor of Social Anthropology at the University of Oslo. His research mainly concentrates on local responses to globalization and identity politics more generally, and he has published extensively on social and cultural diversity, ethnicity, and nationalism. He is currently (2012–2016) directing a major research project on the crises of globalization. Among his books in English are *Ethnicity and Nationalism* (1993/2010), *Small Places, Large Issues* (1995/2010), *Globalization: The Key Concepts* (2007), and *Engaging Anthropology* (2006). In Norwegian, he has published widely in many genres and on a broad range of topics, from evolutionary theory to myth and history.

Ulrik Pram Gad is a Postdoctoral Researcher at the Center for Advanced Security Theory in the Department of Political Science, University of Copenhagen. Current research focuses on Muslims in Western security organizations and on postcolonial sovereignty games in the Arctic. His most recent publications include "Preventing Radicalisation through Dialogue? Self-Securitising Narratives vs. Reflexive Conflict Dynamics" in *Critical Studies on Terrorism* (2012), a volume in Routledge's New International Relations Series on *European Integration and Postcolonial Sovereignty Games* (coedited with R. Adler-Nissen, 2012), a double special issue of *Security Dialogue* on "The Politics of Securitization" (coedited with K.L. Petersen, 2011), and a number of spin-offs from his PhD dissertation *(How) Can They Become like Us? Danish Identity Politics and the Conflicts of "Muslim Relations"* (2010).

Bonnie Honig is Sarah Rebecca Roland Professor of Political Science at Northwestern University and senior research professor at the American Bar Foundation in Chicago. She is the prizewinning author of *Political Theory and the Displacement of Politics* (1993), *Democracy and the Foreigner* (2001), *Emergency Politics: Paradox, Law, Democracy* (2009), and *Antigone, Interrupted* (2013). She has edited or coedited *Feminist Interpretations of Hannah Arendt* (1995), *Skepticism, Individuality, and Freedom: The Reluctant Liberalism of Richard Flathman* (2002), and the *Oxford Handbook of Political Thought* (2006).

Luce Irigaray is Director of Research in Philosophy at the Centre National de la Recherche Scientifique, Paris. A doctor of philosophy, Luce Irigaray is also trained in linguistics, philology, psychology, and psychoanalysis. Her most recent publications include *Sharing the World* (2008), *Conversations* (2008), *Teaching* (2008), *Between East and West: From Singularity to Community* (2005), *The Way of Love* (2004), *An Ethics of Sexual Difference* (2004), *To Speak Is Never Neutral* (2002),

Democracy Begins Between Two (2000), *To Be Two* (2000), *I Love to You* (1995), *Thinking the Difference* (1994), and *Elemental Passions* (1992).

Nikos Papastergiadis is Professor at the School of Culture and Communication at the University of Melbourne. His current research focuses on the investigation of the historical transformation of contemporary art and cultural institutions by digital technology. His publications include *Modernity as Exile* (1993), *Dialogues in the Diaspora* (1998), *The Turbulence of Migration* (2000), *Metaphor and Tension* (2004) *Spatial Aesthetics: Art Place and the Everyday* (2006), and *Cosmopolitanism and Culture* (2012). In addition, he is the author of numerous essays that have been translated into over a dozen languages and appeared in major catalogues, such as the Biennales of Sydney, Liverpool, Istanbul, Gwanju, Taipei, Lyon, Thessaloniki, and Documenta 13.

Mireille Rosello teaches at the University of Amsterdam (Amsterdam School of Cultural Analysis). She focuses on globalized mobility and on queer thinking. Recent publications include a coedited collection of articles on multilingualism in Europe (*Multilingual Europe, Multilingual Europeans, 2012,* with László Marácz), and monographs such as *The Reparative in Narratives: Works of Mourning in Progress* (2010), *France and the Maghreb: Performative Encounters* (2005), and *Postcolonial Hospitality* (2002). She is currently working on a collection of essays on queer Europe (*What Is Queer about Europe: Excentric Readings in History, Politics and Culture*, coedited with Sudeep Dasgupta, forthcoming from Fordham University Press).

Paola Zaccaria is professor of Literary and Visual Anglo-American Cultures and of Cinema Studies and director of the degree course in Science of Communication at the University of Bari. She has translated and edited *Borderlands/La Frontera* by G. Anzaldúa (2000) and produced a documentary about her heritage, *ALTAR: Cruzando Fronteras, Building Bridges* (directors Daniele Basilio, P. Zaccaria, 2009). Her publications include *A lettere scarlatte: Poesia come stregoneria* (In Scarlet Letters: Poetry as Witchcraft, 1995); *Mappe senza frontiere: Cartografie letterarie dal modernismo al transnazionalismo* (Maps without Borders: Literary Cartographies from Modernism to Transnationalism, 1999); *La lingua che ospita: Poetica, politica, traduzioni* (The Hospitable Tongue: Poetics, Politics, Translations, 2004); and *Transcodificazioni* (2005).

Perspectives in Continental Philosophy
John D. Caputo, series editor

John D. Caputo, ed., *Deconstruction in a Nutshell: A Conversation with Jacques Derrida*.

Michael Strawser, *Both/And: Reading Kierkegaard—From Irony to Edification*.

Michael D. Barber, *Ethical Hermeneutics: Rationality in Enrique Dussel's Philosophy of Liberation*.

James H. Olthuis, ed., *Knowing* Other-*wise: Philosophy at the Threshold of Spirituality*.

James Swindal, *Reflection Revisited: Jürgen Habermas's Discursive Theory of Truth*.

Richard Kearney, *Poetics of Imagining: Modern and Postmodern*. Second edition.

Thomas W. Busch, *Circulating Being: From Embodiment to Incorporation—Essays on Late Existentialism*.

Edith Wyschogrod, *Emmanuel Levinas: The Problem of Ethical Metaphysics*. Second edition.

Francis J. Ambrosio, ed., *The Question of Christian Philosophy Today*.

Jeffrey Bloechl, ed., *The Face of the Other and the Trace of God: Essays on the Philosophy of Emmanuel Levinas*.

Ilse N. Bulhof and Laurens ten Kate, eds., *Flight of the Gods: Philosophical Perspectives on Negative Theology*.

Trish Glazebrook, *Heidegger's Philosophy of Science*.

Kevin Hart, *The Trespass of the Sign: Deconstruction, Theology, and Philosophy*.

Mark C. Taylor, *Journeys to Selfhood: Hegel and Kierkegaard*. Second edition.

Dominique Janicaud, Jean-François Courtine, Jean-Louis Chrétien, Michel Henry, Jean-Luc Marion, and Paul Ricoeur, *Phenomenology and the "Theological Turn": The French Debate*.

Karl Jaspers, *The Question of German Guilt*. Introduction by Joseph W. Koterski, S.J.

Jean-Luc Marion, *The Idol and Distance: Five Studies*. Translated with an introduction by Thomas A. Carlson.

Jeffrey Dudiak, *The Intrigue of Ethics: A Reading of the Idea of Discourse in the Thought of Emmanuel Levinas*.

Robyn Horner, *Rethinking God as Gift: Marion, Derrida, and the Limits of Phenomenology*.

Mark Dooley, *The Politics of Exodus: Søren Kierkegaard's Ethics of Responsibility*.

Merold Westphal, *Overcoming Onto-Theology: Toward a Postmodern Christian Faith*.

Edith Wyschogrod, Jean-Joseph Goux, and Eric Boynton, eds., *The Enigma of Gift and Sacrifice*.

Stanislas Breton, *The Word and the Cross*. Translated with an introduction by Jacquelyn Porter.

Jean-Luc Marion, *Prolegomena to Charity*. Translated by Stephen E. Lewis.

Peter H. Spader, *Scheler's Ethical Personalism: Its Logic, Development, and Promise*.

Jean-Louis Chrétien, *The Unforgettable and the Unhoped For*. Translated by Jeffrey Bloechl.

Don Cupitt, *Is Nothing Sacred? The Non-Realist Philosophy of Religion: Selected Essays*.

Jean-Luc Marion, *In Excess: Studies of Saturated Phenomena*. Translated by Robyn Horner and Vincent Berraud.

Phillip Goodchild, *Rethinking Philosophy of Religion: Approaches from Continental Philosophy*.

William J. Richardson, S.J., *Heidegger: Through Phenomenology to Thought*.

Jeffrey Andrew Barash, *Martin Heidegger and the Problem of Historical Meaning*.

Jean-Louis Chrétien, *Hand to Hand: Listening to the Work of Art*. Translated by Stephen E. Lewis.

Jean-Louis Chrétien, *The Call and the Response*. Translated with an introduction by Anne Davenport.

D. C. Schindler, *Han Urs von Balthasar and the Dramatic Structure of Truth: A Philosophical Investigation*.

Julian Wolfreys, ed., *Thinking Difference: Critics in Conversation*.

Allen Scult, *Being Jewish/Reading Heidegger: An Ontological Encounter*.

Richard Kearney, *Debates in Continental Philosophy: Conversations with Contemporary Thinkers*.

Jennifer Anna Gosetti-Ferencei, *Heidegger, Hölderlin, and the Subject of Poetic Language: Toward a New Poetics of Dasein*.

Jolita Pons, *Stealing a Gift: Kierkegaard's Pseudonyms and the Bible*.

Jean-Yves Lacoste, *Experience and the Absolute: Disputed Questions on the Humanity of Man*. Translated by Mark Raftery-Skehan.

Charles P. Bigger, *Between* Chora *and the Good: Metaphor's Metaphysical Neighborhood*.

Dominique Janicaud, *Phenomenology "Wide Open": After the French Debate*. Translated by Charles N. Cabral.

Ian Leask and Eoin Cassidy, eds., *Givenness and God: Questions of Jean-Luc Marion*.

Jacques Derrida, *Sovereignties in Question: The Poetics of Paul Celan*. Edited by Thomas Dutoit and Outi Pasanen.

William Desmond, *Is There a Sabbath for Thought? Between Religion and Philosophy*.

Bruce Ellis Benson and Norman Wirzba, eds., *The Phenomenology of Prayer*.

S. Clark Buckner and Matthew Statler, eds., *Styles of Piety: Practicing Philosophy after the Death of God*.

Kevin Hart and Barbara Wall, eds., *The Experience of God: A Postmodern Response*.

John Panteleimon Manoussakis, *After God: Richard Kearney and the Religious Turn in Continental Philosophy*.

John Martis, *Philippe Lacoue-Labarthe: Representation and the Loss of the Subject*.

Jean-Luc Nancy, *The Ground of the Image*.

Edith Wyschogrod, *Crossover Queries: Dwelling with Negatives, Embodying Philosophy's Others*.

Gerald Bruns, *On the Anarchy of Poetry and Philosophy: A Guide for the Unruly*.

Brian Treanor, *Aspects of Alterity: Levinas, Marcel, and the Contemporary Debate*.

Simon Morgan Wortham, *Counter-Institutions: Jacques Derrida and the Question of the University*.

Leonard Lawlor, *The Implications of Immanence: Toward a New Concept of Life*.

Clayton Crockett, *Interstices of the Sublime: Theology and Psychoanalytic Theory*.

Bettina Bergo, Joseph Cohen, and Raphael Zagury-Orly, eds., *Judeities: Questions for Jacques Derrida*. Translated by Bettina Bergo and Michael B. Smith.

Jean-Luc Marion, *On the Ego and on God: Further Cartesian Questions*. Translated by Christina M. Gschwandtner.

Jean-Luc Nancy, *Philosophical Chronicles*. Translated by Franson Manjali.

Jean-Luc Nancy, *Dis-Enclosure: The Deconstruction of Christianity*. Translated by Bettina Bergo, Gabriel Malenfant, and Michael B. Smith.

Andrea Hurst, *Derrida Vis-à-vis Lacan: Interweaving Deconstruction and Psychoanalysis*.

Jean-Luc Nancy, *Noli me tangere: On the Raising of the Body*. Translated by Sarah Clift, Pascale-Anne Brault, and Michael Naas.

Jacques Derrida, *The Animal That Therefore I Am*. Edited by Marie-Louise Mallet, translated by David Wills.

Jean-Luc Marion, *The Visible and the Revealed*. Translated by Christina M. Gschwandtner and others.

Michel Henry, *Material Phenomenology*. Translated by Scott Davidson.

Jean-Luc Nancy, *Corpus*. Translated by Richard A. Rand.

Joshua Kates, *Fielding Derrida*.

Michael Naas, *Derrida From Now On*.

Shannon Sullivan and Dennis J. Schmidt, eds., *Difficulties of Ethical Life*.

Catherine Malabou, *What Should We Do with Our Brain?* Translated by Sebastian Rand, Introduction by Marc Jeannerod.

Claude Romano, *Event and World*. Translated by Shane Mackinlay.

Vanessa Lemm, *Nietzsche's Animal Philosophy: Culture, Politics, and the Animality of the Human Being.*

B. Keith Putt, ed., *Gazing Through a Prism Darkly: Reflections on Merold Westphal's Hermeneutical Epistemology.*

Eric Boynton and Martin Kavka, eds., *Saintly Influence: Edith Wyschogrod and the Possibilities of Philosophy of Religion.*

Shane Mackinlay, *Interpreting Excess: Jean-Luc Marion, Saturated Phenomena, and Hermeneutics.*

Kevin Hart and Michael A. Signer, eds., *The Exorbitant: Emmanuel Levinas Between Jews and Christians.*

Bruce Ellis Benson and Norman Wirzba, eds., *Words of Life: New Theological Turns in French Phenomenology.*

William Robert, *Trials: Of Antigone and Jesus.*

Brian Treanor and Henry Isaac Venema, eds., *A Passion for the Possible: Thinking with Paul Ricoeur.*

Kas Saghafi, *Apparitions—Of Derrida's Other.*

Nick Mansfield, *The God Who Deconstructs Himself: Sovereignty and Subjectivity Between Freud, Bataille, and Derrida.*

Don Ihde, *Heidegger's Technologies: Postphenomenological Perspectives.*

Françoise Dastur, *Questioning Phenomenology*. Translated by Robert Vallier.

Suzi Adams, *Castoriadis's Ontology: Being and Creation.*

Richard Kearney and Kascha Semonovitch, eds., *Phenomenologies of the Stranger: Between Hostility and Hospitality.*

Michael Naas, *Miracle and Machine: Jacques Derrida and the Two Sources of Religion, Science, and the Media.*

Alena Alexandrova, Ignaas Devisch, Laurens ten Kate, and Aukje van Rooden, *Re-treating Religion: Deconstructing Christianity with Jean-Luc Nancy*. Preamble by Jean-Luc Nancy.

Emmanuel Falque, *The Metamorphosis of Finitude: An Essay on Birth and Resurrection*. Translated by George Hughes.

Scott M. Campbell, *The Early Heidegger's Philosophy of Life: Facticity, Being, and Language.*

Françoise Dastur, *How Are We to Confront Death? An Introduction to Philosophy*. Translated by Robert Vallier. Foreword by David Farrell Krell.

Christina M. Gschwandtner, *Postmodern Apologetics? Arguments for God in Contemporary Philosophy.*

Ben Morgan, *On Becoming God: Late Medieval Mysticism and the Modern Western Self.*

Neal DeRoo, *Futurity in Phenomenology: Promise and Method in Husserl, Levinas, and Derrida.*

Sarah LaChance Adams and Caroline R. Lundquist eds., *Coming to Life: Philosophies of Pregnancy, Childbirth, and Mothering.*
Thomas Claviez, ed., *The Conditions of Hospitality: Ethics, Politics, and Aesthetics on the Threshold of the Possible.*
Roland Faber and Jeremy Fackenthal, eds., *Theopoetic Folds: Philosophizing Multifariousness.*
Jean-Luc Marion, *The Essential Writings.* Edited by Kevin Hart.
Adam S. Miller, *Speculative Grace: Bruno Latour and Object-Oriented Theology.*
Jean-Luc Nancy, *Corpus II: Writings on Sexuality.*
David Nowell Smith, *Sounding/Silence: Martin Heidegger at the Limits of Poetics.*